Academic Politics and the History of Criminal Justice Education

Recent Titles in
Contributions in Criminology and Penology

Domestic Marijuana: A Neglected Industry
Ralph A. Weisheit

Personality and Peer Influence in Juvenile Corrections
Martin Gold and D. Wayne Osgood

Bad Guys and Good Guys: Moral Polarization and Crime
Daniel S. Claster

Innovative Approaches in the Treatment of Drug Abuse: Program Models and Strategies
James A. Inciardi, Frank M. Tims, and Bennett W. Fletcher, editors

Coca and Cocaine: An Andean Perspective
Felipe E. Mac Gregor, editor

Police Under Pressure: Resolving Disputes
Robert Coulson

Punishing Criminals: Developing Community-Based Intermediate Sanctions
Malcolm Davies

Crack and the Evolution of Anti-Drug Policy
Steven R. Belenko

In Defense of Prisons
Richard A. Wright

Police in Contradiction: The Evolution of the Police Function in Society
Cyril D. Robinson, Richard Scaglion, with J. Michael Olivero

Drug Abuse Treatment: The Implementation of Innovative Approaches
Bennett W. Fletcher, James A. Inciardi, and Arthur M. Horton

State Police in the United States: A Socio-Historical Analysis
H. Kenneth Bechtel

Academic Politics and the History of Criminal Justice Education

FRANK MORN

Contributions in Criminology and Penology,
Number 46

GREENWOOD PRESS
Westport, Connecticut • London

Library of Congress Cataloging-in-Publication Data

Morn, Frank.
Academic politics and the history of criminal justice education / by Frank Morn.
p. cm.— (Contributions in criminology and penology, ISSN 0732–4464 ; no. 46)
Includes bibliographical references and index.
ISBN 0–313–29316–3 (alk. paper)
1. Criminal justice, Administration of—Study and teaching (Higher)—United States. I. Title. II. Series.
HV9950.M68 1995
364′.071′173—dc20 94–18557

British Library Cataloguing in Publication Data is available.

Library of Congress Catalog Card Number: 94–18557
ISBN: 0–313–29316–3
ISSN: 0732–4464

First published in 1995

Greenwood Press, 88 Post Road West, Westport, CT 06881
An imprint of Greenwood Publishing Group, Inc.

Printed in the United States of America

The paper used in this book complies with the Permanent Paper Standard issued by the National Information Standards Organization (Z39.48–1984).

P

For Maura

Contents

Preface

Academic criminal justice—the studying and teaching of crime, police, law and legal processes, and corrections—is of recent origin in higher education. Beginning in the 1920s and 1930s, and accelerating in the 1970s, it has become a significant academic mainstay in second- and third-rank colleges and universities.

Considerable semantic confusion surrounding criminal justice needs clarifying. Particularly in the popular mind the phrase frequently means law and legal processes; this historic interpretation is still used in many European countries today, but it is too narrow and does not take into account the academic politicians at the center of this study. In addition, as this story will show, criminologists have long tried to lay claim to the field. Many of the early people in criminal justice called themselves criminologists. The distinction between criminal justice and criminology must be kept clear. The former, indeed, does include criminology but exands to encompass the study of the agencies that combat crime. Although the phrase criminology is used a lot in this history, this work is not about classic criminology, or the sociologically based study of crime and its treatment. This is the history of an academic field that began as law enforcement or police science and developed to encompass issues and agencies addressing crime.

On one hand, the events and circumstances that brought it into existence and propelled it to its present place are unique and revealing. On the other, it has merely revived a plot whose script was written long ago. Most academic disciplines and professions have similar, if not identical, stories to tell. Therefore, to better understand criminal justice education today we need to see how it fits into the historical development of higher education in general and other academic disciplines in particular. That is the purpose of the introductory chapter.

Much discussion and research has been carried out regarding other disciplines. Indeed, some small attempts have been made concerning criminal justice as well. But a very important ingredient—academic politics—has been overlooked or de-emphasized. Simply put, academic politics is the process by which individuals in higher education develop reputations and positions of power to influence and persuade other members of the profession (university faculty, practitioners, college administrators) and the general public to their viewpoints. In this book, academic politicians are seen as important in building an intellectual discipline. The persons involved include faculty members, professors of newly developing fields and old established ones, university presidents possibly in conflict with professors, and academic deans who lean one way or another as battles rage.

ACKNOWLEDGEMENTS

In a project like this, gratitudes are legion. First, the Academy of Criminal Justice Sciences provided me a small sum to help with travel and tape recording of significant persons in the history of criminal justice education. Those who were interviewed (and a list of their names and interview dates appears in the bibliography) were gracious and informative.

Second, the library and archival staffs at various universities were very helpful. The Bancroft Library at the University of California at Berkeley must be credited for making the job of a researcher both profitable and pleasant. Zelma Gelling at the office of the Chancellor's Archives was of great assistance. Also, hidden away in an obscure attic were additional papers relating to the School of Criminology. I discovered these only with the help of Ann Goolsby, a former secretary to the School of Criminology who is still at the University of California; I have used her name as an indicator of those particular files. These files are now in the University Archives, Bancroft Library. Ellin Rowland of the John Jay College of Criminal Justice library archives was very helpful as well.

Third, there were those—such as Gordon Misner,

Richard Ward, Larry Bassi, Robert Culbertson, and Edward Latessa—who let me have access to their personal papers, for which I am grateful.

Fourth, the Center for Studies in Law and Justice at the University of Illinois at Chicago supplied some transcribing and typing in the early stages of this work. Illinois State University provided me sabbatical leave to finish this draft.

Fifth, conversations and debates with friends and colleagues were very helpful. Beverly Smith read the manuscript carefully and critically, for which I am very grateful. Also, I would like to acknowledge and thank Steven Balkin, Patrick McAnany, Joseph Nicol, James Osterburg, John Crank, and Vincent Webb. There were others who were less than friendly. I would like to thank them for their insight as well. In addition, I wish to thank my wife, Dr. Maura Toro-Morn, for both her critical comments and gentle encouragements without which this book would never have been finished.

Of course, the main responsibility for this work and its interpretations is my own.

Chapter 1

Introduction: Academic Politics and Professionalism, 1870–1930

THE UNIVERSITY AND COLLEGE

The earliest pedagogical models for higher education in America were religious ones. Most of the early colleges, those that would become the Ivy League, were connected to particular religious denominations. The goal of education—according to seventeenth, eighteenth, and mid-nineteenth century educators—was the disciplining of the mental facilities. Education was less concerned with stimulating and freeing one's mind than with restraining and disciplining one's character. Hence, fields of study, learned by rote, eventually became known as "disciplines." Latin, Greek, mathematics and moral philosophy became the major mental calisthenics, certainly more important for the workout they gave than for any intellectual outlook they revealed. The ultimate goal, the standard of the educated person, was a "pious life."[1]

As the modern university began to take shape in the late nineteenth century, the religious orientation with its near denominational monopoly of higher education was challenged from several directions. New educators appeared who, like their pious predecessors, saw education as a means to make the student a better person, an enlightened citizen in a democracy. Rather than religion and discipline, however, these humanists emphasized "liberal culture." The ancients remained well-loved but it was their language and culture rather than the religion that prevailed. Considerable emphasis was placed upon literature, philosophy, and Western Civilization courses. Some accepted this as a logical step from pious-man to gentleman.

In many places the humanist or liberal culturalists were successful. Amherst College in the East and Reed College in the West, for example, became dedicated to the liberal culture model. While John Bascom headed the University of Wisconsin (1874-87), an emphasis upon humanities prevailed there. But it was at Yale and Princeton where the liberal culture orientation became strongest. When Woodrow Wilson was president of

Princeton, for example, he saw his university as "not a place of special but of general education, not a place where a lad finds his profession, but a place where he finds himself." Abbott Lawrence Lowell became president of Harvard in 1909 and aligned that university with liberal culture, seconding Wilson's notion that the purpose of education was "the awakening of the whole man."[2] Even science was too narrow, and applied science too vocational, these humanists believed.

Largely because of the influence of Germany, research and scholarship became important components of some universities in the late nineteenth century. Research was an end in itself, and the search for truth was important no matter what its applications were to the modern world. The laboratory, the lecture method, and the seminar became the prevalent pedagogical tools. Because students were considered appendages to their scholar-mentors, teaching became much less important in these institutions than it was to the liberal culturalists. The establishment of Johns Hopkins University (1876) and Clark University (1889) provided institutional models. For some time they stood alone as educational institutions dominated by the scholarship ideal. But by the turn of the century Harvard, Columbia, and the University of Chicago equaled Johns Hopkins and eclipsed Clark.

Initially there was reluctance toward the widespread creation of such intellectual factories. Scholarship brought prestige to a campus, but there were costs as well. Three political groups emerged: students, faculty, and administrators. Most students did not crave a life of scholarship; they wanted a career. They judged professors mainly as instructors, not as researchers. University presidents, also, found it difficult to deal with eccentric genius professors. For most universities the scholarly approach had to be fitted into a campus environment catering to other more immediate needs. Structurally the "graduate school" became the natural home of the scholar. The German-inspired research degree (Ph.D.) increasingly became the badge of the researcher-scholar. Then, of course, pragmatic America wanted practical application for its new knowledge-producing industry.[3]

Liberal culture and scholarship were important, but neither had the power or pervasiveness of the utility orientation. America may or may not have been anti-intellectual. But it was certainly interested in so-called "usable knowledge." According to utilitarian educators and administrators, education must relate to "real life." The vast number of students who went to college even in the 1890s wanted a career. Liberal culture, which may have been an adequate career preparation for many, seemed to be for the rich kids in the Ivy League. The excavating of a tomb in Egypt, albeit interesting, did not seem relevant to a person or a country in the midst of an industrial and urban revolution. Of course, any scholarly program that had a practical, problem-solving impact became the darling of a university president.[4]

The utilitarian emphasis was captured, if not monopolized, by the state-supported institutions of higher learning during the Progressive Era. There was a logic in this because many of them were created or expanded as a result of the land-grant money and philosophy of an earlier generation. In other words, most started with a more technical and mechanical emphasis. This was especially true in the Midwest. In fact, the universities of Michigan and Nebraska were two leaders in the country. The University of Wisconsin, according to the popular journalist Lincoln Steffens, was even "sending a state to college." The university literally extended itself (hence the extension movement) as the entire state became the campus. Progressive governors such as Robert LaFollette in Wisconsin tapped the expertise of these universities for their brain trusts. This "Wisconsin Idea" was used in other progressive states as well and gave impetus to the utilitarian orientation of higher education.[5]

The utilitarian emphasis was best carried out by a new set of university presidents who tried to balance research with some utility. Since the professoriate and the mid-levels of university administration were in formative stages, the president had enormous power. Certain influential people like Charles W. Eliot at Harvard and Woodrow Wilson at Princeton who had supported utilitarianism had left the college arena by the turn of the century, but other prominent individuals were bringing a variety of philosophies and policies to their tasks. Abbott Lawrence Lowell at Harvard, Arthur T. Hadley at Yale, Nicholas Murray Butler at Columbia, William Rainey Harper at the University of Chicago, and David Starr Jordan at Stanford—to name a few—either carried on from previous times or started new careers during the Progressive Era as university presidents. They all had profound impacts upon their institutions and the history of higher education. They were all consummate academic politicians.

A closer look at Benjamin Ide Wheeler, president of the University of California, is instructive. He is particularly important because he was in place at Berkeley when criminal justice education began in its earliest manifestations as police science. Wheeler came from a strong Baptist background in Massachusetts. Educated in classical languages at Brown University and the University of Heidelberg, he published extensively in comparative philology and linguistics. In that sense, he was representative of a mixture of liberal culturalists and scholars in higher education. In 1899 he began a twenty-year career as president and academic politician of the University of California and metamorphosed into a utilitarian. At the outset he demanded and received complete control of the university. During his tenure twenty new academic departments were added and the summer and extension divisions expanded. In addition, he dominated the establishment of new professorships and guarded against too much "individualistic intellectualism." He maintained that "the drift of the times is away from the theories of the doctrinaire toward the capacity for correct and effective action." The chief of police at Berkeley and eventual founder of the criminal justice education movement at the University of California, August Vollmer, undoubtedly agreed. Although his expressing of Pro-German sentiments in 1919 forced Wheeler to step down, he continued to influence the University of California for several years in an advisory capacity.[6]

One early solution that brought scholarly status and practical utility to the university was the professional school.

PROFESSIONS AND THE PROFESSIONAL SCHOOLS

The professional school, dedicated to training practitioners for a particular occupation that had achieved professional status, seemed a useful compromise between scholarship and careerism in higher education. Since so many in criminal justice education have argued for such a model, a word on its history is appropriate here. Furthermore, especially at the dawn of most professions, academic politics was an important factor. Not only did academics contend with their own "real world" practitioners, but many politicians in the professional school had political skirmishes with scholars in other parts of the university. Four examples are illustrative: military, medicine, law, and divinity.

Military

One of the earliest professional schools in America was the United States Military Academy. A word about it seems appropriate because so many early criminal justice educators tried to develop a "West Point of Law Enforcement." In addition, its early history included some of the problems common to professionalism and professional schools in America.

In the immediate post-Revolution era Americans had a profound respect for citizen soldiers (the militia), and an equal distrust of professional armies. The former were seen as "democratic" and the latter as "aristocratic." Some attempts were made at a national school for military officers in the late eighteenth century, but it was not until 1802 when the United States Military Academy was formally established at West Point, New York. Thomas Jefferson was very important in this process because he wanted an institution to ignore the classics and concentrate on science and mathematics. In fact, in the early years West Point was used to train the Corps of Engineers exclusively.[7]

The Military Academy had a slow start for the first twenty years of its existence. It was not until the mid-1820s, under the superintendency of Sylvanus Thayer, that West Point's academic reputation reached prominence. In part, this was due to the popular distrust of creating a privileged professional military class. Most of the presidents up to Andrew Jackson favored the idea, but large numbers of citizens felt it to be an un-republican institution. A pamphlet, *The Military Academy at West Point, Unmasked*(1830), complained of the Academy's "tendency to introduce and build up a privileged order of the very worst class—a military aristocracy—in the United States."[8] The author was Alden Partridge, Thayer's predecessor at the institution. Almost every state petitioned Congress to abolish it. Many Jacksonians, in keeping with their dislike of government monopolies like the national bank, tried to get rid of it as well.

In spite of growing opposition to the Academy, Thayer began to strengthen the scientific curriculum and introduce other academic departments. Students earlier might have graduated after attending only a few months of classes. Thayer introduced a four-year program and a requirement of an additional year of service. The college was run like a military company. First year students, the "plebs," underwent great pressure and social abuse. Those faint-hearted who came just for a free education usually dropped out at this point. Classes were small with students taking part in active learning. While some were reciting aloud, others demonstrated their knowledge on the chalkboards. Yearly examinations were awesome with attrition rates highest among the plebs. Class lists were prepared based upon merit, and those with the highest place were selected for the Corps of Engineers. Those at the bottom were assigned to the infantry. Due to Thayer's reforms, West Point was the best engineering school in the country throughout the mid nineteenth century. After the Civil War, as the country came to respect things military, the reputation of West Point grew.[9]

West Point demonstrates two conflicting trends that translated to policing a century later. First, there was a desire to professionalize the leadership ranks of the military. Second, at the same time the public disliked the notion of a professional army. They felt that the qualities making a good soldier—honor, courage, loyalty—could not be taught in the classroom. Nonetheless, in Europe and some places in America the military academy was one educational model for criminal justice.

Medicine

In America the absence of a restrictive professional group, like the British Royal College of Physicians, permitted unbridled expansion of medical schools. Between 1800 and 1910, for example, over 450 medical schools sprang up in America, most of them giving diplomas for a fee. A small number of eastern based physicians who had received some quality education, the self-styled "regular" doctors, fought this cut-throat competition and created the American Medical Association (AMA) in 1847 as an institutional expression of their concern. Only by defining what was orthodox could they discredit the unorthodox. In terms of expertise, however, these "regulars" had little advantage over the "irregulars." Medical theory and technology were in such a state that the practitioners of homeopathy and herbalism had as much claim to successful treatment as did the "regulars."[10] In fact, the fastest-growing group of medical practitioners throughout the nineteenth century were abortionists and patent medicine distributors.[11]

Throughout the last half of the nineteenth century the "regulars" gradually gained dominance. First, they became involved in the public health movement springing up in large urban areas. Second, as the hospitals slowly became more important after the Civil War, the "regulars" captured positions through their medical schools and made sure the "irregulars" could not gain a foothold in these important institutions. Third, they became very active in leading crusades against the abortion clinic and patent medicine industries. Finally, advances in the 1890s revolutionized medicine, making it more a science and less an art. Until the 1890s only three medicines actually cured diseases: quinine was used for treating malaria, mercury for syphilis, and digitalis for heart disorders. In 1895 an antitoxin was discovered for the nineteenth century's greatest killer, diphtheria. Now the "regulars" indeed had greater claim to successful scientific treatments.[12]

Although the number of so-called quacks had been reduced, the number of doctors still remained high by the turn of the century. Prominent on the agenda of the AMA was the removal of numerous proprietary schools of medicine, sometimes called "sundown institutions" because they emphasized evening instruction. In 1906 the AMA's Council on Medical Education studied the problem. In 1910, the Flexner Report on medical education warned that current methods of medical education would result in enormous overproduction at a low level. Consequently, a crusade to stiffen medical requirements and eliminate the proprietary schools resulted. Medical elites hoped to lower the quantity and raise the quality of medical practitioners by reducing and controlling medical schools. In 1900 there were 160 medical schools. By 1910 there were 133 and by 1920, 85. Medical professionalization, therefore, was a mixture of monopolization and quality control. However, it is interesting that as the number of medical schools decreased, similar strategies had the opposite effect in the legal profession.[13]

Law

Between 1800 and 1910 fully 171 law schools were founded, and most opened during the last third of the nineteenth century. This was an educational institutionalization of a process that had largely followed informal apprenticeship forms earlier; indeed, most instructors in the early law schools were practicing lawyers who gave only part-time attention to their academic responsibilities. Although President Charles Eliot of Harvard was proud of his appointment in 1873 of the first full-time law professor—a man who had never practiced law—practitioners of the law remained the main teachers of the law. By the turn of the century another university president, David Starr Jordan of Stanford, would bemoan the problem of "pettifogging law schools and an untrained bar." As far as Jordan was concerned, too many law teachers were still in active practice rather than focusing their ambitions and energies on the law school.[14] As the case method of instruction developed during the last decades of the century, however, things began to change. An instructor could no longer teach by recitation and anecdote only, methods that required minimal readiness. Intellectual effort and preparation were forced upon the teachers; and in the larger law schools at least, the part-timers were slowly pushed out and a legal professoriate emerged.

It was in the early twentieth century that the modern academic legal professor developed. Indeed, as if to sound the gavel and open the decade, the Association of American Law Schools began in 1900. From the beginning, however, this new organization and its members were confronted by a series of challenges, the most important of which were the growing differences between legal educators and practitioners. First, academic lawyers, being so new, needed to find their place in the world of law. In the nineteenth century advocacy was the main function of lawyers. They were to be above special interest, to be free and independent, to be knights in the courtroom. By the twentieth century, however, corporate lawyers emerged; and they seemed to be greater supporters and defenders of special interests, spending more time in the boardrooms than the courtrooms of America. Legal educators still trained people to practice law, but many—most notably people like Felix Frankfurther—hoped their students would use the law to better society. Such a mission, in fact, was all the more appropriate during the Progressive Era when society seemed ready and willing for reform.[15]

This sense of public responsibility and identification with political reform gave a more liberal quality to law professors, whereas their students largely chose career paths that were conservative. Indeed, the "Cravath System," a practice well established by 1910, was one in which law firms recruited recent graduates and retrained them at entry levels. Apparently the most successful practitioners had little faith in the educators. Conversely, law professors believed the practitioners had lost their independence.

Second, the American Bar Association (ABA) was taken over by the same corporate lawyers. Although law teachers and their special organization, the Association of American Law Schools, met in conjunction with the ABA between 1900 and 1914, the academics never felt accepted. In total disregard or ignorance of academic calendars, the ABA moved its annual meeting times from August to October in 1914. True to its years of feeling separate from the ABA the Association of American Law Schools officially separated.[16] The bifurcation of educator and practitioner thus seemed complete.

Law professors and legal practitioners were driven apart by differing definitions of the appropriate mission of law and lawyers in American society. However, they were driven together with mutual concern over the lower levels of the legal profession. Numerous "diploma mills" arose between 1890 and 1910 to provide inexpensive legal education. While daytime schools increased by 60 percent, nighttime schools did so by 350 percent. Some argued that the night schools, providing legal education to less affluent working students, prevented elitism in the law profession. Others, particularly law professors, felt that these schools, filled with part-time students and part-time teachers, simply lowered educational standards. Students were not taught the law, it was felt, but were given a quick credential to operate within a profession for which they were ill-prepared. Not only the law schools but the entire profession was demeaned. So a political alliance was struck between educators and practitioners to cleanse and control the profession. When the Alfred Z. Reed report, *Training for the Public Profession of Law*, appeared in 1920, it was hoped that it would do for legal education what the Flexner Report had done for medical education.

The legal establishment hoped that in the name of a united profession, law school education would be restricted and regulated. Now the American Bar Association and the American Association of Law Schools would unite to control admission standards, educational requirements and facilities, and bar standards. The Reed Report, however, was a disappointment. In a democratic society, it advised, such avenues of upward mobility should not be discouraged. Diversity and democracy, rather than monopoly and control, were healthier for the profession and the country. The crusade ended and the alliance between elite practitioners and educators soon fell apart. As late as the 1920s, therefore, most states required nothing more than a high school education for admission to the bar.[17]

During the 1920s the legal elites splintered anew. During this period business became supreme and so did the business lawyer. Even one presidential candidate, John W. Davis, was a famed corporation lawyer. However, the New Deal era did shake the elites and increase the already-present enmity between legal teacher and practitioner. Government service under Franklin D. Roosevelt provided a "new practicality" for the legal scholar, one with some social worth beyond making money. The brightest students were trained and encouraged to serve in Washington rather than on Wall Street. For a time, professional power shifted from corporate to government lawyer. With the New Deal, then, the legal academics successfully challenged the legal practitioners for control of the profession.[18] Of course, how long this would last depended upon the political and social climate of America.

Divinity

Another academic profession and professional school that evidenced friction between educator and practitioner was that of theology. It also illustrated the dual directions a profession might take depending upon the type and stature of the educational unit in which its professional school resides. Religion, or divinity, was one of the earliest academic professions, going back to the medieval university. Most colleges established in Colonial America were sectarian. As these early colleges joined with new ones to develop the modern university, they ceased to pay much attention to religion. At first their place was taken by a variety of Bible schools and seminaries that remained independent of the university; they became a "minor profession."[19] These places, like their law school equivalent, were practitioner-oriented. Study of scriptures was an act of faith rather than an act of intellect. Instead of expanding intellectual boundaries, their purpose was to draw clearer lines of difference between denominations. Since student bodies needed no conversion, emphasis was placed upon elocution: the means of conveying the message was more important than the message itself. Any kind of intellectual criticism was anathema.

Some universities compartmentalized religious studies into divinity schools that had different problems resembling those of other newly-born academic professions. Of major concern was faculty-student relations. At the sectarian school the practitioner taught only what the student wanted to learn: how to be a good preacher and pastoral shepherd. In the divinity school, on the other hand, most faculty were interdisciplinary scholars who wanted to replicate themselves. Young people heading for the pulpit were taught textual criticism of the scriptures, comparative religions, theology, archaeology, and history. It was obvious to many that the management of a "living congregation" would not be learned in divinity school. Students had to either convert to a scholarship that might border on agnosticism or learn the preaching craft in spite of their teacher.[20]

According to H. Richard Niebuhr's study, *The*

Advancement of Theological Education, those divinity students who had considerable practical experience felt out of place in the university. Their storehouse of experience and practical wisdom was inappropriate to the divinity school. Furthermore, there was a status structure within the interdisciplinary divinity schools. In medical schools and to a lesser degree in law schools, the practitioner teacher and the scholar teacher had equivalent status. With rare exception in divinity schools did the preacher possess the stature of the professor. More important individuals in tangential disciplines—say, a professor of archaeology or history or philosophy teaching in the divinity school—had greater status than those having a doctorate of theology.[21] In short, the disciplinary parts were viewed by many as greater than the whole. Divinity schools became a smorgasbord of specialties, as did many schools of the minor professions such as education and social work, ostensibly providing a feast but in danger of loosing individual flavors and adequate digestion in the vast array. Of course, such development would have been less likely without the parceling up of information into academic disciplines.

DISCIPLINES AND "SCHOOLS"

The compartmentalization of knowledge grew apace with the rise of the modern university. Specialization of knowledge, rather than its more renaissance generalization, became important. Amateurism, which had previously connoted a love of knowledge, became a negative feature meaning unskilled and unprofessional. At first the borderlines were perforated and the content amorphous. The role of the early academic professionalizer and politician was to bring clarity and definition to that ambiguity. Universities, following early notions of bureaucracy, had broad divisions. Departments aided the bringing together of people with overlapping interests, skills, and perspectives into an intellectual community. Frequently, departments were built around the perspective and reputation of one person, who was probably a successful academic politician. In fact, the university department might serve to amplify and extend his influence. Even university presses, publishing facilities on a university campus, were developed as vehicles for the particular university's scholars. If a scholar's views and energies transcended his locale, an intellectual "school" might develop giving the scholar and his university even more prestige.

Such a school would be an assembly of independent scholars led by one person whose intellect, personal charisma, academic vision, and missionary zeal inspired and motivated a set of disciples to go forth and germinate other departments with the same intellectual outlook, thereby creating a vast network of scholar-students. Although there was indeed an intellectual core, there was also considerable tolerance for individual creative freedom and disciplinary backgrounds. In fact, in the social sciences (with the exception of economics) there would be abundant interdisciplinary crossfertilization. Such schools, however, rarely lasted beyond the lives of their founders, making way for new people and their own intellectual methodological configurations to respond to changing times.[22] Columbia University and the University of Chicago were two major institutions of higher education that basked in the glory of their departments, schools, and scholarly stars. Students radiated out from these departments to establish new ones elsewhere and shape broader concepts called disciplines.

Humanities

Those fields of study commonly called humanities (art, history, modern languages, music, literature, and philosophy) began professionalizing in the late nineteenth century. Actually, there were some earlier signs with the forming of the American Oriental Society (1842) and the American Philological Association (1869). But most came later. Some later examples were the Modern Language Association (1884) and the American Philosophical Association (1901).

With rare exception (and history will be that exception), the humanities were never too powerful on the university campus. There were several reasons for this. First, there were considerable internal tensions within each of the cultural areas. Many clung to older notions that all the humanities programs needed to do was cultivate and civilize the student. Others wanted to apply the rigors of German scholarship to the arts, and there was not always a logical fit. Furthermore, academic domination of the humanities was never firm. Art and drama schools, historical societies, music conservatories, and museums (to name a few) challenged the universities as centers of practice and scholarship in the humanities. Finally, even though a consensus formed around phrases like "esthetic values" and "higher civilization," there was no real sense of interrelationship between the various fields. At least the social sciences lay claim to being "scientific." Certainly for the natural sciences—and in a myth-making way for the social sciences too—the thread called "science" loosely bound them together. This was not true for the humanities; and in the rush for political place and power in the university, the humanities were relegated to a minor position.[23]

History was an exception. The most important person whose research and ideas translated into political power for the discipline was Frederick Jackson Turner. After the publication of his paper "The Significance of the Frontier in American History" in the early 1890s, Turner's ideas permeated historical scholarship and the popular mind for generations. He even established a quantitative ("scientific") methodology long before most of the social sciences did. From his academic base, first at the University of Wisconsin and later at Harvard, he had considerable power within his university and those places where his students taught. For decades he controlled the resources of research and publication in American history.

Other historians—such as James Harvey Robinson, Walter Prescott Webb, Carl Becker, and Charles Beard—were quick to take advantage of history's exalted position and established relationships and alliances with the National Education Association. In 1913 this association launched a Commission on the Reorganization of Secondary Education. In its *Report*, published in 1918, it made clear that the social sciences, which were rejected as basic components of secondary school curriculum, had not achieved political power. On the other hand, history (which did have several years' head start) achieved a prominent place and impacted upon secondary and college education for decades to come. Therefore, the importance of history in the classroom was largely due to the impact of Turner and the political acumen of certain history professors during the early years of its academic professionalization.[24]

Social Sciences

The social sciences (anthropology, economics, political science, psychology, and sociology) did not exist as distinct disciplines before 1870. In fact, many of their pioneers—men like Carroll D. Wright, director of the Federal Bureau of Labor Statistics, and John Wesley Powell, a geologist and ethnologist who directed the Smithsonian Bureau of Ethnology until 1902— had little to do with higher education. But considerable change, challenge and conflict occurred in late nineteenth-century America to make social issues and problems more relevant. In a nineteenth-century interdisciplinary way, professors in traditional areas of study began offering topics of interest within the more advanced courses in moral philosophy. Apparently there were enough of these teachers and courses to call into creation the American Social Science Association by 1865. The shaking-out of these disciplines, what some scholars call the "organization of knowledge," came about in distinct phases between 1870 and 1920.[25]

During the first phase, generally but not exclusively in the 1870s, small numbers of academic pioneers with a social science interest were dissatisfied with their place within the university. Economics, for example, was generally associated with historical studies. Charles Dunbar held a chair in political economy but taught jurisprudence. At Yale, Francis A. Walker ostensibly taught political economy, but it was largely industrial history. Not until 1876 did Daniel Coit Gilman, president of Johns Hopkins University, set up a "professorship of political and economic science."[26] For much of the nineteenth century, psychology was part of philosophy or biology. Early psychologists—such as William James at Harvard and G. Stanley Hall at Johns Hopkins—spent considerable effort drawing distinctions between themselves and the host disciplines.[27]

In addition, social problems generated by the industrial and urban revolutions of the late nineteenth century gave rise to the earliest sociologists. Herbert Spencer's Social Darwinism held sway for much of the post-Civil War generation. This ideology had the tendency to stifle debate and public policy over social problems. It also explained society in biological terms.[28] Therefore, Franklin H. Giddings, Edward A. Ross, Charles H. Cooley, and Albion Small, to name a few, had to spend considerable energy breaking their earlier ties to biology.[29] Also a humanist uproar over a scholarly course on political science at Amherst College forced the departure of German-trained John W. Burgess for Columbia University, where he established a preeminent department in 1876.[30] In short, a few social scientists were beginning to redefine themselves in such ways as to prepare for the founding of new disciplines. Theirs were acts of academic politics.

Younger scholars, trained either in Germany or in research universities such as Johns Hopkins or Clark, came upon the scene in the 1880s and early 1890s to mark the second generation of discipline-builders. This group needed to differentiate further themselves by founding national organizations. In 1884 historians spun off from the American Social Science Association, taking political economists along with them to create their own historical association. At the second meeting of the American Historical Association, Richard T. Ely—like his colleague at John Hopkins, Herbert Adams, had done two years earlier—assembled a variety of scholars, ministers, and social reformers and established the American Economics Association. The "old economists," those of the political economy approach of the 1870s, mostly remained outside the new organization. Meanwhile, the "new economists," divided between social reformers and pure scholars, vied for control. The social reformers dominated until the 1890s.[31] G. Stanley Hall established the first psychology lab in America in 1883 and initiated the *American Journal of Psychology* four years later. By 1892, when the American Psychological Association was founded, there were 18 laboratories in American universities and over a dozen holders of Ph.D. degrees in experimental psychology.[32] As late as the 1890s, however, there was no sociology as a discipline. Most sociological research took place in the settlement houses, called laboratories of social science by Robert Woods of Andover House in Boston. Social Darwinism still held such political and popular appeal that academic sociology needed to await a different social climate in which to grow appreciably. John Burgess continued to build a political science program at Columbia, and by 1886 he established the *Political Science Quarterly* as a forum for his students.[33]

The third and most active phase of academic politics and professionalization began in the 1890s and continued in various ways in all the social sciences into the 1920s. The drama of separating from mother disciplines and creating token unity through national associations now gave way to internal consolidation and heated professorial politics. Certainly, an important early endeavor involved defining more clearly the thrust of each new discipline. For many of the new disciplines, laying claim to being a science was important. Was the field in question a *social* science or a social *science*? History, influenced by the heavy quantitative style of Turner, in a surprising way was very "scientific." A group of historians with an economic interpretation gave history an even more scientific appearance.

Psychology was one of the earliest to wrestle with this issue while it was undergoing great growth. There were four departments of psychology in American universities by 1904; there were 35 by 1912. About one hundred Ph.D. degrees were awarded by 1904; that number doubled by 1917. Many of the formative years of psychology and the American Psychological Association were taken up in disassociating from philosophy, one of its parent disciplines. High on the agenda of the "new psychologist" was making the field more scientific. Joint meetings with the American Society of Naturalists and the American Association for the Advancement of Science announced to the profession its close connections to science. James McKeen Cattell, one of the pioneering "new psychologists," used his position as editor of the *Popular Science Monthly* and *Science* between 1910 and 1918 to publicize psychology as a science. But for some it was not scientific enough. John B. Watson launched a "behaviorist revolt" and in 1913 complained that psychology was unscientific and that it needed to emulate the natural or physical sciences even more. Other social sciences would lay claim to scientism, but not as early or to the degree of psychology.[34]

In the last analysis there are two disciplines—political science and sociology—that had the greatest impact upon criminal justice and that illustrate best the practice of academic politics.

Political Science. By the turn of the century two political science programs dominated: those at Columbia and Johns Hopkins. Most of the professors at Illinois, Michigan, Minnesota, Missouri, Pennsylvania, Princeton, and Texas, for example, were graduates of Columbia or Johns Hopkins. At this time questions arose about the nature of the new field. The "old political scientists" felt that history and political science were inseparable. Woodrow Wilson's book *The Study of Administration* (1887) was early in pointing to other directions. Now, others suggested a break with history and thus challenged the definitions drawn by the dominate departments.[35] In conjunction with the New Orleans meetings of the American Historical Association and the American Economic Association in 1903, a group of political scientists unaffiliated with Johns Hopkins and Columbia formed the American Political Science Association. Not all members were academics. In fact, by 1912 only 20 percent came from higher education; the rest were lawyers, businessmen, and librarians. In 1906 the Association's official journal, the *American Political Science Review*, began to compete with Columbia's *Political Science Quarterly*. By 1914 there were 38 institutions in America with distinct political science departments. There were some political science components in either history, economics, or sociology in 89 colleges. Departmental independence was achieved at Harvard in 1911, Minnesota in 1913, Northwestern in 1915, the University of Southern California in 1916,

Kansas in 1917, and Stanford in 1918. In effect, the new association arose to wrest power from the two predominant departments. But another university was about to come on the scene to dominate and give additional meaning to political science.[36]

After obtaining a doctorate at Columbia University, Charles E. Merriam joined the University of Chicago in 1900; with his *American Political Theories*, he promised to be a conventional scholar. Then, in the years 1909-11 and 1913-17 Merriam was elected city alderman from Chicago's Seventh Ward. In 1911 he even campaigned to be mayor. The University of Chicago president, Harry Pratt Judson, disliked such unscholarly activity and refused to name Merriam as chairman of the newly formed political science department. In fact, Merriam's scholarly ideas were shaped by his participation in politics. He became an academic politician only after flirting with being a "real world" one. In his essay "The Present State of the Study of Politics," Merriam set forth a new political science, one in which history was subordinated to statistics and psychology. He claimed that political science should solve real problems and serve society. The irrationality of city politics suggested that methodological debates and theoretical speculation should give way to the practical concerns of governance.[37]

Merriam impacted upon political science in three ways. First, from leadership positions he spread his notions on the science of politics. In 1923 a new president of the University of Chicago appointed him chairman of the department. An impressive production of doctorates followed shortly thereafter. For example, until 1920 thirteen political science doctorates came out of Chicago. Between 1920 and 1940 the number increased to 80 and the University of Chicago displaced Columbia and Johns Hopkins as leader in the field. Then, in 1925 Merriam became president of the American Political Science Association and used that position to further spread his ideas.[38]

Second, Merriam established relationships with philanthropic organizations such as the Rockefeller Foundation and the Spelman Fund. Philanthropy existed to provide moneys, especially if research had practical value, but competition for this money stiffened as the number of professors increased. Some cooperative effort was needed, thought Merriam, to control that competition. The humanities (through the American Council of Learned Societies) and the natural sciences (through the Natural Research Council) had organized to obtain funding for research by the early 1920s. With political skill and powerful friends in philanthropy,

Merriam was able to establish the Social Science Research Council in 1923 to regulate the distribution of research money toward social problems. Thus, he was able to set the research agenda for many political scientists for years to come.[39]

Third, Merriam came to think of political science (to him it was now political sciences) in an interdisciplinary way. Some doubted that the social sciences had matured enough for such interdisciplinary cooperation. Certainly, individuals in history and economics had reservations. Nonetheless, Merriam felt that the social sciences should come "together to consider the fundamental social problems in which they are all concerned and which cannot be effectively solved without their joint consolidation and action." So just at a time when the disciplines were separating themselves, Merriam was asking them to come back together.[40]

In one regard his notions held up for a while with public administration, but centrifugal forces were at work. As early as Woodrow Wilson's *The Study of Administration* in 1887, there was some concern over the management of government. Concern over public corruption and inefficiency during the Progressive Era made such studies even more relevant. In 1912, the year that Wilson was elected president of the United States, the American Political Science Association formed a Committee on Practical Training for Public Service. Two years later this committee presented its *Prepared Plan for Training Schools of Public Service* and acknowledged the importance of political science training for government service. A Society for the Promotion of Training for Public Service resulted, and through its journal (*The Public Servant*) it began campaigning for professional schools of public administration in 1916. Political science, guarding its small university domain, was reluctant to create professional schools that might compete for students. Any experimentation with academic public administration in the 1920s, therefore, was relegated to political science departments as an applied field of study.[41] Only with the coming of the New Deal would academic public administration display enough vitality and independence from political science to warrant the establishment of the American Society for Public Administration in 1939. Until that time, however, it fit nicely into Merriam's notions of practical political science.[42]

Sociology. As the new disciplines "narrowed down" they left the three D's—studies of the defective, dependent, and delinquent classes—to a large number of charity workers. Interest in these social problems was compelling, especially against the backdrop of the industrial and urban revolutions of the late nineteenth century and the social engineering mindset of the "Progressives" in the early twentieth century. Before it had a distinct intellectual content or methodology, sociology entered the university system with a reputation as a "science of leftovers."[43]

Between 1889 and 1900 nearly one hundred colleges or universities introduced courses in sociology, most of which were in divinity schools. The persistence of Social Darwinism was frustrating, but at least the critical perspective of the Progressive Era offered some solace and opportunity. One of the most important pioneering departments of sociology was formed at the University of Chicago in 1893. William Rainey Harper, the first president of the University of Chicago, was committed to building an educational empire based upon research useful to society. Although Herbert Baxter Adams (a historian) and Richard T. Ely (an economist) were first recruited, the chairmanship of the new department went to Albion Small. Born and raised in Maine, Small attended Colby College, the Newton Theological Institute, and the Universities of Berlin and Leipzig before earning a Ph.D. in history from Johns Hopkins in 1889. For the next three years he was president of Colby until Harper called him to Chicago.[44]

At first it was not clear what the new department of sociology was to be. Small felt that it should study contemporary society through an interdisciplinary approach. History and economics had an important place in the curricula and were taught by Small. Charles H. Henderson lectured on social work. Frederick Starr taught anthropology, and Marion Talbot—a pioneer in the "home economics" education movement—lectured on sanitary science. Courses in philosophy, psychology, political science, comparative religion, and household administration could be taken as well. There was a particularly strong relationship with the divinity school, especially after Shailer Mathews gave that school a pronounced sociological orientation. John Dewey of the School of Education was also a close friend to these early sociologists.[45]

Charles H. Henderson's lectures on social work were very popular in the early days at the University of Chicago. This popularity signaled a major problem for sociology at the University of Chicago and nationwide. In speaking of the institutionalization of American sociology, one student commented:

> The identification of "sociology" with practical or applied sociology and social reform was the majority view even in academic circles and made the task of scientific and academic legitimacy a very delicate and difficult one for the early academic sociologist.[46]

In the nineteenth century social work was done by individual or organized charities. A number of schools of social work developed to teach these "friendly visitors." The New York Charity Organization Society established a six-week Summer School in Philanthropy in 1898. Graham Taylor of the Chicago Commons settlement house and Julia Lathrop of Hull House set up the Institute of Social Sciences in 1903; five years later it became the Chicago School of Civics and Philanthropy.[47] While Henderson was at the University of Chicago from 1893 to 1915, the sociology department had strong ties to social work. Henderson and Small helped form the Bureau of Charities in Chicago at the turn of the century, and by 1912 Henderson was president of United Charities. When Henderson died in 1915, however, the sociology department moved away from such applied activities and was taken over by the social workers in the School of Civics and Philanthropy. There Sophonisba Brickridge and Edith Abbott were doing much in professionalizing social work; in 1920 that school became a School of Social Service Administration at the University of Chicago, further defining and distinguishing sociology from social work.[48]

After moving away from social work the University of Chicago's sociology department achieved nationwide prominence for its scholarship between 1915 and 1935, which had considerable influence on the development of the discipline everywhere. It became the Chicago "school" of sociology. In a sense, the sociology professors at the University of Chicago became an academic political machine.

Using the city as their laboratory, these sociologists—first under Robert Park, W. I. Thomas, and Ernest Burgess—produced students and studies in urban sociology. Already, Small had established the *American Journal of Sociology* as an outlet for research. Then the University of Chicago Sociological Series was started, with Park and Burgess collaborating on a textbook that became so famous among students that it was simply referred to as the "green bible." The University of Chicago Press began to publish what would become classics in the discipline: *The Hobo*, *The Negro in Chicago*, *The Gang*, *The Polish Peasant in Europe and America*, and *The Jack Roller*, to name a few. Although Clifford Shaw and Henry McKay were at the Chicago Institute for Juvenile Research, they maintained a close relationship with the sociology department. Edwin Sutherland, who received his Ph.D. from the department in 1913, returned as a research professor in 1930 and laid the groundwork for his theories and textbooks on criminology.[49] Like political science, the early years of sociology were dominated by the discipline-builders and academic politicians at the University of Chicago.

CONCLUSION

The years 1870-1930 were important formative times for academic professions in America. The modern university arose in response to the increased complexity of the human experience. Knowledge became specialized and fields of study divided and subdivided. In various degrees the ancient professions—such as medicine, law, and divinity—continued to evolve and professional schools developed. Other fields of knowledge began a course of action—professionalization—that led to academic disciplines. In turn, these new discipline-builders wanted a measure of power and status within the university structure and in the wider intellectual community. Professorial politics became important as key individuals set up national associations, promulgated their ideas about the new field of knowledge, and used their academic departmental base to create the discipline.

The process was like establishing a frontier. As Frederick Jackson Turner was declaring that America's geographic frontier had closed by the turn of the century, an intellectual and academic one was opening. There was some nudging and positioning in the staking of claims, but in a sense all new arrivals were legitimate just because they were present. Later, as the map filled up, turf became more closely guarded and legitimization became a difficult process. Academic politics became more heated. Against this historical framework the rise and spread of criminal justice education may best be understood.

Chapter 2

Progressivism and Police Education, 1910–1935

For most historians the opening decades of the twentieth century seemed unique and important enough to be designated the Progressive Era. Reforms and reformers existed before this time—the Abolitionists and the Populists quickly come to mind—but the progressives arrived at the turn of the century with an agenda and ideology that changed much of American society for decades to come. It is not our purpose to delve deeply into this period here. Some elements of that movement need highlighting, however, because widespread social reform (which included considerable activity in criminal justice) and the origins of criminal justice education at the college level owe much to progressivism.

First, to justify both the thrust of this chapter and the viewpoint of the entire book, a word about criminal justice is needed. By the beginning of the twentieth century, and indeed beyond, the phrase "criminal justice" referred to the criminal law and court processes. Only rarely was it given broader meaning. Criminology, which was still in an embryonic state, would be housed eventually in the developing discipline of sociology. However, enough ambiguity existed over the word "criminology" to allow a host of nonsociologists to lay some claim to it. Such activity led to numerous academic political battles. It is the thesis of this book that early developments at this time eventually led to the academic criminal justice movement seen in the context of police training and education. Some may disagree with law enforcement education as the genesis of academic criminal justice, but the historic evidence and lineage are indisputable.

PROGRESSIVISM

The industrial and urban developments of the post-Civil War era had dislodged and disrupted many traditional values in America. Old elites felt displaced and out of control as "robber baron" industrialists and political bosses held sway. Many workers tried to gain some control over their lives through the organized labor movement. Farmers did much the same through the Grange and Populist parties. Lower-class urban dwellers attached themselves to the political machine. In those labor and agricultural movements the middle class had few places. And in America the rise, power, and exertions of the middle class are closely connected to agencies and activities of criminal justice. In short middle class professionals or a variety of specialists just outside the professional ranks became the bedrock of progressivism.[1]

Progressivism got its earliest start on the local level, moving next to the state and federal realms. Taking cues from Lincoln Steffens's *The Shame of the Cities*, municipal reformers attempted to wrest control of their city governments from the political machines, reorganize city government along "scientific" lines, and use government as a means of economic and social reform. Tom Johnson and Newton D. Baker, for example, made Cleveland one of the best-governed cities in America. Other reform mayors, however, found themselves powerless because trails of power and corruption led to the state capitals. Joseph W. Folk, mayor of St. Louis, was stymied until he became governor and broke boss rule statewide. Hiram Johnson of California, Robert M. LaFollette of Wisconsin, Charles Evans Hughes of New York, and Woodrow Wilson of New Jersey likewise worked to purge their states of corruption. Initiative and referendum were invented to circumvent reactionary state legislatures, direct primaries were pushed to stop boss selection of political candidates, and female suffrage was supported to bring purity to politics. When national problems were exposed by muckraking literature (written by such people as Ida Tarbell, David Graham Phillips, Lincoln Steffens, and Upton Sinclair), aggressive presidents like Theodore Roosevelt and Woodrow Wilson brought progressivism to the federal level.[2]

Actually there were many progressive movements. Nonetheless, two convictions were commonly shared. First, it was believed that special interests had held too much power for too long, and the people (i.e., the middle classes) needed to assume greater authority.

Hence the "trust-busting" activity of Theodore Roosevelt, William Howard Taft, and Woodrow Wilson. Second, the new middle-class government needed to be stronger and more active in serving the public welfare. Hence laws regulating the working hours of women and children, and crusades against vice.

In addition, a definite mindset gained prominence that became a long-lasting legacy of the Progressives. Fundamental to progressive thinking was the belief that organizations did not live apart from the humans who constituted them or who were serviced by them. Of course, the very personalized boss machines of the nineteenth century did too. Now, however, the person in the organization needed to be an expert. Expertise became panacea. Herman Metz, a reformer and comptroller of New York City, articulated well the Progressive position: "The practical man knows *how*. The scientific man knows *why*. The expert knows *how* and *why*."[3] A well-trained expert staff might uplift any organization in particular and society in general. The organization should be divided into areas of expertise, bureaus of skilled specialists, and be led by a "public man" who oversaw and directed the bureaucracy and educated the wider public on the necessity and beneficence of the organization. Above all the "public man," the bureaucrats, and the organization must be efficient.

At no time in American history had people been so enamored with the concept of efficiency. In 1895 Frederick W. Taylor ushered in the "scientific management" movement with a paper, "A Piece-Rate System: Being a Step Toward a Partial Solution of the Labor Problem," presented before the American Society of Mechanical Engineers. By 1911, with the publication of *The Principles of Scientific Management*, Taylor was the darling of the Progressives. It was thought that all organizations and processes should be taylorized, a process totally impossible until the principles of nonpartisanship, strong executive leadership, and the separation of politics from administration were attained. And of course, those were the goals of progressivism.[4]

In terms of the agencies of criminal justice (corrections, courts, and police), the progressive ideas held out considerable promise. The earliest applications of the progressive design occurred in the rise of the juvenile court, probation, and parole.[5] But there existed no clearer example of organization in need of reform during the early twentieth century than the police.

POLICE AND PROGRESSIVISM

With rare exception the history of policing nineteenth-century America was characterized by corruption, inefficiency, and partisan politics. But Cincinnati was different, and genuine attempts at reform occurred there as early as 1886. Due to a political scandal, Philip M. Dietsch came to power as a reform chief and quickly put the police department on a military basis. A short-lived Police School requiring 72 hours of instruction for all officers was inaugurated in 1887. Such reform lasted until the "do-gooders" were turned out and the old "politicos" were restored. Some 25 years went by before other departments began to follow the Cincinnati model.

Generally, police personnel viewed their occupation as a job and not a career. Occasional fraternal and "benefit" societies sprung up, but even the largest—the New York Benevolent Association, established in 1891—-had little impact. Patrolmen on the beat continued to exercise enormous discretion with no formal training and little organizational control. Police chiefs, who were largely figure-heads or politicians, deferred much power and authority to captains and ward bosses at the precinct level. Big-city policing, then, was largely feudalism.

It was during the Progressive Era, with chiefs having more monarchial designs, that the modern era of policing began. Police chiefs sought to gain control of their own organizations and in so doing invented the idea of professionalism. By this they meant managerial efficiency and control, achieved in part by more compliant, more effective subordinates. Police training and education now seemed more relevant and important.[6]

Some attempts at forming a national organization of police chiefs had been made in St. Louis in 1871. However, it was not until 1893, when a group of police chiefs met in Chicago to form the National Police Chiefs Union, that police administrators institutionalized a growing professional consciousness. The organization was primarily a social group until 1901 when Richard Sylvester, police chief of Washington, D.C., took over. Sylvester directed the organization, now known as the International Association of Chiefs of Police (IACP), until 1915 and turned it from an assembly of cronies to that of a forum for serious debates. For example, the IACP was in the forefront of pressuring police departments to adopt the Bertillon and, later, the fingerprinting identification systems. In addition, Congress was lobbied to create a national bureau of identification. Concern over the portrayal of crime and crime fighting in the infant motion picture industry led to endless discussions on the "Keystone Cop" phenomenon. Considerable anxiety and self-examination arose over police brutality, expressed as the "third degree" issue. Although a magazine, *The Detective*, and the annual proceedings were already published, a move to establish an official journal began. Clearly, the earliest attempts at professionalism came from administrators looking for administrative solutions to problems facing the police, a development that would get further impetus and support during the Progressive Era.[7]

Police training fit very nicely into the Progressive perspective. Once the chiefs gained some control over hiring officers, a process that grew rapidly from 1915 to 1920 with emergent civil service principles, the subordinates needed to be made "experts." The pool of prospective employees had never been great. In the past, political affiliation and loyalty had been more important than physical and mental qualities. One study of aspirants for police positions in San Jose, California, in 1917 found that only 3 out of 30 had I.Q.s over 100.[8] Twenty years later a sociologist expressed the opinion that 75 percent of all American police officers were unfit for their work.[9] In fact, in an early expression of the Peter Principle, it was claimed that the better officers left policing early, leaving the less fit to move up the bureaucratic ladder.[10] Nonetheless, Progressive police chiefs wanted to impose their standards on their subordinates. Thus middle-class reforms—efficiency, professionalism, and education—were to be thrust upon the working classes. In a trickle-down process, chiefs and other managers would modernize procedures and operations, in hope of improving police activity on the streets.

Other developments paved the way for police reform during the Progressive Era. A Bureau of Municipal Research was organized in 1906, and until 1921 (when it became the National Institute of Public Administration) it conducted numerous studies "evaluating" police departments against the standards of Frederick W. Taylor and the gospel of efficiency. Between 1913 and 1921 seventeen major city police departments were examined. This became the favored research technique for many progressive chiefs and "college cops," mixing research with the utility of evaluation. Early writers such as Leonard Fuld and Raymond Fosdick created models of research as well.

Change was slow and spotty in spite of the IACP and the Bureau of Municipal Research. Much policing during the Progressive era remained decidedly unprogressive.

But one exception was Philadelphia. During the first decade of the twentieth century the City of Brotherly Love was thought to be one of the most corrupt places in America. It was one of the more shameful cities described by Lincoln Steffens in *The Shame of the Cities*. In 1911 a reform mayor, Rudolph Blankenburg, came to power. He appointed George D. Porter director of public safety and James Robinson superintendent of police. This triumvirate set out to remodel the police department along military lines. A patrolman's manual was published and made required reading in the recently established School of Instruction. Four week-long courses were set up for all recruits, and both written and oral examinations were required at the end of the session. In addition, weekly quizzes on the patrolman's manual were conducted at the precinct station houses. The two-platoon system, in which an officer was required to serve 18.5 hours street duty and 11.5 reserve duty, gave way to a three-platoon system. Officers now had an 8-hour shift, and officials claimed that crime rates went down after this reform. Prohibitions against political activity were instituted as well. After the department was made administratively "sound," officers were used as agents of reform and a crusade against vice resulted. The golden age of police progressivism in Philadelphia occurred between 1911 and World War I. Most of the reforms were undone by a new chief, Smedley D. Butler, in the 1920s. For example, the School of Instruction, was unhesitatingly abolished and officers were told to learn their job on the job. But by that time attention was turning to California and the work of another reform police chief, who became the father of the police education movement.[11] His legacy was more long-lasting.

AUGUST VOLLMER

August Vollmer was born in New Orleans to German parents in 1876. When his father died in 1884 the family moved back to Germany but returned to Louisiana two years later. Vollmer then received his formal and formative education at a vocational school in New Orleans, learning bookkeeping, shorthand, and typing. Concern over the wide-open permissive nature of New Orleans apparently compelled the Vollmers to move to the quiet and respectable university town of Berkeley, California, in the 1890s, where "Gus" opened a coal and feed store. Vollmer spent one year in the Philippines during the Spanish-American War as a military policeman. By 1900 he was back in Berkeley working as a letter carrier. There is some evidence to suggest that he became something of a celebrity in 1904 for his dramatic prevention of a train wreck. Such notoriety, plus his hard-working and honest character, did not go unnoticed. In 1905 he was prevailed upon to run for the office of city marshal, a successful feat he duplicated in 1907. When Berkeley created a police department in 1909 Vollmer was made chief, a position he held until 1932.[12]

Shortly after Vollmer became city marshal the political machine of Abe Reuff in San Francisco was caught up in scandals that brought it down, vividly demonstrating the dangers of politics in city government.[13] Of course, Berkeley was not San Francisco or even nearby Oakland. In fact, those two neighboring cities siphoned off much vice and crime, acting as negative models of urban living. Berkeley remained an island of respectability and intellectual liberalism (a perfect, if not artificial, environment) in which experiments in progressive policing could occur. In these formative days Vollmer may have been more of reflector of his environment than a formulator of police policy. The fact that community expectations, heavily dominated by the University of California, acted as a catalyst for his reforms has been overlooked.[14]

As chief Vollmer instituted several reforms that placed him in the tradition of the progressive chiefs in the IACP. His deputies were given bicycles for greater mobility and speed in making their rounds. To decrease response time and increase administrative control, an electric alarm system was introduced. Clarence D. Lee, formerly a secretary in a San Francisco business, became one of Vollmer's officers and reformed the record-keeping activities of the department.[15]

In 1908 Vollmer opened a police academy with Walter Peterson, an officer from the Oakland police department. They taught police methods to the Berkeley officers. By 1911, according to Vollmer's report to the mayor and city council, six subjects were required of personnel: first aid, knowledge of state laws and city ordinances, principles and rules of evidence (two separate courses), treatment of juvenile cases, and the rights and duties of witnesses.[16] This was one year before Philadelphia's School of Instruction was set up, in effect making Vollmer the father of the police academy movement.

Professors at the University of California, where president Benjamin Ide Wheeler held sway with his expansive ambitions and practical orientation, also saw how their ideas might be put to use in the "real" world. A. M. Kidd, a professor in the law school, joined Vollmer to teach criminal evidence. William Helms, a parasitologist, taught sanitation law. Then, in 1916 Vollmer established a formal relationship with the university by offering a series of courses for his officers during summer sessions.[17]

The summer-session arrangement with the university, which lasted throughout the 1920s, marked an early phase of Vollmer's thinking about education. The lines between training (as found in his police school at the station) and education (as found in the university) were blurry, both for Vollmer and for the educators and administrators at the university. Indeed, they remained so for generations to come.

In 1917 Vollmer and Albert Schneider, a professor of pharmacology and bacteriology at the university, set forth a plan for a police school. It was at the same time that Progressives in Washington had passed a law subsidizing vocational training in secondary schools. Perhaps Vollmer and Schneider were anticipating the extension of such support to higher education as well, which indeed occurred in the 1930s. At this point their planned school at the university was limited to in-service people, those currently working as police officers. A tentative list of fourteen faculty members was created, all of whom (with the exception of Vollmer) were connected to the university.

Much has been made of Vollmer as the father of police education, and his contribution must not be discounted, but the sympathetic position of the university president and the cooperativeness of the faculty were instrumental. Vollmer's level of education, which he obtained in a vocational school in New Orleans, probably made him unduly respectful—if not awestruck—of the prompting of the professors and administrators at the university. In short, the earliest beginnings of police education at Berkeley were more an act of academic politics than a visionary invention of Vollmer. Proposed courses in physics, chemistry, and biology indicate the input and impact of the professors. Police organization and procedures were a minor part of the plan. The world war got in the way, however, draining attention, energy, and resources. The proposed police school died in the breech in 1919 and any further curricular experimentation had to await the 1930s.[18]

Vollmer built his reputation as a police reformer throughout the 1920s. With considerable rapidity he attained national stature. The modernization of the Berkeley police department continued. A fingerprinting system, handwriting classification scheme, and early polygraph apparatus were introduced in 1921. Vollmer installed the first aluminum street markers in America in 1924. Two years later a study of a more efficient distribution of patrolmen on their beats was under way.

Vollmer became president of the International Association of Chiefs of Police in 1922 and used this position to articulate his ideas on progressive policing. He spoke out for more modern equipment in policing (surely the 1920s was a time of technological revolution for policing), a greater emphasis on crime prevention, and a more sophisticated system of record keeping. Not only were more police academies and schools needed but so were universities to study criminal behavior. In other ways, however, Vollmer was out of step with many chiefs. Raising recruitment standards of police officers was easier in the Berkeleys of America than in the Chicagos. Using European models of police professionalism, Vollmer's advocacy of lateral entry—with command officers achieving positions without going up through the ranks—fell on deaf ears.[19]

So far, Vollmer had been mainly interested in providing training and education to those in his police department. One shift in his thinking occurred in the 1920s as he began to advertise in the university newspaper for college students to come to work for the police. Some of these "college cops" were George Brereton, William F. Dean (who later achieved fame as a general in the Korean War), Walter A. Gordon, John D. Holstrom (who later became the Berekley chief of police) V. A. Leonard, William Wiltberger, and Orlando Wilson. V. A. Leonard remembered that the entrance examination for the department was harder than any he took on campus. Other "college cops" proved that education was not necessarily a panacea, as some turned out to be incompetent. Leonard recalled that the person testing highest in his group lasted only a few weeks on the job. He did not like doing "dirty duty" and felt he knew more than his superior officers (this may point out a basic problem with highly educated, intelligent people doing menial tasks). Of course, most of the "V-Men," as they called themselves, were college students working their way through school. The police professionalizers had to convince their personnel as well as the public that policing was indeed a profession.[20] Nonetheless, a majority of the students turned cops worked out well enough—some even making dramatic career changes due to the experience—to give Vollmer and his followers confidence. Increasingly, they felt that by coupling training and education individual officers would do better work and, most important, the occupation would be elevated into a profession.[21]

Perhaps taking cues from the Bureau of Municipal Research, Vollmer conducted numerous survey studies of police departments throughout the 1920s. In those days such surveys were the chief research of the would-be police scholar. More important, they provided an opportunity to spread the gospel of police professionalism. As early as 1915 Vollmer conducted a study of the San Diego police department. Studies of New Haven (1926), Chicago (1927), Kansas City, Missouri (1928), Minneapolis (1930), and Gary, Indiana (1930), followed. Vollmer spent a year as chief of the Los Angeles police department, where he reorganized and modernized its administration. A police school within the department was soon set up. Ties to the University of Southern California were established and courses on police administration were given in the extension division. On the whole, however, the time in Los Angeles was frustrating for Vollmer as politics and corruption would not go down. The uniqueness of Berkeley was proved, and Vollmer eagerly returned to northern California in 1924.[22]

Due to his growing reputation as an expert on policing, Vollmer was selected in 1929 to work on the National Commission on Law Observance and Enforcement, commonly called the Wickersham Commission. Much of the work was to be done in Chicago, a place already familiar to him through his survey of its police department two years earlier. Charles Merriam, always eager to build up his academic empire, offered Vollmer a place in the political science department at the University of Chicago. Vollmer represented an enlightened practitioner who could add luster to the department by embodying Merriam's ideas of proper and practical political science. Merriam even supplied two research assistants from the political science department, David Monroe and Earle Garrett, to help prepare Vollmer's monograph on law enforcement in America.

Merriam, however, did not want to establish a police school. In fact, he was not interested in having Vollmer lecture to students, although a small seminar was established. Instead, Merriam wanted "to put the university in the position where it can act, on request, in a consulting capacity on police matters." But, in thinly disguised promises that encouraged Vollmer, Merriam felt that the University of Chicago might become "a great center for the scientific study of police work, with the whole country as our field of action." New and better police methods would result because "a great research institution can make a real contribution to actual problems if it has the right personnel."[23] All this fit into Merriam's growing interest in policy approaches to political science. But such promises did not materialize, and Vollmer left in 1931 exhilarated with ostensibly sympathetic scholars like Merriam, Ernest Burgess, Herman Adler, and Raymond Moley.

During his time in Chicago, Vollmer helped organize the Regional Peace Officers Association, the Illinois State Identification Bureau, and the Chicago Academy of Criminology. In addition, he inspired several students who went on to form the Council of Police Science at the University of Chicago. It was made up of numerous Chicago policemen and regular students (as well as faculty members like Edwin Sutherland from sociology and Leonard White from political science) who were still hopeful that Chicago would become a center for police students.[24]

In some ways the Traffic Institute program at Northwestern University modestly tried to fill that role when it was established in 1933, but soon the University of Chicago abandoned its experiment with police studies. One of Vollmer's disciples, William Wiltberger, was in Chicago at the time and was angry over the fickle nature of the University of Chicago. "I am really surprised at that Chicago University bunch," he wrote in 1932.

> I am convinced that they are not as much the friend of the police officer as they profess to be. I have not had any talks with [Leonard] White or [Charles] Merriam but I have with the rest of them down there and I have found they "know" all about the police and crime game. They seem to have nothing but criticism even for the best which is being done by the profession. They think that Social Work should be in the foreground and the crime agencies in the background.
> Well it is the old story which you know better than I do. It is the old stigma of the Administration of Criminal Justice profession no matter how it progresses.[25]

Shortly after his return to Berkeley, Vollmer retired from the police department and took a long working vacation throughout Europe. In the meantime the Wickersham reports were published, adding to Vollmer's credibility as one of America's leading police personalities.

Actually the Wickersham reports—though they comprehensively covered crime, police, courts, and corrections—dichotomized policing. A popular version of one of the reports, *Our Lawless Police*, pointed to the problems of police brutality. It was largely negative and critical. The crime-infested 1920s suggested the inability of police as presently constituted to prevent crime. On the other hand, Vollmer's *The Police* was a restatement of his progressive ideas. It was more upbeat and positive. In response to the Wickersham reports, the Rockefeller Foundation in the early 1930s granted the

Bureau of Public Administration and the political science department at the University of California funds to further develop police studies.[26] Very early, then, the political science discipline was laying academic claim to police education. However, as would happen for the next forty years, semantics got in the way and for lack of a better word the police science offerings were often labeled "criminology." This simple act opened all kinds of political battles with sociology.

During the fall of 1933 a group of Berkeley faculty members (A. M. Kidd of the law school and Herman Adler seemed to be the leaders) met to develop the criminology offerings. Not only the stature of Vollmer but also the economic Depression was having an impact. On one hand, fewer students could afford to go to the university. Adding another timely field of study might entice enrollments. On the other hand, jobs were so scarce that people who might not otherwise enter or continue college might attend for lack of alternatives. In these times of job scarcity students were even more job-sensitive, thus making police science inherently attractive. Then there was policing itself. Traditionally policing was a working-class occupation, appealing to people who were not overly concerned about schooling or ideas of professionalism. Now, with other more attractive jobs drying up due to the Depression, there was a middle-class labor pool available that might be more receptive to entering police work and clamoring for greater status. For example, in 1940 it was reported that more than half of the 300 police recruits in New York City had college degrees.[27]

A four-fold program resulted at the University of California. The "criminology with emphasis on the technical aspects" was relegated to Vollmer, who became a professor of police administration in the political science department from 1931 to 1937. Vollmer's elevation, a political act in itself, suggests the importance of real life experiences over academic credentials in an earlier era. Kidd taught the "legal aspects" and Adler the "social aspects." An Institute of Criminology was contemplated, but had to await a better economic situation.[28] In the meantime, Vollmer began to build an academic career. More police surveys quickly followed: Santa Barbara (1934), Portland, Oregon (1934) and Piedmont, California (1935), were studied at this time. *Crime and the State Police*, a study done with Alfred Parker, was published in 1935. In next year Vollmer's principal work, *The Police and Modern Society*, appeared.

By attaching himself so closely to the academics, Vollmer lost some support from the police ranks. Thomas

Hunter, one of his early students who graduated in 1935, remembered "derogatory comments from unenlightened law enforcement people attributing [Vollmer's] efforts to mere publicity grabbing."[29] Certainly, Vollmer's ideas had changed. Training was still important and police academies within police departments remained essential. But now that he was an educator, college education assumed greater importance for him. He was not always clear on what form that education should take; some disciples went out with a general idea and created programs unique to their college environments and their individual interpretation of Vollmer. It seems, however, that Vollmer wanted a professional school, something like those for medicine and law. In this way the police would become true professionals at least at the upper and mid-administrative levels. Of course, a hidden agenda (one not even clear to Vollmer but soon to come anyway) was the creation of an academic profession: professors of police science. Several V-Men went out and created police programs elsewhere, thereby forging a new academic discipline and profession.[30] None of these disciples was closer to Vollmer in intellect and attitude, than O. W. Wilson.

ORLANDO W. WILSON

Wilson was born to strict Norwegian parents in Veblen, South Dakota, in 1900. The family moved to California and Wilson went through the San Diego educational system before attending the University of California to study engineering in 1918. Family financial difficulties soon forced Wilson to look for work, and he landed a job with the Berkeley police department from 1921 to 1925. Due to problems with engineering, Wilson switched to economics and after graduating in 1925 set out to find work in the business world. Policing at this point in his life was a means to an end. August Vollmer had other ideas, however, and he pressured Wilson in the fall of 1925 to take a job in Orange County, California, as chief of the Fullerton police department. It was a disaster[31]

The Fullerton department was small, having only seven officers and an operating budget of $27,500. Mimicking Vollmer, Wilson quickly put reforms into in place. A crime reporting system was inaugurated, the two police cars were removed and a policy of paying officers to use their own cars was started, and an in-service training session for personnel was begun. In short, Wilson tried to transplant Berkeley to Fullerton, a process that was not successful. In addition, Wilson's public relations with the town were not good. Several of his speeches to civic-minded groups seemed too liberal, if not radical. The five-member standing committee in charge of overseeing the police department responded to public pressure and asked Wilson to resign in December 1925. He had held the job for only three months.[32]

Disillusioned with police administration, Wilson remained in the Los Angeles area for the next three years working for the Pacific Finance Corporation. In 1928 Vollmer convinced him to try policing once again, this time in Kansas. Wichita, Kansas, was for Wilson what Berkeley was for Vollmer. It was there, between 1928 and 1939, that Wilson salvaged a police department and his own reputation. First he cleansed the force of corruption; over 20 percent of the personnel left during the first year. In the name of efficiency, and to further break any chances of subculture collusion among the officers, Wilson introduced a principle for which he would be associated for years: the use of one-man rather than two-man patrol cars. In keeping with his Vollmerian notions of professionalism, he drew up a "square deal code," a code of ethics that his biographer thinks was the legitimate source of the IACP's "Law Enforcement Code of Ethics" which appeared in 1952. But certain steps indicated that he and Vollmer did not agree on everything. Wilson was much more impressed with the military model of policing than was Vollmer, and the Wichita police soon appeared in more army-like garb. Appropriately enough, however, his greatest innovations were in police training and education. This compelled Wilson's biographer, with some exaggeration, to call Wichita the "West Point of Law Enforcement."[33]

Very early Wilson instituted an in-service program that eventually expanded to six weeks of instruction. In addition, on each shift one-half hour before the men went on the streets there was "roll call training." To signal the seriousness of such activity, weekly quizzes were given in the squad room. Like Vollmer at Berkeley, Wilson made use of nearby colleges to give the officer courses that were not readily available in the academy format. It seemed to Wilson that the most needed courses (criminal law, evidence, criminal investigation, identification procedures, patrol practices, traffic control, and police administration) appropriately belonged to the political science discipline, and he got them adopted in that department at the Municipal University of Wichita (later called Wichita State University) in 1936. He then developed a police cadet program, which allowed nonpolice (or pre-service) students taking those courses to work part-time for the

Wichita police department.[34]

Loyal to the progressive agenda, Wilson began a crusade against vice as soon as the department was reformed. Bootleggers, gamblers, and prostitutes were driven out of the city. Many civic leaders (possibly patrons of the vice lords) felt the chief was too aggressive and uncompromising. By 1938 considerable support existed among city commissioners to rid the city of Wilson. At threats to cut his salary, terminate numerous reforms, and appoint disloyal subordinates to key positions Wilson was convinced that politics and policing were mixing to his disadvantage. To clear the air and gain some personal bearings he took a year's leave of absence and moved to Chicago in 1939 to act as consultant for the National Institute of Public Administration. Taking cues from his mentor, August Vollmer, while in Chicago Wilson conducted police surveys of Peoria, Illinois; Hartford, Connecticut; Huntington, West Virginia; and San Antonio, Texas, before a call came from Berkeley.[35]

August Vollmer retired from the University of California's political science department in 1937. David Barrow, chairman of the department, and A. M. Kidd wanted not only to keep the police studies component alive but also to expand it. With the support of the university president, Robert Sproul, Vollmer's few courses in the political science department became a full major in 1939. The "group major" idea—an emphasis within a host department or discipline, which had characterized the offerings in the university throughout the 1930s—was abandoned in favor of a freestanding department status. This was a significant development, and it testifies to the academic political skills of Vollmer. More importantly, it suggests the power of his professorial brethren at Berkeley.

With Vollmer's lobbying it was agreed that the likeliest candidate to head the new department would be Orlando Wilson, who accepted the position and moved to Berkeley in the summer of 1939. In the fall of that year Wilson, A. M. Kidd, and Paul Kirk set forth their "recommendations for the development of a criminology program" at the university. The foundation course of the program would be "principles and problems of criminology," an academic course similar to that being developed by people like Edwin Sutherland in which the theories of criminology and the agencies of criminal justice would be woven into an integrated whole. This was to be followed by "investigation and identification," taught by Wilson. "Public safety," a traffic engineering course, acknowledged the importance of the automobile in policing. "Legal relations," a history of criminal law with discussions on the tricky issues of search and seizure, would be taught by Kidd. "Criminological microscopy" and "forensic medicine and toxicology" showed the importance of criminalistics (a phrase coined by Paul Kirk for science as a part of the investigative process) in policing. Finally, "criminal psychology and psychiatry" rounded out the recommended program.[36]

CONCLUSION

Although modern policing arose in the mid-nineteenth century, it went through a politicized period until the Progressive era. The founding of the International Association of Chiefs of Police (IACP), in 1893, marked the beginning of the professionalization of police leaders. The general social and political climate of progressivism lent support to their movement. They in turn created a new ideal of policing, one in which the mission of policing shifted from maintaining order to fighting crime. These new professionalizers—most notably August Vollmer in Berkeley, California—introduced the police academy and police higher education as essential in their own professionalization. Vollmer was the first and most successful in making law enforcement a field of inquiry in higher education. But the university environment at Berkeley, particularly its administrative ranks, must not be dismissed. Henceforth, criminal justice (or criminology, as it was initially called) would depend upon the kindness of such strangers. By 1940 Vollmer had his favorite student and a fleshed-out program in place at the University of California. But World War II temporarily stalled developments at Berkeley. In the meantime other V-Men were finding places and developing police science programs along lines they felt were in keeping with the Vollmer model.

Chapter 3

V-Men and Models of Police Education, 1935–1950

It would be wrong to think that all meaningful developments in police education occurred only in California. Wichita State's program, begun by O. W. Wilson, continued modestly. As interest waned (or changed substantially) at the University of Chicago, it increased at Northwestern's Traffic Institute after 1933. Edwin Sutherland and James Robinson consulted with O. W. Wilson about a possible police science course at Indiana University in 1936.[1] In that same year the universities of Alabama, Washington, Harvard, and Purdue began offering two or three courses in policing.[2] During the next year, Frank Boolsen, a Vollmer protégé, was at the University of Toledo.[3] Perhaps one of the most important developments outside California in these early years was in Michigan.

Oscar G. Olander, head of the state police in Michigan, had been familiar with Vollmer's ideas and pressured for a police school in the 1920s. One was finally started in 1930 but succumbed to the Depression three years later. Olander continued his crusade, however. In addition, LeMoyne Snyder, whose father had been president of Michigan State College from 1896 to 1915, was a medico-legal adviser for the state police. He was interested in a training mechanism for those interested in forensics, or science as applied to criminal investigation and legal matters. Finally, Donald Bremer as head of the Michigan State College police used his personal friendship with the school president as leverage for the promotion of a police program. Furthermore, Michigan State College was a land grant college, one given money from the federal government to offer the more technical and mechanical sciences. It seemed an appropriate place for experimenting in vocational training of police officers.

In the fall of 1935 the police administration program was begun with 39 students enrolled. With the exception of one lawyer and one medical doctor, the courses were taught by state police personnel. Students concentrated in the physical sciences, with a required four years of military training (there was an active ROTC, or reserve officer training corps, at the college). Arthur Brandstatter, one of the first generation of students in the program, was especially impressed with the eighteen-month "field training" that followed the study on campus.[4] One historian of this field of study would claim that "from 1935 until World War II, the Police Administration Program was the closest approximation to a police West Point program ever to be developed in the United States."[5] Vollmer was ambivalent, as can be seen by his response to similar innovations being developed by one of his disciples in California.

WILLIAM WILTBERGER AT SAN JOSE, CALIFORNIA

The California state college system was taking form during the late 1920s and early 1930s. The first so-called Normal School in California (a school mainly for the teaching of future teachers) opened in San Francisco in 1857 but was moved to San Jose—about 50 miles to the south—in 1871 to protect the predominantly female student body from the evils of the big city. A branch of the California State Normal School at San Jose was established in Los Angeles 10 years later, and it soon became the Los Angeles State Normal School, then later UCLA. Another branch was opened in Chico in 1887. By the turn of the century independent state normal schools were at San Diego and San Francisco. Santa Barbara's State Normal School of Manual Arts and Home Economics was opened in 1909. Fresno and Humboldt followed shortly thereafter. By 1921 there were seven state normal schools in California when the legislature renamed them all as state teacher colleges and allowed them to give baccalaureate degrees. In 1935 the word "teachers" was dropped from the titles and the state college system was born.[6]

Dropping the word "teacher" from the college letterhead, however, did not change the central focus. Throughout the 1930s the schools remained trainers of teachers. But in doing so they took on a curricular profile quite different from the main research universities such as the University of California. Since so many students were preparing to teach in high schools, these colleges began offering areas most likely to be found in secondary education, some of them with a very vocational orientation. Art, commerce, English, home economics, industrial arts, mathematics, modern languages, natural science, physical education, social science, and speech began to appear. Although a few were found in the university, most were unique to the state college system.[7]

In addition, these colleges were different demographically. First, as university tuition became too expensive for most during the Depression, many students chose state college over university training. This caused a boom in student population in the teachers colleges. Second, they were self-styled "people's colleges" with no barriers to admission. All one needed was evidence of high school graduation, and that was waived if one was over 21 years of age. In addition, several state colleges (e.g., Fresno and San Jose) had junior colleges connected to their campuses. Funding for state colleges came from the state, and there might be certain limitations in experimenting with curricula. On the other hand, junior colleges were financed from local sources and had considerable leeway in developing programs.[8]

The junior colleges were a spinoff of the same process that was making the universities research institutions. The junior college idea originated among the German-trained academics of the late nineteenth and early twentieth century, who saw the first two years of college as being more closely akin to secondary education than to the more research-oriented universities. Unsuccessful attempts were made at the universities of Michigan, Minnesota, and Pennsylvania to draw clearer distinctions between the first and last two years of college education, but William Rainey Harper at the newly formed University of Chicago was most successful. Harper divided the undergraduate program into Senior College and Junior College in the late 1890s. The Senior College was closely affiliated with the graduate school. Although it was affixed to the university, the Junior College at the University of Chicago had its own faculty, curriculum, and student government. With such a model it was small wonder that Illinois was one of the first to form a distinct two-year college, the Joliet Junior College, in 1902.[9]

The philosophy behind the junior college movement was to offer programs unique to the needs of the community. Therefore many vocational courses, otherwise not found in the university, found a home in the junior college. Most were "terminal," or not transferring to the university. The lines were clear: there were some transferable courses in the junior college so that students could move on to a four-year institution, but greater legitimacy of pure vocationalism existed there. And the university laid claim to more academic research programs, but was unsure where the line might be drawn between a professional and a vocational program. In between was the state college.[10]

In the western states the state colleges had a more active role and greater impact on the future of education. One college president, Wilson Compton of Washington State College, described this environment later:

> If on the Atlantic Coast one were to ask,"which are the leading colleges and universities?" the list would be rather long before it included any except private institutions. In the middle West the list would be more evenly divided. The further west one goes, the more dominate becomes the place of the state colleges and universities.[11]

In the formative years the junior college closely connected to a state college did give the ambitious college president great opportunity in bringing new programs to his campus. San Jose State was particularly bold in developing two-year technical courses in ceramics, commercial art, interior decorating, accounting, merchandising, secretarial work, child training, costume design, homemaking, drafting, aeronautics, photography, radio engineering, and journalism. Of course, police science too.[12]

In addition, a "mission" was developing that was quite different from that found in the university, something that would later haunt Vollmer and the V-Men. In 1936 the George-Dean Act supplemented the earlier Smith-Hughes Act and expanded federal money to vocational education in colleges. Many colleges, ever ready to cash in on federal largess, began offering vocational education for selected "semi-professions." Although the universities had to maintain the academic standards of scholarship and research, "the state college, closely in touch with the activities and needs of its community [began] to provide training for newer types of employment."[13]

As early as 1924 the California Crime Commission had studied the problems of crime in the state and the weaknesses of its existing crime-fighting organizations. One of its recommendations was that the State Bureau of Criminal Identification and Investigation arrange for police schools to upgrade personnel. This became law in 1929. T. W. MacQuarrie, president of San Jose State, came under enormous pressure from Vollmer and Earl Warren (at that time the prosecutor of Alameda County, in which Oakland and Berkeley were located) after the law's passage. In 1931 a two-year program was established at San Jose State with George Brereton, one of Vollmer's students and "college cops" in the Berkeley police department, chosen to head the experiment.[14]

The early days of the program at San Jose reflected Vollmer's ideas and Brereton's inclinations. Although Brereton was a member of Vollmer's cadre of college cops, he had received his education in history, even getting a master's degree in that discipline in 1926. He was working on a doctorate in history when the call came from San Jose. In fact, his favorite course at San Jose would be history of policing. Brereton wanted a mix of academic and practical courses because his program was "not planned to develop specialists in any one of the more technical fields, but rather to instruct the basic elements of the profession."[15] Others disagreed.

By the 1930s a California Plan for Peace Officer Training had been developed by the governor. Instrumental in establishing this plan was John C. Berwick, chief of the Bureau of Trade and Industrial Education in the California Department of Education. Before the annual convention of the California Peace Officers Association in 1936, Berwick questioned the value of existing textbooks and courses in criminology. Such "dead stuff" should be avoided, he maintained. Practitioners must be in complete control so that "the academically trained schoolmaster does not try to teach our boys a lot of 'cold storage' knowledge that will be of no value to them in peace officer work," he asserted. Curriculum, therefore, should not come out of the colleges but out of the operating agencies.[16] Existing federal funds for vocational training were to be utilized to establish "zone schools" and technical institutes connected to the junior colleges throughout the state. In short, the more vocational aspects of police education were being relegated quite early to the junior college. Ironically, in 1938 Brereton was made the first Supervisor of Police Officer Training in charge of administrating these schools.[17] In the meantime his place at San Jose was being taken by a man who would have been far more comfortable heading up the more vocational-trainer aspects of police education. Indeed, William Wiltberger would soon restructure Brereton's program.

Wiltberger came to California from Illinois in 1920. He worked for three years in Vollmer's police department as he studied economics at the university. In 1923 he was back in Illinois working briefly with Herman Adler at the Illinois Institute for Juvenile Research and studying for a year at the University of Chicago. From 1925 to 1927 he was the chief of police at Evanston, home of Northwestern University just north of Chicago, where he tried to replicate Vollmer's reforms at Berkeley. Northwestern's dean of the law school and president of the university, John Wigmore and Walter Dill Scott, respectively, responded favorably to Wiltberger's suggestion that the International Association of Chiefs of Police use the Northwestern facilities each summer for a police school. The offer was held up in the IACP, however, and never came to fruition.[18] Genealogy was established, though, as Franklin Kreml, a founder and first director of the Northwestern Traffic Institute in the 1930s, was one of eighteen Northwestern students who began work for the police under Wiltberger.[19] By 1927 Wiltberger was back in Berkeley doing graduate work in political science at the University of California when he was called to St. Petersburg, Florida, to be Director of Public Safety. But politics forced him to resign that position in 1934; he quickly accepted the offer to take over Brereton's job at San Jose State.

In terms of police education, Wiltberger was one of Vollmer's more thoughtful and acerbic disciples. Before moving to San Jose, Wiltberger and Vollmer were in sync. For example, as early as 1931, when Vollmer was taking his place at the university and soliciting opinions on the ideal police curriculum, Wiltberger spoke up for the professional school model. "We need to bring together the contributions from all other fields and bring it together in its proper relationship," he declared in 1931. "And after all is said and done, I cannot see any other way out for a proper course in the whole field of Criminology than to have a School of Criminology such as we have of Law, Education, etc."[20] However, he advised his mentor two years later, "if we have to choose the curriculum fundamentals of another field, I would much rather choose the field of public administration."[21] In short, it was the police executive—and those who might aspire to be police managers—who should be the target population for police education. Of course, this opinion was aimed at the University of California and was given before Wiltberger moved to San Jose.

The lack of success of police education thus far, Wiltberger told a representative of the American Bar Association, was due to the fact that college and university presidents lacked interest and understanding of the problem.[22] As any aspiring academic politician might do, Wiltberger pledged to Vollmer that he was going to keep the college president, T. W. MacQuarrie, involved "because after all any school or department succeeds in special enterprises as much as the President is interested in the same."[23] This particular president was "a practical man, a vocational expert," Wiltberger acknowledged, and the history of the program would be impacted upon accordingly.[24] In this particular case police education was one of several weapons a college president would use to establish empire.

Another key figure at San Jose was John Black, the city chief of police. Black not only taught part-time at the school but provided students opportunities for practical experience in his department. In addition, Black did "all that he could within his power to sell the police school program to leaders in the community," declared Wiltberger. "This type of operation is necessary to the success of any police school training program in college."[25] Black also hired many of the graduates. In fact, for the year 1935-36 only San Jose junior college graduates were hired into his department.[26]

Such developments in San Jose seemed appropriate especially since they were in the context of the junior college. Then in 1935 the San Jose junior college and the state college combined facilities. This enabled the president, with sleight of hand, to allow federal money earmarked for the junior college to be used by the four-year institution. A baccalaureate degree was soon offered by the Police School. This arrangement would last, to the benefit of the Police School, until 1940 when the state attorney general, Earl Warren, forbade it and thereby drove the junior colleges and the state colleges apart.[27]

With the new school it became clear to Wiltberger that heretofore "everyone in this field [had] been groping in the dark."[28] As he saw it there were only two possible paths to follow. An educational institution could graduate people who knew the tasks and techniques of a job so that they could go out immediately and do it; or it could graduate people who were inadequately trained but who had an academic background in general education. Wiltberger chose the former over the latter, thereby establishing a model that I call the "Wiltbergerian model," replete with far-reaching ramifications for police education for decades to come.[29]

The threefold mission of any such police school, Wiltberger felt, should be to train people to do police work, to act as a placement service for its graduates, and to be a center of service for the various police departments in the area. He wanted to divorce this program from all the ordinary collegiate red tape.[30] To him the new school was to resemble a police department.[31] For example, the head of the school was to be a "director" so as "to get away from academic inference."[32] "It may be necessary for a policeman to bump his head at the University of California," he lectured Vollmer, "but not at the other colleges in this state." With the fervor of a fundamentalist prophet he proclaimed,"I am going ahead with this four-year program based entirely on the point of view of a training program for the policeman on the beat, and mark my word, it will go over in a very short time."[33]

In addition, he felt he had to distance his program from the social sciences. Earlier, while still working in Chicago, Wiltberger was asked to collect police exhibits for the Chicago World Fair to be held in the late 1930s. These exhibits, he was told, were to be located in the "social science" division of the fair. As he traveled the country talking to police officials, he found the phrase "social science" to be a liability. "It was necessary, in connection with this project in order to meet the ridicule which existed in the police field, to set up a distinctive police section and use the name police exhibits profusely." In fact, he felt one of the weaknesses of Vollmer's plan at Berkeley was a too close affiliation with the social scientists, because "policemen will not take to such training programs which bear the name of social science or social aspect."[34]

Curriculum in the new four-year police program was to be arranged around the functional divisions of a police department: patrol, identification, records, traffic, criminal investigation, and administration.[35] Admission to the school would be guided by the same criteria as that of recruitment into any police department. Since employment opportunities for women remained limited, in spite of the policewomen's movement of the Progressive era, females were not allowed into the school. Maximum age for entering students was twenty-eight. Minimum requirements for height (5'9") and weight (150 lb.) were the same as for most police departments; exceptions were made "only for those already in the service or those who can furnish a definite prospect of employment in police work." All prospective majors needed letters of recommendation from their local chiefs of police. Once they were admitted, students were to wear a uniform.[36]

Who should teach in such a school? Wiltberger understood the inefficient nature of the "school of hard knocks." And as an academic he could not deny the importance of traditional educators.[37] Nonetheless, instructors were to be selected on the basis of experience. Even for nonpolice courses such as law, direct experience was necessary. The best lawyers who might teach in the school, for example, should have practical experience in criminal justice agencies such as prosecutors' and defense attorneys' offices. "It is more important that emphasis be placed on the selection of qualified experts than upon the academic degrees they may hold," Wiltberger declared in 1937.[38]

Some curricular changes were needed as the two-year program became a four-year one. Wiltberger used what he called the "inverted approach," that is, teaching highly technical courses early and reserving the more academic ones for the last two years. This allowed the school to make the transition more easily from junior college status, where those courses were already set up, to the four-year program. The approach had several advantages, Wiltberger felt. It allowed those not ready for the rigors of regular college an opportunity to gain some experience, as they might have done in a junior college. Also, it offered a rude awakening to those enamored with the romance of crime and crime fighting by quickly introducing them to the more mundane aspects of police work. It also allowed the school the opportunity to obtain federal money for vocational education.[39]

Therefore, the first two years of the police school resembled the junior college offerings of a few years earlier. Two years of physical education were required. Considerable typing, report writing, and police gunnery were involved. In addition, a student patrol was set up to give students experience in policing at the college. Eventually field work at the local police department was required, because "we not only give the students theory, but plenty of actual practice in the field work and on the job," Wiltberger proudly proclaimed in 1935.[40]

It was in the upper division, the last two years of courses, that creative license was taken. At first, classes such as law and evidence, traffic, forensic chemistry, and police administration found a natural home. Existing academic courses, it seemed to Wiltberger, were filled with extraneous material. To have students take a variety of courses from the traditional disciplines, forming something like an interdisciplinary "group major," made it too difficult to fit in everything that the students needed. Wiltberger's solution was to change and adapt the traditional courses to the police field. The hard sciences were more easily adapted, and new courses such as "police chemistry" and "police physics" quickly found places in the curriculum. These were basic chemistry and physics courses with all the examples and problems geared to crime and criminal investigation. By definition, however, they had to be at the most elementary levels of science.

One of the most successful courses was public speaking. Such a course had been introduced earlier with mixed results. Now, however, in conjunction with the chairman of the public speaking department, Wiltberger created a public speaking course just for police officers. The chair of the public speaking department agreed "that this was the only practical approach to effectively teach police students the art of public speaking, which would be of the most value to them."[41] For a policeman to know what he needed in the other disciplines would require too many years of school, and Wiltberger would have none of that. "I have become so mad over trying to cram this work into four years that I am not going to attempt to fool any longer with the general academic work of courses in these fields," he wrote to Vollmer in 1936.[42] Courses in "police sociology" and "police psychology" did appear, but by far the curriculum was filled with specialized courses that had no academic precedent.

As Wiltberger's ideas emerged, he and Vollmer increasingly disagreed. But the emerging discipline (if it can be called that) was unchartered enough, and Vollmer was magnanimous enough, to allow for such differences of opinion. Like all pioneers trying to make sense of their mapless environment, they took license with the terrain. President T. W. MacQuarrie remained a strong supporter of the police school. In fact, in terms of academic politics the president was essentially dictating to Wiltberger. In a report made to the University of Minnesota on police training in 1937, MacQuarrie defended and praised that program.[43] But Wiltberger's teaching style was criticized; his defense revealed more about his ideas of police education.[44]

The fundamental problem, according to Wiltberger, was that many in the college simply did not understand or appreciate the unique attributes of vocational studies in academic settings. After he heard that students were lamenting his teaching techniques, Wiltberger complained that they were too "imbued with the big idea of note taking and organization of their notes from other academic instructors" and consequently failed to see the value of constant grilling. "Thus we have the old conflict between academic teaching, of covering a whole lot of points, and the vocational and police method of grounding men over and over in important or fundamental techniques so they are sure to have it," he declared self-assuredly. In a critique of Wiltberger's teaching, MacQuarrie had cautioned that "if we were going to put all police department methods in a college—it would be a police department school and not a college." Therein lay the rub, and Wiltberger, perhaps foreseeing the future as well as reflecting on the immediate past, felt as early as 1936 "that most of our troubles in the school had come from adhering too much to academic methods rather than vocational and pure police methods."[45]

Thus the Michigan State and, most importantly the San Jose State programs of police education were in place. The trainer-vocational model was to become very strong in the junior colleges and state colleges, particularly in California. On one hand, this model impacted several generations of police professors and practitioners. On the other, it bacame an obsticale to many professionalizers later as they tried to create a new academic discipline. In the meantime, while Wiltberger and his program faced a crisis as World War II neared, one more V-man was creating another model in the Pacific Northwest.[46]

V. A. LEONARD AND WASHINGTON STATE COLLEGE

Between 1925 and 1932 V. A. Leonard was a part-time student at the University of California and a full-time police officer in the Berkeley police department. In 1933 a mixture of economic and academic problems forced Leonard to return to his home in Texas where he spent a year working on a book, *The Police Communication System* (1937). He then settled into his new job as Superintendent of Identification in the Fort Worth police department. While he worked his way through the ranks in the police department, Leonard earned baccalaureate and master's degrees in criminology and public administration from Texas Wesleyan (1939) and Texas Christian (1940). In 1941 he applied for a position as chief of police in Pasadena, California. While anxiously awaiting a decision on that job, Leonard was approached by Vollmer and pressured to head a new police program at Washington State College in Pullman, Washington.

Competition between the University of Washington in Seattle and Washington State College in Pullman had always been keen and a bit one-sided. It was commonly accepted in Pullman that the academic community of the state wanted to keep Washington State College an agriculture experimental station and reserve the more scholarly education for the university.[47] President Earnest O. Holland, however, was of a different mind set. As president of Washington State College for nearly a quarter of a century, he became a possessive parent of the institution. Throughout the 1920s and 1930s he supervised the construction of forty buildings on campus. One aspect of his building program was the introduction of police science. Actually, the University of Washington had introduced some police courses in its political science department as early as 1936, even winning some praise from Wiltberger.[48] But it never grew beyond a few courses, and Holland felt he could easily upstage it. Shortly after August Vollmer suggested Leonard for the job, Holland started a publicity blitz and by September 1941 the entire Northwest was aware of a new police science curriculum at Washington State.[49] This was academic politics at the highest level.

The new program, called "police science and administration," received special attention from the "the prexy," as Holland was called by the faculty. From the beginning it was a freestanding program, situated in no other college or department, and Leonard was answerable only to the president.[50] Money and equipment flowed easily into Leonard's budget.[51]

The first term was spent designing the curriculum under the watchful and approving eye of Holland. By December 1941, five courses had been devised that reflected Leonard's model of police education. A crime lab course, "aspects of technological crime detection," was the first and easiest to set up. After all, the hard sciences continued to impress the early founders. To be so scientific was to gain easier access and acceptance in the academic community, it was felt. Shortly thereafter, a "police quarters" was under construction to house a chemistry laboratory and photography facilities. Later, Leonard would bring one of the original Keeler polygraphs to Pullman, eventually donating it to the Smithsonian. A course on communications, a favorite of Leonard's ever since he had written a book on the subject, and another on traffic control were introduced. "Social aspects of crime prevention" was a course on criminology that duplicated some offerings in the sociology department.[52]

It was the fifth course, "Police I," a general police administration course open to the general student population, that Leonard felt was his greatest innovation. Looking back in 1945, Leonard confided to Vollmer that two things he did at Washington State

> will prove of value to the other fellows in this business after the war—two things which I believe explain our staying qualities when others closed their doors for the duration—establishment of Police I as a service course available as an open elective to the entire campus, and the emphasis on crime prevention in the curriculum, both of which have served to draw young women into the classes.[53]

When a fellow V-man, Willard "Huck" Schmidt was re-establishing the program at San Jose State in 1946, Leonard advocated the importance of Police I. "It is the type of course that takes hold in the student body," he told his old friend.[54]

> Time and time again I have students express the opinion that the course should be required of all students at the institution for graduation in every department. That, of course, is another matter, but it does indicate how the subject material can be made to capture the imagination and afford the opportunity for important indoctrination. I consider that Police I as a survey course deserves a substantial share of the credit for the success of the total program here.[55]

This might have been done out of necessity, as the war drew away large numbers of males from the classrooms. One reason for the demise of the San Jose State program during the war was its one-sided maleness.[56] In the first year Police I had twenty students, all of whom were men. In the next year four females were a part of the 48 students. By 1944 the course had 39 women and one man enrolled.[57]

Nonetheless, Leonard's course made transitions from a vocational trainer to a general or liberal education offering. In fact, Leonard even thought of breaking out of the law enforcement mold that had dominated developments thus far. For example, early in 1943 he began negotiating with Richard McGee, Supervisor of Washington's Public Institutions (who became important later for the School of Criminology at the University of California) about adding a prison component to the program. Internships, or field experiences, stemmed from these talks with McGee and promised positions for student trainees in the correctional system.[58] Those modest changes were precursors of later important innovations. Still riding the crest of enthusiasm in 1943, Leonard published a promotional article in *Public Safety* declaring his program at Pullman to be the "West Point of the Police Field."[59]

At heart Leonard remained a policeman. "It was a real treat to get out and mix with the fellows again," he declared after visiting over forty Washington police departments in the autumn of 1943.[60] Like his mentor at Berkeley, Vollmer, he thought a professional school, modeled perhaps after engineering or medicine, was the ultimate goal because a profession could not exist until a professional school existed.[61] When Pennsylvania State University contemplated a police program, Leonard advised them that the Washington State students

> understand that we are not training them to enter the service as chiefs of police. They understand there is no substitute for experience and that they will be expected to begin at the bottom of the enterprise and move upward through the regular channels of promotion. Ultimately, some of these men will rise to positions of responsibility in the service where they can influence policy, and it is then that the real implications of

> professional training in this business will begin to emerge in tangible form.[62]

One of Leonard's students was even more revealing. "After a few years in the field, if I keep quiet about being a college man, I should learn enough to win the confidence of the men I work with. Then I can start applying my college training," he confided.[63] Thus, more than others at this time Leonard and his students understood the problem of educating a "professional" for an occupation in which experience rather than education was the key to advancement.

Leonard began to build an empire at Pullman in several ways. First, expecting a growth in the program after the war he added new faculty. Donald McCall, a criminalist or crime lab specialist from the Portland police department, was hired in 1944, ending Leonard's one-man show.[64] Second, Leonard began dreaming of expanding into the graduate school. A professional school, which was the favored option, was out of the question for a two-man department, although Leonard did get some encouragement along these lines from the president. So he went in another direction. "When the Ph.D. is included in the Department's offerings, we can then say that police training has arrived," he wrote to Vollmer in the summer of 1944.[65] This too was a bit ambitious for two professors, neither of whom had doctorates themselves. A master's degree program was another thing, however, and in November 1944 graduate credit was given the police program. Now a master's degree could be awarded, the first going to Mei-Ko-Wang from China in 1946, and "another cornerstone on the road to academic recognition of the police field" had been reached.[66] Even the very powerful dean of the College of Sciences and Arts, C. C. Todd, was impressed with the rapid growth of the police program and its apparent strength.[67]

Third, as the numbers of students increased, recruitment and retention of faculty raised new and perplexing questions. William Beall, an expert on criminal investigation and police communications, joined Leonard and McCall in 1946 but left in to the following year. Leonard fretted over the difficulty of obtaining the right kind of police professor. In the postwar era, he felt, traditional professors would be "a dime a dozen," but it was "an entirely different matter to sally forth in the search for a man with that rare combination of both police and academic background who possesses the qualities that make a teacher."[68] Doctorates in the field were nonexistent and when Felix Fabian joined the department in 1950 he was told to obtain a Ph.D. as quickly as possible. That badge of academic respectability was even appropriate for Leonard. After vacillating between the University of Texas and Ohio State University, Leonard moved to Ohio in 1946 to take a doctorate so that when he returned to Pullman he could "move police administration into the rightful spot in the sun."[69]

Fourth, a scholarly literature was needed. Following Vollmer and Wilson's lead, Leonard conducted a police survey of the Seattle police department in 1945, even thinking of making it the basis for a future Ph.D. thesis.[70] Aside from Vollmer's book *The Police and Modern Society* and several monographic police surveys, scholarly works were scarce. Such a literature was necessary if police science and administration were to become a respectable academic discipline. While working on his doctorate at Ohio State University, Leonard heard that O. W. Wilson was working on a book about police administration, a topic Leonard was developing for his own thesis. In 1947 he asked Vollmer to use his influence to have Wilson abandon the project because it was impractical for more than one member of the Berkeley group to study the same subject.[71] Wilson did not back off, however, and throughout 1948 and 1949 the two were in a footrace for publication. Wilson's book, *Police Administration*, was published in 1950 and soon became a classic. Leonard's thesis, *A Theory of Police Organization and Administration*, was also put in book form and was finally published as *Police Organization and Management* in 1951.

Leonard became an editor of a Police Science Series in the early 1950s. His aim was a five-foot shelf filled with a police science library covering "the field in authentic and professional fashion and which will, in addition to its other values, furnish the text and library support in organized form for a police curriculum."[72] Leonard's tastes were catholic, with even a comprehensive history of policing being contemplated.[73] Certainly, an examination of the over forty projected titles reveals his views on the emerging field of police education. Most were to be a link to the past, with titles such as *Techniques of Police Supervision*, *Police Records Administration*, and *Auto Theft Investigation*, to name a few. Thirty percent of the list addressed forensic sciences, once again showing the importance of the physical sciences. But some titles indicated a broader vision. For example, *Psychology for Law Enforcement Officers*, *Psycho-Analytic Approaches to Problems of Crime*, *The Family and the Police Officer*, and *The Police Officer and the Schools* were to be written.

According to Leonard himself, he and his program had

been treated like a "spoiled child" under President Holland.[74] By 1945 Holland was retired and his place taken by Wilson Compton. At first Compton suggested that the program be renamed "criminology" and changed from an independent department to a school status.[75] However, an Appraisal Committee appointed to evaluate the various programs in the fall of 1945 suggested that it be absorbed into the College of Sciences and Arts, where Leonard knew it would "have to compete with a constellation of departments for the support and attention of the dean."[76] Postwar academic politics was already changing the nature of Leonard's favored placement at Washington State.

In spite of such administrative jockeying, the program grew as men returned from the war. In September 1945, for example, 79 registered in the police program, 21 of whom decided to declare it their major.[77] Enrollments were so great the next year that it was necessary to postpone opening the college for two weeks in order to accommodate the increasing number of students.[78] A total of 148 persons took courses in the police program in the fall of 1947; the number increased to 160 in the spring.[79] Growth continued, and by 1950 Leonard could claim that only nine other departments had more majors.[80]

Even though the number of students increased and the program achieved some legitimacy on the campus, Leonard began to look beyond Pullman. Competition between eastern and western Washington increased, and Leonard saw that the times of growth and expansion had passed.[81] Even the University of Washington got into police education anew in 1948. Ironically, instead of going academic or professional, as one might have expected, the university brought in Gordon Sheehe from the Northwestern University Traffic Institute to create an in-service program. It was to be headquartered on the Seattle campus and would offer extension courses throughout the state. Leonard did not feel threatened. "[Sheehe] is so thoroughly saturated with the Northwestern University technique that the prospects for a degree curriculum at UW are temporarily remote to say the least," wrote Leonard.[82]

CONCLUSION

There was something more profound in Leonard's restlessness. "The thing I would enjoy most during the next ten years," he wrote Vollmer late in 1949, "would be the planting of new programs and I believe it is in that direction that I can render the greatest service."[83] More than most of the V-Men, with the possible exception of Vollmer himself, Leonard was ceasing to be a *Police* educator and was becoming a police *Educator*. Although creating a professional police—be it managers or street cops—remained important, Leonard was breaking through to a new level: the profession of the police educator itself. Such a career turn called upon a new set of skills, that of the academic politician. It was at this point Leonard and Wiltberger most dramatically parted ways. After the war Wiltberger never returned to education and at heart remained a trainer of cops; bordering on being an ideologue, Wiltberger had a too thin a skin to be a good academic politician. Although Leonard remained at Washington State College, he represented a new development in police education—the development of a police professoriate.

Therefore, two individuals and the institutions they headed personified the earliest trends in police education. The way in which they played academic politics also differed. As is often the case, the person who inspired and stimulated the movement—in this case August Vollmer—remained ambiguous and inscrutable. It was left to the disciples to clear the air. Of course, it was not a large jump from teaching future administrators of police departments to focusing on the administration of police science programs in colleges. It took a similar mindset, to be sure. As short as the jump was, it remained necessary to make it before other disciplinary developments could occur. For the greater institutionalization of this trend we must return to Berkeley, California.

Chapter 4

Berkeley Renaissance, 1945–1960

Developments at the San Jose State and Washington State colleges were encouraging, but Berkeley remained the Mecca for police education and August Vollmer its Mohammed. Although he was retiring, Vollmer could take comfort in knowing that his favorite disciple would be settling into the University of California with some promissory notes for the near future. "We believe that work in this field is of immense practical importance to the state, that it can properly be treated on a University level, and that this University is strategically situated to assume leadership in the field," wrote President Robert Sproul to O. W. Wilson in 1939.[1]

There had been a flurry of development in the late 1930s and early 1940s, but as strained international relations moved to outright war after Pearl Harbor, the situation bode ill for the immediate future of higher education in general and male-dominated police education in particular. Not only most students but many professors—O. W. Wilson and William Wiltberger, to name just two—transferred from college campuses to military camps. Nonetheless, August Vollmer and his V-Men had tremendous faith in the future and the role of the University of California in developing the new academic profession. One sign of that optimism occurred at Vollmer's home shortly after Pearl Harbor.

Seven V-Men came together at Euclid Avenue in Berkeley on December 30, 1941, with enthusiasm and concern over the future of police education. Robert L.

Drexel, chief investigator for the San Jose, California, District Attorney's office, was there. So was Benjamin W. Pavone, chairman of the Peace Officers Training Division of San Francisco Junior College. Frank Yee, a student of Vollmer's and a police administrator from China, was present and lent an international air to the deliberations. O. W. Wilson and V. A. Leonard were there, both excited—and perhaps a little nervous—over the future of their programs. Finally, William Wiltberger and Willard Schmidt came from San Jose with ideas of their own about the nature and development of police education and educators.[2] Years later Wiltberger remembered this meeting vividly, even the seating arrangements. Either as a self-proclaimed chief apostle (or chief protagonist), Wiltberger sat directly opposite Vollmer; other people in a self-perceived subordinate ranking fanned out from Wiltberger's left and right in a semicircle.[3]

But things did not go well, and Wiltberger left the Berkeley meeting feeling upstaged by Wilson and Leonard. It was clear to him that they had caught Vollmer's ear and that his place was slipping there, as it was in San Jose State. Frankly, he had never learned to play academic politics well. Long and bitter letters followed, especially to Leonard, criticizing many aspects of the meeting.[4]

To be sure, some of this animosity was due to Wiltberger's personality and feelings of being left behind. But Vollmer's ambiguity and uncertainity—plus his own natural evolution in thinking—as to what the field was to become, left disciples to interpret and squabble. Years later, in a letter scolding Vollmer for not writing down his ideas for posterity, Wiltberger discussed his own pugnacity. Perhaps reminiscing more over the past than seeing clearly into the future, Wiltberger could see

> someday where O. W. [Wilson] and I will have a knock-down and drag-out fight over what you said once and what you meant. I broke one chair over his head one day in my office. I don't want to break any more furniture. I don't care about his head. You know as well as I that many of us got a piece of your ideas and not always the whole picture.[5]

For that reason a Vollmerian school at the University of California became all the more important. It would be an institutional manifestation of Vollmer's ideas on criminology.

SCHOOL OF CRIMINOLOGY AT THE UNIVERSITY OF CALIFORNIA

Creating the School

During the war, Vollmer's plans for a school of criminology at Berkeley were put on the back burner. In effect, his attention was directed to Pullman, Washington, and the work of V. A. Leonard. In the immediate postwar period, with Wilson still in the military, much of the work at Berkeley was done by Paul Kirk, a renowned scientist and criminalist, who was teaching the "technical aspects of criminology." Kirk felt that there would be a postwar flood of students in criminology, a view not shared by many of his colleagues across campus, and that even though it was too late to be a pioneer in the field, the university should become a strong competitor. Playing a fairly strong card, Kirk recommended that a criminology department be created in 1946, otherwise the program as it currently existed should be discontinued entirely.[6] George Brereton, a former V-man and now head of the California Department of Justice's Division of Criminal Identification and Investigation, agreed and sent letters of support to President Robert Sproul.[7] By the end of 1946 the presidential levels of the university believed the criminology program should be strengthened.[8] The faculty, however, did not agree.

Apparently university politics had become different during the postwar period. Faculty, particularly the scientists, had become very powerful due to the war; in many ways their research projects and expertise were instrumental in winning the war. After all, the leader of the project that developed the atomic bomb, J. Robert Oppenheimer, was a Berkeley professor. Their standards of appropriate disciplines and scholarship and university governance were different from those of the more political and practical university presidents. Even though many university presidents still had power, they now increasingly had to share it with faculty in general and faculty committees in particular. Therefore small curricular battles became one part of larger academic wars.

A "Committee on Educational Policy upon Criminology" concluded its study and made a report in January 1947. Its views would haunt the School of Criminology for twenty-five years. In terms of classic disciplines, criminology "lacks character and supplies no need which is not or will not be sufficiently met by majors in Sociology, Economics, Political Science, and the Natural Sciences," declared the committee.[9] In fact, this was not even criminology as it was being developed at places such as the University of Chicago. It was police administration and crime detection and the term "criminology" was misleading and inappropriate. The problem was rank vocationalism. Paul Kirk wrote to O. W. Wilson, who was still in the army at the time, to warn him that "some things, such as the nature of our purpose and plans, will not suit you I know. We are going to have to go over lightly on anything that looks [like] vocational training."[10] Already the Graduate Council had turned down a request by A. M. Kidd for a master's degree in criminology, declaring it to be an applied field worthy only of a professional degree. As an undergraduate program, the committee feared, criminology might attract students of mediocre ability who would more easily be caught up in academic fads and fashions. Although the committee was less than enthusiastic about creating such a program at all, there was one redeeming compromise. Criminology might be construed as professional training for graduate students with the only acceptable administrative home being in a professional school; but it certainly did not fit into the College of Letters and Sciences.[11]

President Sproul responded to the faculty challenge by creating another committee, the "Committee to Consider and to Make Recommendations on the Report on Criminology of the Committee on Educational Policy," and loaded it with friends of criminology. In a sense, the issue of criminology at Berkeley became a test of political power between the president and the faculty. The Kidd committee (made up of A. M. Kidd, Paul Kirk, O. W. Wilson, August Vollmer, Milton Chernin, and John D. Hicks) was hardly an impartial faculty body. It was packed by the president to overcome or politically respond to the report of the Committee on Educational Policy. The Kidd committee requested a professional School of Criminology. But in an attempt to test the waters, it requested that the School be allowed to have undergraduates as well. Faculty and high-level members of the administration—such as the graduate dean and the academic vice president, who had more direct linkages with the faculty—sided with the original report of the Education Policy Committee.[12] However, President Sproul—ever the friend of Vollmer and perhaps testy over such faculty recalcitrance—reminded the academics that the schools of Architecture, Business Administration, Public Health, and Optometry allowed undergraduate enrollment. A compromise was struck and a new School of Criminology was created that allowed students to enter in their junior year. But in one final blow the Board of Regents, as it approved the School in

1948, did not allocate any money until a Dean of the School was appointed, thereby precipitating another crisis. Actually the creation of the School of Criminology must be seen as one of the early battles between faculty and administrators over who should control the future and quality of the university. Although truces occur, that war would break out time and again. All too often criminology was the disputed territory, a symbolic as well as a substantive battleground.

Appointment of the dean was crucial not only to the start up of the School but to the direction it would take. In addition, it highlighted differing interpretations of criminology among the faculty and, more important between the faculty and the president of the university. Four candidates soon emerged and the "Committee to Advise on the Appointment of the Dean of the School of Criminology" divided.

Milton Chernin and Edward Rogers felt that the function of criminology was to do research on the causation of crime. They believed that there existed already sufficient knowledge into the system and agencies dealing with crime and criminals, hardly a heady task for the scholarly potential of the university. The real challenge to scholar and practitioner alike was the understanding of crime causation. The School of Criminology should address both problems: efficient agency administration and the causes of crime. But the emphasis and the dean should be directed to the latter. Either Thorsten Sellin from the University of Pennsylvania or Sheldon Glueck of Harvard University were likely candidates in the opinion of Chernin and Rogers.[13]

A. M. Kidd and Joseph Harris viewed criminology differently. For them, the main function of the School of Criminology was the training of those engaged in the agencies directly related to fighting crime. Kidd believed that any idea that crime would be eliminated once its causes were found was

> the nostalgic belief of professors trained in the basic and applied sciences, but it has no place in criminology. University departments of sociology, psychology, social welfare, and government agencies are pouring out studies literally by the thousand[s]. Their effect on crime is barely perceptible. Crime marches on. There is no need for a School of Criminology to carry on in basic and applied sciences.[14]

Besides, the academic audience was assured, surprisingly little was known about policing. Effort should be directed to where it might do the greatest good, that is, fighting crime in the most efficient way. O. W.

Wilson should be the dean, declared Kidd and Harris, because "little success can be hoped for unless the university program is administered by men who know the subject practically and have the confidence of the [agency] officials that progress can be made."[15] The selection was deadlocked between two poles: Sellin or Glueck on one hand, and O. W. Wilson on the other.

The organization and development of the School of Criminology was stymied over an issue that would continue to perplex criminology and police educators throughout this period: What was the basic nature of criminology? However, the committee agreed on two things. Perhaps the School should not be limited to one of the two perspectives, but the dean should determine the emphasis. Sellin or Glueck might be expected to focus on crime causation, whereas Wilson would concentrate on improving the system. The second decision of the committee suggests a caving-in to the president. That is, the committee reported the two alternatives and allowed the president to decide.[16]

As might be expected, the deanship levels of the university favored Sellin or Glueck. The president, however, not only sided with Wilson but even narrowed the mission of the School. In short, he had to guarantee other disciplines that the new upstart would not gobble them up. For example, earlier O. W. Wilson had created a model curriculum that incorporated corrections and crime causation.[17] Now the emphasis was to be on police administration because

> the [areas of] correction[s], probation, parole and the like could very well be handled through the existing Schools of Social Welfare, with the emphasis in Criminology being in Police Administration and Crime Detection.[18]

On February 24, 1950, O. W. Wilson was made dean of the School of Criminology. Now Wilson became the focal point for the School. But the role of Kirk and Kidd in establishing that program had been enormous and has been underestimated. More important, the part played by the president—and the importance of academic politics on all levels—became tantamount, yet has been entirely overlooked.

The Wilson Years

When the School opened in 1950 it offered two options: law enforcement and criminalistics. Shortly thereafter, Austin MacCormick joined the faculty and made corrections a component—contrary to original plans. In effect, the president and the School "pulled an end run" on the faculty and expanded the mission of the School. Students in their first year were required to take criminal investigation, police administration, physical evidence, legal medicine, and legal relations. In the second year police planning, traffic engineering, detection of deception, and crime and delinquency were required. Two regular faculty members (Wilson and E. O'Neil) were aided by eight "joint appointments," or those who had appointments in other departments. For example, Paul Kirk at first kept his position in the chemistry department. Two part-time lecturers or those who had full-time jobs elsewhere were on staff as well. The chief of the Berkeley police department, John Holstrom, was a lecturer for much of this period. Although no one mentioned it, the system was inexpensive, a delightful proposition for university bureaucrats. The salary of joint appointees was spread between two departments, and lecturers could be paid less because of their part-time nature. From 1951 to 1954 four regular faculty and an average of ten joint appointments and four lecturers staffed the School. In 1954 Douglas Kelley joined the faculty, and in the following year Kirk moved over entirely from the chemistry department. At no time throughout the 1950s did the regular faculty surpass five, and in fact by 1960 it was down to three. One important appointment was approved in 1958 to bring Joseph Lohman into the faculty, but at the last moment he decided to stay in Chicago. Lohman became very important to the School later on, as we will see. Consequently, in keeping with its original mandate, the bulk of the teaching in the School during the 1950s was done by part-timers who were more professionally than academically oriented.[19]

O. W. Wilson was a policeman, and the perception among the academic community at Berkeley was that the School of Criminology was a police school. Indeed, Wilson maintained high visibility as a student of policing. For example, between 1950 and 1960 he conducted management surveys of 32 police departments and published his book *Police Administration*. In addition, in 1956 he chaired a committee for the Police Officers Research Association of California (PORAC) that developed a code of ethics for law enforcement.[20]

Contributing to this "cop shop" perception was the distribution of the students in the School. A tally of enrollment in 1951 showed that the 99 majors in the School were divided between undergraduate (77) and graduate (22). Undergraduates clustered in law enforcement (40) and criminalistics (17) rather than corrections (20). There was also a large number of students taking criminology as an undergraduate elective, an increase from 671 to 738 in 1951.[21] Because of the curricular format, these students took a disproportionately high number of police courses. The media did not help. The *San Francisco Examiner* published an article on the School of Criminology in 1957 emphasizing its role as a "World Leader in Crime Prevention Work." Of the 166 majors in 1957, fourteen were foreign students, "nearly all of them ranking police officers in their own countries," announced the *Examiner*[22]

However, graduate students in the School tended toward corrections. Actually corrections had some advantage over police studies. Police administration was based upon public administration. And police surveys, a research and publication activity of the police scientist, hardly seemed scholarly for most academics. Corrections could lean upon public administration as well, but it was also attractive to the sociologist and psychologist looking for a natural laboratory—the prison—for research. Furthermore, the police professor and the professional school orientation seemed more vocational. On the other hand, correctional specialists rarely put all their energies into training wardens and parole officers. So during the 1950s the correctional aspects of the School seemed more research-oriented and academically respectable than the law enforcement component.

No doctorate was available until 1964, but master's degrees are indicative. Of the 19 master's degrees awarded by the criminology component of political science between 1928 and 1950, 15 were in law enforcement. Between 1950 and 1963, however, 41 master's degrees were given; 13 were in corrections and 8 in policing. Sixteen were given in criminalistics, again showing the power and respectability of science. Four graduate degrees were given in criminology as defined in a sociology department.[23] In 1959 Wilson could claim that 53 percent of the master's degrees awarded by the School had to do with penology.[24] So there were actually two acts being played upon the same stage. At the undergraduate level—where the traditional academics wanted to minimize enrollment in the School anyway—the police program was thriving. On the graduate level corrections was stronger.

As early as 1953 Wilson petitioned University officials for a council of advisors to help bridge gaps between criminology on the campus and in the community. There was already a form of "Kitchen Cabinet," called the MOB by Wilson, but this new advisory council was be official.[25] The list of people, headed with the name of August Vollmer, leaned heavily toward the police. Names of chiefs of police throughout the Bay Area abounded. But so did the names of district attorneys and correctional officials, as Wilson responded to the growth of corrections in his school.[26] These influential professionals in the community, headed by Richard McGee who was now director of the California Department of Corrections, was not called into session until 1959, when the School of Criminology had to fight for its life.[27]

Academic Politics and the School

Clark Kerr, university chancellor from 1952 to 1958, had never been a supporter of the School of Criminology. In fact, John Holstrom was convinced that Kerr wanted to destroy the School. Shortly after Kerr was made chancellor, Holstrom's police officers were accused of harassing university students. Both Wilson and Holstrom felt Kerr was an "academic elitist" having no appreciation for professional education outside law and medicine, who felt police education should be relegated to the state college system.[28] However, university president Robert Sproul restrained Kerr for much of the period. But when Sproul retired in 1958, Kerr was elevated to the presidency. The political map had changed and now the anti-School forces began to surface again.

Early in 1958 an Academic Advisory Committee was set up to investigate the School of Criminology. It reported that the School should reduce those professional courses bordering on vocational training. Next an Educational Policy Committee, chaired by Robert Brode, was asked to more fully review the School and its place in the university. When it determined that an even more in-depth study was needed, the Cline Committee was set up in the summer of 1958.

At issue was the appropriate role of a professional school in a research institution. Indeed, research and scholarship into the causes of crime was important; but until a magic bullet was found to cure the disease of crime, the first aid or tourniquet became very important—or so Wilson felt as he defended his school. Criminology must be an applied field; and just as good physicians were best trained by skilled practitioners, so were good criminologists. "Professional training cannot be provided exclusively by instructors who use knowledge from a book in lieu of actual experience in the field," he concluded.[29] Four years earlier, O. W. Wilson had given a featured speech on a "General Philosophy for Criminology Programs" that summed up the prevailing Vollmerian ideas throughout the period. According to Wilson,

> While the essential difference between vocational and professional training undoubtedly is the distinction between training in techniques and skills, and training in basic theories and principles and their application to practical problems dealt with in the field, the distinction in criminology must be one of primacy rather than exclusion; in criminology, professional training must include some training in skills and techniques that are purely vocational in character, and vocational training must include some understanding of basic theories.[30]

Of course the School was practical and it was wrong to compare it to the College of Letters and Arts; it was a professional school, Wilson adamantly reminded the university.

But that was precisely the problem, according to Wilson. "On one hand, we have the traditional pure scholar," he wrote to Leon Radzinowicz. "On the other, the realist who is concerned with immediate problems and their solution and who is represented by the professional schools, although with a growing support in other areas within the university faculty. The pure traditionalist would probably root out of the University every professional school including those of medicine and law."[31] Indeed, the medical and dental schools were conveniently located off campus across the bay in San Francisco.

From the summer of 1958 to that of 1959 the Cline Committee went about its investigations. Leon Radzinowicz, the famous British criminologist who was just setting up his Institute of Criminology at Cambridge University, was quizzed and unintentionally hurt his old friend's program. After praising the creation of the School, Radzinowicz pointed out that changes in academic scholarship had occurred but had gone unnoticed by the School. Trying to smooth over his criticisms, Radzinowicz told Wilson later that perhaps a time had been "reached when more fundamental reconstruction of the school was necessary so as to reflect the broader changes in the rest of the related bodies."[32] Other damaging testimony came from Richard McGee, chair of the School's Advisory Council. McGee felt that the School had not turned out as many graduates in corrections as he had hoped. In addition, two universities, Columbia and the University of Michigan, responded negatively when asked about the appropriateness of a School of Criminology at the university level.[33]

In the summer of 1959 the Cline Committee made its

report, and it was devastating. There was no clearly defined field of criminology, it declared. Furthermore, the existing undergraduate offerings were unsuitable for a university. Criminology was too vocational, lacking any central academic discipline. Criminology was too multi-disciplinary and "the students are not—cannot—be disciplined in so many sciences." Instead of broadening student perceptions, the School was so diluted of academic rigor that poor students were salvaging a degree out of the university when they should have gone to a state college. Finally, there was no scholarly tradition or tendency on the part of the faculty. Police surveys, being too descriptive, were no excuse for scholarly research. It looked as though Vollmer's dream, just three years after his own death, was to die as well.[34] In a fit of despondency over ill-health Vollmer had committed suicide in 1955; was his School of Criminology about to do the same in 1959?

Immediatelly following publication of the Cline Report, Wilson called the Advisory Council into session. Defending the fact that he had never summoned the members before, Wilson claimed that all earlier problems were administrative issues inappropriate for the Council. However, now—speaking with all his strength and conviction for over an hour—Wilson discounted the Cline Report as filled with "ambiguities, half-truths, misrepresentations, obscenities, and innuendoes."[35] Then Wilson and MacCormick presented a written report refuting every charge and criticism of the Cline Report.[36] The Advisory Council was won over (a remarkable feat considering it had been ignored since its inception) and went quickly into action.[37] In fact, from the autumn of 1959 through the winter of 1960, Richard McGee and the Advisory Council were much more active and important to the history of the School than O. W. Wilson. In many ways it was shaping up to be a "town" versus "gown" battle. McGee began marshaling support from the agency practitioners of the state.[38] Then in October 1959 the Council presented a position paper to the chancellor and Academic Senate attacking the Cline Report as sloppy and biased. The School, according to the Advisory Council, should not only be retained but expanded, giving greater emphasis to corrections.[39] President Clark Kerr, seen by Wilson as a weak man who would respond to such pressure from the community, indeed caved in and appointed a new committee to review the Cline Report. This new committee—jokingly referred to as the "committee on the committee"—set aside the Cline Report, but also recommended that the School be radically reformed.[40] However, a lesson was implicit. Academic politicians, although bold on campus, can be easily intimidated by real-world activists.

Reformation of the School, and indeed of criminological education in the state, began dramatically. Even the word "criminology" was taking on a different meaning, emphasizing the more sociological and psychological aspects and methodologies of studying crime. Law enforcement and crime detection as primary definitions were conspicuously absent. There would be no undergraduate major in law enforcement at the University of California. Instead, the California State College system was encouraged to take over police education. Criminalistics training should be done at the State College as well, but due to the level of existing cost-outlay and development it would continue at the university for a few more years. Crime causation, an area of research and scholarship within many social sciences (such as sociology and psychology), should remain in the parent discipline. It was corrections that seemed most suitable for the School at the undergraduate level. On the graduate level there were to be two tracks: a professional degree (on the master's level) and a research degree (at the doctoral level). The professional degree was to be temporary, disappearing as the state colleges took over. What was to emerge was a professional school that was not to look or act like a professional school. Such an arrangement became something of an academic "catch-22" and would lay the School open to attack later. However, the research degree was to be the mainstay because ample opportunities could be found "in the giant social laboratory created by our systems of probation and parole."[41] Could O. W. Wilson and the other V-Men adjust to such a radical restructuring of Vollmer's school? Within a month of these policy changes it all became moot because O. W. Wilson left Berkeley.

In January 1960 a professional thief implicated several Chicago policemen in a burglary ring. Mayor Richard Daley, reacted to the so-called Summerdale scandal, fired the police commissioner and brought in a group of police specialists to form a recruitment committee. O. W. Wilson was on that committee. By the end of February, Wilson was named Superintendent of Police in Chicago; and for many, the next seven years were regarded as the golden era in Chicago policing. The *San Francisco Examiner* took this opportunity to jibe the University of California and its arrogant intellectual ways. Wilson's appointment proved that "the contention that such a school [of criminology] is essentially non-academic and as such does not fit into the long-range plans of the university, is substantially outweighed by the school's value to society," editorialized the *Examiner*.[42]

Contempories and historians alike have misinterpreted Wilson's move to Chicago as motivated by self-sacrifice and public service. On the contrary, in light of the previous two years of political turmoil and the unraveling of the School of Criminology in Berkeley, the Chicago position seemed a face-saving godsend. O. W. Wilson could no longer fit into the School of Criminology, and as early as mid-January there was considerable talk among university officials hoping he would not return.[43] Thus by 1960 O. W. Wilson and August Vollmer's dream of police education at the University of California was at an end. By exorcising that spirit the School was saved, for a season.

Much of 1960 was taken up in the search for a new dean. Almost immediately people like Milton Chernin renewed debates of a previous decade suggesting Lloyd Ohlin as a replacement for Wilson.[44] Apparently the faculty was not up for the fight, because Ohlin's name quickly disappeared. This was due to the Advisory Council, particularly Richard McGee, who entered into every discussion regarding the School. This council, though wanting higher academic standards, was not ready to turn from the community and the hoards of practitioners who were to be consumers of the product of the School. What was important was to replace Wilson, an academic *practitioner* with an *academic* practitioner. Both elements were needed, but the emphasis must change. Opinions swung to Joseph Lohman. Although he had only a master's degree Lohman had a definite sociological perspective that quieted the academic's concerns. When he was interviewed for the job, Lohman agreed that Wilson's narrow police training concepts had overshadowed the School. Much of this kind of vocationalism, claimed Lohman, should be left to other colleges or be placed in university extensions or institutes.[45] Most of all he recognized the importance of the Advisory Council and cultivated its approval and support.[46] With little debate or controversy, Joseph Lohman officially became the dean in 1961.

By that time the curriculum had changed substantially, most notably with the aid of Richard McGee and the Advisory Council. McGee had been especially active in suggesting courses. For example, he championed juvenile delinquency to be part of the core instead of an elective. Research methods and statistics became requirements.[47] New courses—such as criminology, the etiology of crime (sociological), the etiology of crime (psychological), criminal law in action, corrections, criminal careers—began to appear. Lohman aggressively sought grant money and soon the faculty increased. A three-man research team was started in 1962 and expanded to 19 people involved with six different research projects by 1964.[48] Soon a doctorate in criminology appeared. The School of Criminology survived but in a different form; some things were gained but others had to be given up. Police education, the priority for Vollmer and the V-Men, became a casualty to academic politics. A new generation of "criminologists" would be trained at Berkeley who would have different perspectives from the Vollmerites. In equally dramatic ways, similar struggles were playing out in the new professional organization.

SOCIETY FOR THE ADVANCEMENT OF CRIMINOLOGY

When William Wiltberger and Willard Schmidt arrived at Vollmer's home for that December 1941 meeting, they came with a provocative notion. Apparently, in the late 1930s Wiltberger and Schmidt at San Jose State had come up with an idea for an organization. Schmidt, who had worked with Wiltberger in the Berkeley police department years before, remembered the two-hour debate in the San Jose Police School office. One proposed name for the organization, the Association of Police Educators, had been dropped as to broad because it would bring instructors into the organization from police academies. Another name, the Association of College Police Educators, might bring in too many college administrators, and by that time Wiltberger had had his fill of college presidents who criticized his teaching skills. Finally, the organization of two settled on the Association of Heads of College Police Schools, and August Vollmer proclaimed the idea "bully." V. A. Leonard liked the concept too, because "such an organization will open the way for a formal approach to any number of problems and will afford the means for directing national attention to the fact that professional training for police service at the University level is sound public policy."[49] Wiltberger and Schmidt's idea became the main item of discussion at the December 1941 meeting.

Almost immediately Vollmer and Wiltberger split over the fundamental direction of the proposed organization. The San Jose contingent felt that association membership should be restricted to heads of college police schools. Vollmer, on the other hand, with strong support from Wilson and Leonard, felt "that we should include outstanding professors in the social sciences and criminology," a position that was given face acceptance but was modified in the bylaws by limiting membership to those working in police training programs in accredited colleges. Wiltberger suggested and won approval for a threefold classification system with distinctions drawn amongjunior colleges, state colleges, and universities, thus allowing for differing program development. Though lip service was given to research on police subjects, the immediate purpose was to stimulate the formation of police training schools in colleges across the country.[50] The organization was to be called the National Association of College Police Training Officials. A second meeting was to have been held at Pullman, Washington, where V. A. Leonard wanted to solidify his position with his college president and show off his facilities.[51] The war got in the way, however, and little occurred except occasional letters between Vollmer and Leonard.

In 1946 there were new attempts to revive the organization at a meeting held at the Durant Hotel in Berkeley. At this time the name was changed to the Society for the Advancement of Criminology. William Wiltberger saw that the name change was significant and complained. "My interest is in turning out expert police officers, not criminologists," he confided to Vollmer in 1949. For Wiltberger, "changing the name of that organization was the bunk."[52] What he did not realize was that criminology at that time was still vague enough in the popular and academic mind to act as a vehicle for the academic legitimization of police education. No less a figure than Thorsten Sellin, in his famous *Culture, Conflict and Crime* (1938), felt that criminology had a hybrid quality. It was not a discipline, he wrote, but a meeting place of numerous disciplines that happened to share a common interest in topics relevant to crime.[53] Ten to fifteen years after Sellin uttered those thoughts, the viewpoint was increasingly inappropriate for the more academic and sociological criminologists. Although it is not clear, perhaps Wiltberger foresaw a struggle in which the more mainstream criminologists might try to bring clarity to their own field and carve out a place for themselves in the academic world at the expense of his own position.

Indeed, the new organization tried to walk the tightrope between two extremes. On one hand, Wiltberger's concerns were addressed as the new organization limited membership to "persons engaged by accepted universities and colleges to instruct or supervise in *professional* and *vocational* training programs in Criminology"(emphasis in the original).[54] On the other hand, in-service people (Wiltberger's people) had to be held in place as well. V. A. Leonard, disliking the strictly in-service vocational program being established at the University of Washington by Gordon Sheehe, warned that "if we let the bars down to include in-service training we will have neutralized the main objective of the association."[55] That objective was to perpetuate criminology as defined by Vollmer, Wilson, and Leonard. Such discussions and concerns were relevant given the status of police higher education in the late 1940s and 1950s.

The Michigan State College program revived in 1947 when Arthur Brandstatter returned from the military. In a short time he headed up the department and was connected with it for nearly thirty years. Under Brandstatter's guidance a criminalistics curriculum was added in 1947. A prevention and control of delinquency section (1948), highway traffic administration program (1952), and correctional administration and industrial security components were added by the end of the decade. A graduate degree program was begun in 1956.[56] Brandstatter and his program fit nicely into President John A. Hannah's quest for a university with utility. Every year over 200 professors were managing "education projects" in foreign countries. The police systems of South Korea and Vietnam had been organized by the Michigan State police professors. So vigorous was Brandstatter that he opened up himself and his department to attack from some Michigan State professors and students for creating a "Lilliputian police state" at East Lansing, Michigan.[57]

Indiana University reorganized its department of police science and administration in 1949. The more in-service component was turned over to a newly created Center for Police Training, thereby making clearer distinctions between the academic and the vocational. Donald Kooken headed that department until Robert Borkenstein replaced him in 1958.[58]

However, most of the developments in police education occurred in California. Donal MacNamara headed the program at the University of Southern California until 1953, when his place was taken by John Kenney. The Fresno State and San Jose State programs revived and thrived after the war. However, Fresno emphasized corrections over law enforcement, according to one 1951 survey.[59] Los Angeles State College set up a Police Science and Administration program in 1949 based upon a policy of interchangeable courses. The same instructor taught identical courses at daytime and nighttime to accommodate the ever-shifting work schedules of police officers. Such a system would be used by other colleges, especially the more urban ones. By 1960, Los Angeles State enrolled 700 students in its police courses.[60] In addition, Sacramento State College began to expand its evening courses in policing to the regular daytime program in 1952.

Administrators of these state college programs, responding to such growth and the prodding of the V-Men, sought to instill a degree of uniformity in their offerings as the 1950s drew to a close. By 1960, five educators—Frank Boolsen at Fresno State, Allen Gemmage at Sacramento State, A. G. Germann at Long Beach State, G. Douglas Gourley at Los Angeles State, and Willard Schmidt at San Jose State—formed the California State Law Enforcement Program Administrators in order to coordinate their programs. They decided that the first two years should provide a broad liberal arts education, plus vocational training appropriate for a police patrolman. The next two years would broaden the liberal arts orientation but also prepare those aspiring for police supervisory positions in agencies or for graduate work at the University of California.[61]

The growth and development of police programs within California junior colleges (or community colleges as they were becoming known) was even more apparent. Since the police program at San Jose had moved from junior college to state college status, there was only one junior college in California with a law enforcement component in 1947. By 1950 there were six, and then thirteen in 1957. According to the calculations of Richard Myren, the number had grown to thirty-six by 1962.[62] In many ways, Visalia junior college was representative in the 1950s.

John Kenney started the police program at Visalia in 1947, but he soon moved on to the University of Southern California. Richard Hankey, a product of the Los Angeles junior college system himself, had studied under Vollmer in the late 1930s. From 1939 to 1944 he was a member of the Berkeley police department. At first Hankey was reluctant to become involved in college teaching, but Vollmer prodded and prophesied in 1948 that "the professional police training school is certain to grow in numbers in this country and you fellows, who have the requisite educational background, will be much in demand in the not too distant future."[63]

For much of the 1950s Hankey made Visalia, later to be renamed the College of the Sequoias, a showplace of the Wiltbergerian tradition of police education. Hankey's program was intensely practical, and in-service training became his specialty. By 1951 all courses at Visalia were offered in the late afternoon or evenings so that the police people of Tulare County could attend.[64] Soon Hankey was traveling throughout California as an advocate for the in-service model of police education, and he became the main resource person on in-service training for the Society for the Advancement of Criminology.[65] Apparently the Society was appreciative of his work, or still of two minds about the role of junior college police training in the organization, because Hankey was made its president in 1956, the only junior college educator to ever hold that position. In the following year he left Visalia for a state college position in Los Angeles, but his program and ideas were kept alive by his successor, Edward Farris.

The in-service movement had considerable vitality throughout the 1950s. Older models such as the Northwestern Traffic Institute expanded their offerings to over 20 courses during this decade.[66] The Case Western Reserve University's Law-Medicine Center began offering courses for the police officers of suburban Cleveland in 1953.[67] The Southwestern Center for Law Enforcement Education began at the University of Oklahoma in 1954; it was noted for its special seminars on auto theft, the polygraph, and jail security.[68] The Police Training Institute at the University of Illinois was opened in that university's extension division in 1955.[69] In February 1949, Joseph Lohman, chairman of the Illinois Division of Corrections and future dean of the School of Criminology at Berkeley, suggested to David McCandless that the South should have a police training institute. In January 1951, the Southern Police Institute at the University of Louisville was opened under the direction of McCandless.[70]

In California the in-service programs were even greater. In 1959 a Standards and Training bill was passed requiring that a portion of all moneys collected through bails and fines be set aside for the purpose of police training programs. In that same year the California State Department of Justice created a commission of Police Officer Standards and Training (POST) to establish rules and standards for all police training. Any department affiliated with POST could send people for additional training and be compensated by the state. Twenty-three junior colleges were certified by POST to operate police training programs.[71]

The Wiltbergerian model had spread like wildfire, but not without opposition. As usual, V. A. Leonard offered a counter-position. "In-service training was never intended, nor can it be expected to train a man professionally for a given field. The basic function of in-service training is to keep professionally trained men abreast of new developments in the field."[72] This became a point of consternation as well for the Society for the Advancement of Criminology as it was seeking its identity.

After an energetic start in 1946, the Society for the Advancement of Criminology became sluggish.[73] O. W. Wilson, president of the organization for the last half of the 1940s, was either still in the military or busy setting up the School of Criminology at the University of California. Although both he and Vollmer felt that the School and the Society were closely connected—two sides to the same coin—the School took precedence. Throughout the 1950s Vollmer's disciples held office as president, giving the organization a distinctive police and California orientation. Douglas Kelley, of the School of Criminology, was president in 1950. Frank Boolsen, William Dienstein, Richard Simon, Richard Hankey, and John Kenney, all V-Men, quickly followed as presidents. The chain was not broken until 1959 when Marcel Frym, a legal scholar, became president and a symbol for dramatic changes.

During the 1950s the organization was small and informal. In 1953 there were 32 members.[74] As late as 1957, Jack Kenney remembered, the meeting at the University of Southern California was small enough to be held in the university president's conference room.[75] This is a telling remark, indeed, pointing up the importance of the college president—a person who would turn over his own conference space to a bunch of police professors—in the early days of police education. During this period all meetings were held at those universities where a police program existed and the president was amenable. Donal MacNamara joined in 1949 and remembered the Society to be little more than a social group, a "back-scratching" crowd. Little was done except have a luncheon, a speech, a group discussion, and a dinner. There was little resemblance to a traditional scholarly professional organization.[76]

Throughout the decade, clinging to the legend of August Vollmer and the future of the School of Criminology, the Society was a West Coast operation. When Douglas Kelley tried to establish an affiliation with the International Society of Criminology in 1950, for example, it was made clear to him that everyone thought he presided over a California organization.[77] After all until 1955 all meetings were held at Berkeley. The next two meetings (1956 and 1957) were held in Fresno and Los Angeles. Regional divisions were set up by 1954, and Arthur Brandstatter became vice president in charge of the midwestern region. Donal MacNamara left the University of Southern California for a position in New York in the early 1950s and began setting up his own satrap as vice president of the eastern area.[78]

Both Brandstatter and MacNamara worked to break the West Coast hold on the Society. Certainly, they were much more skilled and energetic than the current president, William Dienstein, who was busy working on an advanced degree at Stanford University. "If the Society is to progress," Dienstein wrote to David McCandless in 1954, "it will be necessary to get some go-getters in the offices—not like me. The organization needs some spark which it apparently had not had so far."[79]

One of Brandstatter's assignments as vice president for the midwestern region was conference arrangements for 1954. He pressured Dienstein to move the upcoming meetings from the West Coast. In addition, he wanted to restructure the format of the conference into a three-day meeting. Each regional vice president would be in charge of one of the day's activities.[80] But Dienstein stalled and Brandstatter was frustrated. "I don't see how I can go ahead with plans for the SAC [Society for the Advancement of Criminology] annual meeting without knowing when and where it will be held," he scolded the president. Finally, in obvious frustration, Brandstatter relented and suggested the meeting be held in the West.[81] Dienstein now went into action and the seventy members of the Society were polled as to preference for the annual meeting; and Denver was the compromise selection.[82] But it was too late to set up a formal meeting, so Dienstein had to settle for a "section status" within the American Association for the Advancement of Science, which just so happened to be meeting in Berkeley anyway.[83]

Brandstatter's Midwesterners and MacNamara's Easterners were increasingly frustrated, not to mention financially strapped, by always having to travel to the West Coast for annual meetings. Consequently, attendance at national meetings by those outside California fell, which made the Society appear less and less national. By the mid-1950s the Society was threatened with schism, being on the brink of becoming a confederation with equally strong and competing eastern, midwestern, and western groups. Only nineteen people attended the Fresno meeting in 1956, thirteen of whom were from California colleges.[84] In 1958 a meeting was held at the University of Arizona, but the president warned that "any further east would create innumerable hardships."[85] The Society remained western-locked until 1959, when President Marcel Frym successfully prevailed to hold it in Chicago. Once the California grip was broken, it would be another six years before the meetings moved there again. At last a very important professionalization process had occurred. The regional character, the particularly California monopoly, had been put aside and the Society made attempts at being a national rather than a regional organization.

Organizations certainly must be known by their goals and emphases. As the name implies, throughout this period the Society for the Advancement of Criminology was concerned with issues of education—not so much the "science of criminology" as the spreading of Vollmerian programs of criminology into higher education. Douglas Kelley, for instance, felt the major problem during his administration was the integration of police training programs into the Society.[86] As early as 1953, President Frank Boolsen worried that certain elements in the organization might "have forgotten the fundamental purpose of SAC [was] to promote and foster criminological training and to discuss problems common to all the programs."[87] Boolsen asked James Enochs, a specialist in state college curricula for the California State Department of Education, to address the 1953 meeting on "Standardization of Criminological Curricula." Lively panel discussions followed on the issues of "transference of students" and "course content."[88] Regional vice presidents were appointed during the next year, and their main job was standardize all two- and four-year programs in their regions. For example, all police science and administration courses were to be categorized as criminology.[89]

But by this time criminology as an academic discipline was searching for an identity quite different from that of the police professors. The period from the 1930s to the 1960s was something of a golden age for criminology, as names like Edwin Sutherland, Clifford Shaw, Henry McKay, Thorsten Sellin, Robert Merton, Howard Becker, Edwin Lemert, Marvin Wolfgang, and Richard Quinney attest. These were sociologists who emphasized social science, particularly theory building and quantitative research techniques. Although crime and the agencies of criminal justice were of interest, emphasis for most of these men was on juvenile delinquency and corrections. Consequently, their political and professional associations were largely in sociology, where they had to compete with many other academics. By the 1950s many of these sociological criminologists were looking for other organizations in which they might play academic politics to better advantage.

By the end of the decade the Society was being redirected, a job done by two persons: John Kenney and Donal MacNamara. Actually Kenney was a V-man, caught between cherished old ideas and compelling new ones. Kenney had been a Berkeley police officer and student at the University of California before moving to Los Angeles and eventually taking a degree from UCLA. His specialty was police administration, but when he began teaching at the University of Southern California he came under the influence of criminologists such as Marcel Frym and Peter Lejins.

During Kenney's presidential term (1957-59) there was an attempt to broaden not only the geographical but also the ideological focus of the Society.[90] For example, with a slight margin of victory in July 1957 the name of the organization was changed to the American Society of Criminology. Such a name change was significant, suggesting a different direction for the organization than originally intended. Educational issues remained somewhat important, but there was a decided shift from promoting criminological programs in colleges to that of studying the science of crime and crime prevention.[91] Even educational issues became more scientific. Concern over the "hit-and-miss" development of many criminology programs prompted Kenney to write "A Proposal to Study the Teaching and Research in Criminology in the United States" in 1958. This was a curricular issue, to be sure; but unlike so much previous discussion, the main focus here was empirical research.[92] In addition, Kenney wanted a special meeting to identify areas of research and areas of possible support from foundations.[93] A publications committee was set up to investigate the proliferation of books and articles of dubious scientific merit making their way into the literature under the guise of criminology.[94] A stronger affiliation with the American Association for the Advancement of Science was promoted in order to gain status.[95] And the August Vollmer Award was set up in 1959 to recognize outstanding research in the field of criminology. Donal MacNamara admitted that this was done as a ploy to seduce prominent persons to join the Society.[96] The first award was given to Marvin Wolfgang. Such refocusing had a quick impact, as ninety new members joined in 1958. Every year thereafter more new criminologists joined, further alienating the Vollmerites.[97]

Perhaps there was no more pivotal person in this process than Donal MacNamara. Although he had spent three years at the University of Southern California, MacNamara was an Easterner. He was not a Vollmerite. Instead, he had studied police administration under Bruce Smith at Columbia University. MacNamara eagerly returned to New York in 1953 and soon became vice president of the Society for the eastern region. His region became increasingly strong and independent, having affiliations with the American Sociological Association, the Society for the Study of Social Problems, the American Correctional Association, and the International Association of Chiefs of Police.

Consequently, as the "national" meetings saw sparse attendance in the West, MacNamara had well-attended regional meetings in the East. In fact, there were so many sociologists and psychologists interested in criminology in Boston, New York City, and Philadelphia that the eastern region took on a direction of its own.[98] MacNamara felt that the Vollmerites were "fringe people" who stood in the way of making criminology an acceptable academic discipline. "The police science instructors had no academic prestige or acceptance," he recalled. For MacNamara it was not a matter of West versus East, or of police versus corrections. It was simply the difference between scholarship and teaching.[99]

MacNamara became president of the American Society of Criminology in 1960 and started a three-year crusade (Richard Hankey later remembered it as "ramrodding the Society") to build the scholarly reputation of the organization.[100] A new journal, *Criminologica*, first appeared in 1963 as an outlet for scholarly publications. At previous annual meetings, considerable discussion on the nature of criminology had occurred.[101] Marvin Wolfgang (one of the more famous academic criminologists in America, who was serving as a vice president of the Society) made it clear that occupational affinity did not necessarily make one a criminologist. This was a dramatically different definition from the one earlier proffered by both Vollmer and Wilson. Instead, a criminologist was one who used a "scientific approach to the study and analysis of the phenomena of crime and criminal behavior." Wolfgang's interpretation did not go unchallenged, but it was clear that the debate did not include the Vollmer people or their perspective.[102] The police professors through hard academic politics were being pushed out of the organization they had created.

CONCLUSION

Higher education, and the professionalization of academic disciplines and professional schools, is a highly competitive enterprise. Ultimately, it is boldly academic politics. Campus tranquillity masks considerable infighting and struggles for power. Basking in the protective environment of the late 1930s and the 1940s, criminology—as defined by August Vollmer and the V-Men—became entrenched in California. For similar reasons it grew elsewhere as well. There had been some academic struggles initially, but friends in high places helped the developments at the University of California.

But now the School and its concomitant Society were more visible and open to criticism by other academics, earlier preoccupied by the Depression and the world war, who did not think police education should occur at the university or that the destiny of the field should be controlled by such blatant vocationalizers. By the early 1960s, therefore, the V-Men had been squeezed out of the School of Criminology and the organization they had established in 1941. Furthermore, the semantic standard by which they had been known was being more clearly defined to their exclusion. These police professors had to start anew the search for their own identity and their proper place within higher education. That search would be greatly aided by social and political forces let loose in the 1960s.

Chapter 5

The International Association of Police Professors, 1963–1970

By 1963 the American Society of Criminology (ASC) had seen a decade of considerable changes. Following Donal MacNamara, who had been a driving force in the late 1950s and president of the Society from 1960 to 1963, leadership of the organization became even more dominated by sociologists. People such as Walter Reckless (1964-66), Gerhard Mueller (1968), Bruno Cormier (1969), Marvin Wolfgang (1970), and Simon Dinitz (1971) were presidents throughout this period who seemed alien to the tradition of Vollmer and Wiltberger. Concern over agency operations seemed less important to the new members and leaders. In fact, it was not until 1970 that a former president, Walter Reckless, advocated that criminological studies make greater allowances for the way the system operated.[1]

Finally breaking the western monopoly of the 1950s, the Society now established an eastern one. When Felix Fabian and John Kenney attended the Denver meeting in 1961, they recognized that they were the only representatives of the "old group."[2] With the exception of the Berkeley meeting in 1965, all ASC convention sites were in the east. Even San Juan, Puerto Rico (1971), and Caracas, Venezuela (1972), were chosen for annual meetings, perhaps to give the organization a sense of international significance, before the West Coast was seriously considered again. In those days conference location predetermined the kind of people who would attend and shape the organization (with the exception of a few extremely active and committed academic politicians). Californians, with their law enforcement and vocational orientations, were being left out.[3]

The police professors of the 1950s felt that much

going on in the ASC was arcane. William Melincoe, a Vollmerite teaching at Sacramento State College, felt the police people had been pushed out by the sociologists.[4] Harry More, from Washington State, thought the ASC was too corrections-oriented.[5] Indiana University's Robert Borkenstein argued that the ASC had nothing to do anymore with law enforcement.[6] Edward Farris saw the endless debates on the nature of criminology as silly academic stuff. "Why worry about that?" he asked. "You've got a problem with crime and we ought to resolve that!"[7] Even Jack Kenney, who was partially responsible for the revolution that had occurred in the Society, became concerned that "the sociologists and psychologists were getting beyond meeting the needs of the professional people."[8] In short, a number of displaced police professors were sufficiently alienated from the Society they had helped to found that they contemplated forming a new one. These thoughts and complaints found expression at Pullman, Washington, the academic home of V. A. Leonard.

After serving for over twenty years at Washington State, Leonard decided to retire and return to Texas in 1963. Earlier he had given up the chairmanship of the department to Donald McCall, who along with fellow faculty members Felix Fabian and Harry More decided to commemorate Leonard's retirement. Jack Kenney from Long Beach State College and Douglas Gourley from Los Angeles State College made the trip to Pullman. So did Edward Farris, who was eager to talk about his new program at New Mexico State College. Robert Borkenstein came from as far away as Indiana University. A few, like Borkenstein, had no other motive than to pay homage to Leonard.[9] However, others had hidden agendas. Jack Kenney remembered going to Pullman with the specific intent of forming a new organization.[10] Although unable to attend, William Melincoe had been pushing for an alternative to the American Society of Criminology for some time, and he fully expected something new to come out of the Pullman meeting.[11]

Once these old friends and colleagues had paid their respects to V. A. Leonard, discussion turned to common problems and concerns. Memories have faded as to who actually first suggested a new organization. Fabian thought it was Douglas Gourley.[12] Farris thought he had done it.[13] Melincoe had sent a letter hinting at it. Clearly, a variety of people from a variety of places were ready for such a move. Consequently, when the idea of a new organization was introduced hardly any opposition existed and it was effortlessly formed. Thus was born the International Association of Police Professors (IAPP).

Perhaps the word "international" was a bit grandiose, even though one person at the Pullman meeting was from the National Police College at Taiwan. However, it did allow the Vollmerites to make a sly statement clearly distinguishing themselves from the American Society of Criminology, and suggesting closer attachments to the International Association of Chiefs of Police. In this case imitation was more than a form of flattery. Administrative practitioners in policing it was felt were more appropriate models for police education than any theorizing criminologists. In addition, emphasis was put on "police professors." In looking forward they glanced backward twenty years or more to reinstate and reemphasize a commitment to police science and police education. For them the criminal, and the causes for his deviance, were less important than the agencies of crime fighting. The social, cultural, and political climate of the 1960s would boost their concerns onto the national scene.

"COMING APART": AMERICA IN THE 1960S

Clearly, crime and disorder have been a historical constant in America. Urban disorders called into existence the modern police.[14] Employee theft inspired the rise of private police.[15] Labor disorders forced the beginnings of the state trooper systems.[16] Prohibition and gangland wars gave rise to the Wickersham Commission and the police education movement. Such public awareness and political concern, however, was not as consistent as the problems. Too many things got in the way—industrial growth, western expansion, wars and depressions—for developing any consistent crime policy, which then became instead increasingly crisis driven.

But in many ways the 1960s became a measuring rod. Not since the 1840s-50s and 1920s had a decade been associated with crime. It was a time of sensational events magnified by the mass media. Political assassinations were sprinkled across the period. Medgar Evers, a regional representative of the National Association for the Advancement of Colored People, was murdered in Jackson, Mississippi, in 1963. President John F. Kennedy, and then the prime suspect in his killing, were both shot down before startled national audiences later the same year. Thereafter, in almost frightening succession, political celebrities fell to assassins. Two extremists, Malcolm X (previously a leader in the Black Muslim movement) and George Lincoln Rockwell (head of the American Nazi Party) were killed in the 1960s. Spokesmen for moderation, such as Martin Luther King, Jr., and Senator Robert Kennedy, also fell shortly thereafter. In addition, bizarre murderers such as the Boston Strangler, Charles Whitman, Richard Speck, and Charles Manson, revealed the madness in society.

Beginning in 1963 the reported incidence of serious crime against persons and property rose at alarming rates. After twenty years of slow increases, crime in all categories shot up rapidly, increasing 203 percent between 1960 and 1974. Robbery alone, in this era of the "mugger," rose 310 percent. Several factors contributed to such increases. The baby boom generation, those born after World War II, had reached the crime-prone years of age 15 to 30. An unpopular war in Southeast Asia caused many youth to distrust authority figures ranging from presidents to police to parents. Abundant media coverage heightened public awareness, concern, and fear of crime. Racism, always a prevalent characteristic of American culture, was at work as well, for it was "crime in the streets" more than "crime in the suites" that aroused the greatest outrage. Street crime (such as assault, homicide, robbery, and rape) tended to concentrate among the lower classes and was used to justify unresolved racist anxieties. Even though most victims of crime lived in the urban ghettos, the middle classes protested most loudly (through public opinion polls) about crime in the streets. Drug use expanded greatly, both within a growing defiant youth culture and among ghetto residents. The Summerdale scandal in Chicago (1960) reminded Americans of police officer susceptibility to crime. Subsequent revelations in Denver, Buffalo, New York City, and Indianapolis strengthened public impressions of the "tarnished badge." Clearly, events of the 1960s showed the weaknesses in policing. At the very time that demands for greater police expertise were occurring, the Supreme Court stepped in to make policing even more difficult.

Beginning in 1961 the Court applied many constitutional restraints previously restricted to the federal policing establishment to state and local agencies. For example, in *Mapp v. Ohio* the Warren Court, as part of its "due process revolution," declared that evidence obtained through unreasonable searches might be excluded from trials. After *Gideon v. Wainwright* (1963) insured indigents of their right to counsel in the courts, legal representation moved step by step into police activities. The *Escobedo* decision (1964) ruled that when an investigation went from "general inquiry" to focus on a "particular suspect," legal counsel could be present. According to the *Miranda* ruling (1966), upon arrest—but prior to questioning—suspects had to be warned of their constitutional rights to remain silent and to have an attorney.

On one hand, such decisions interfered with the efficiency of police work. The Warren Court was accused of "coddling the criminals" and "handcuffing the police" by hard-line crime control advocates who saw an already hard job become more difficult. On the other hand, such decisions made the police more responsible and accountable to the rule of law. As Samuel Walker suggests, these decisions brought police procedure into public view, and expectations about the quality of police performance increased.[17] Supervision and training became all the more important. In short, the police needed to be more professional. Maybe more education could accomplish that.

Perhaps even more jolting to middle-class sensibilities than crime was disorder. From 1964 to its peak in 1968, mob activity seemed the most threatening challenge to American society. In the last analysis, crime has a life largely independent of policing. But modern policing, going back to the reforms of Robert Peel in England in the 1830s, was built upon maintaining order in the streets.[18] Now, it seemed, the keepers of the peace were involved in and maybe responsible for the riots across the land. At first, much disorder was connected to the tactics used by the civil rights movement. Peaceful sit-ins, pray-ins, and lay-ins posed problems even for the most enlightened police department. How did one gently remove inert humans from public places and thoroughfares without appearing overbearing? Some departments, such as in Birmingham, Alabama, simply did not care; they turned police dogs and fire hoses upon demonstrators before the incredulous eyes of television audiences.

The pent-up frustrations of low-income people surfaced in New York City; Rochester, New York; Philadelphia; and Jersey City, New Jersey, in 1964 as civil disobedience turned into destruction. In the summer of 1965, the worst racial disturbances to date swept the Watts area of Los Angeles. Thirty-three cities witnessed some form of race riot in 1966; the next year was even worse. Twenty-three people died during five days of rioting in Newark, New Jersey, in 1967. One week later Detroit erupted, and forty-three people died in the week-long chaos. Then in the spring of 1968, in the wake of Martin Luther King, Jr.'s, death, rioting began anew. To borrow a phrase from a popular history of the period, the United States seemed to be "Coming Apart."[19]

The National Advisory Commission on Civil Rights, referred to as the Kerner Commission, was established in 1967. Racism, reported the Commission, underlay these years of disorder. In addition to unemployment, inadequate housing, and paltry social services, most Black Americans too often received unequal justice within the agencies of criminal justice. In fact, as in Harlem and Philadelphia (1964), Watts (1965), San Francisco and Atlanta (1966), and Newark and Detroit (1967), police actions to a large degree were responsible for escalating the disorder. As if to validate the Kerner report, in the next year the Chicago police ran amok during the Democratic Convention melee.

America was faced with a perplexing problem. Policing is the most visible attribute of government, the most tangible expression of authority. To jeer and call the police "pigs" in a larger sense was a vote of no confidence for government itself. Indeed, attacks on the police might be harbingers of graver things to come. Clearly, long-range social solutions were needed, but political ones were a quicker fix.

The political issue of "law and order" was first used by Barry Goldwater during the 1964 presidential campaigns. Goldwater was defeated, but shortly thereafter President Lyndon Johnson declared his own "war on crime" by creating the Office of Law Enforcement Assistance (OLEA) in 1965 to dispense federal grants to law enforcement agencies. In a little over two and one-half years, OLEA doled out $21 million for training and research, much of this money went to colleges to fund law enforcement education. In addition, Johnson created the President's Commission on Law Enforcement and Administration of Justice, the first such national crime commission in 35 years. After a two-year study by a panel of distinguished people, nine task force reports and a general report, *The Challenge of Crime in a Free Society*, were issued in 1967. Additional research money was needed, declared the Commission, and agency personnel needed more training. Another boost to the police professoriate was the Commission's recommendation that police recruits have a college degree.

The Commission took a "systems" approach to crime and crime-fighting agencies. The administration of justice should be seen as an interrelated whole, with the police, courts, and corrections impacting upon each other. This new intellectual construct would have profound impact upon both criminology and police education in the future. As early as 1952, the American Bar Foundation, a research arm of the American Bar Association, had been set up to study the administration of justice in America. Frank Remington, a law professor at the University of Wisconsin, headed pilot studies in Michigan, Wisconsin, and Kansas in 1956 and 1957. Some 2,000 small field reports were amassed into a seven-volume Pilot Project Report. In addition, a series of scholarly works edited by Remington came out beginning in 1965 with Wayne R. LaFave's *Arrest: The Decision to Take a Suspect into Custody*. The philosophy of the Foundation was to regard the agencies of justice as a total system, with decisions made at one point reverberating elsewhere. Certainly the phrase "criminal justice" had been used earlier, but it referred most often to the legal system and the court process. Now it was to be a new umbrella under which policing and corrections would join the legal system. The lawyers in the Foundation were simply extending their conceptual definitions more broadly. As any buff of geography or Western history knows, the frontier pioneer has a grave responsibility: to give place names. Those tags—even if they are not always appropriate—have a tendency to linger. The work of the American Bar Foundation had a great impact upon the President's Commission on Law Enforcement and Administration of Justice. The phrase "criminal justice" increasingly became part of the public vocabulary, particularly in the 1970s.[20]

President Johnson responded to the Commission by forging the Omnibus Crime Control and Safe Streets Act, which passed into law in 1968. Title I of the act replaced OLEA with a new agency within the Department of Justice called the Law Enforcement Assistance Administration (LEAA), which had charge of dispensing block grants to the states for policing. Much of the money went for crime-fighting hardware and bizarre weaponry. More germane to our concerns, however, was another agency within LEAA.

The Law Enforcement Education Program (LEEP) sought to upgrade policing through education. After all Americans have always placed great faith in higher education. But direct governmental aid to education has been associated with a sense of crisis. For example, in 1862 the federal government used the Morrill Act to encourage acquisition of the agricultural and mechanical skills needed during the Civil War crisis. In 1917 the Smith-Hughes Act, which gave aid to vocational education, saw easier passage due to the war in Europe. Victory in World War II was attributed to technological and scientific achievements as much as to military skills. The G.I. Bill of Rights resulted in 1944 to insure the growth of technology and science in American culture. The launching of the Soviet satellite Sputnik in 1957 shocked America into reevaluating its educational system. The National Defense Education Act followed in 1958. Significantly, the word "defense" in the title points up the connection between crisis and government involvement in higher education. To carry the military metaphor further, a war on crime declared in the late 1960s ushered in another federal excursion into higher education.

Indeed, in spite of the previous thirty years of Vollmerian police education, most officers had little education. Fewer than 10 percent of American policemen had been to college, according to a December 1968 issue of *Fortune* magazine.[21] *Time* magazine reported in October 1968 that police recruits in Detroit came from the bottom 25 percent of their high school graduating class.[22] Clearly, in-service police personnel needed more education, a challenge taken up by LEEP.

Between 1969 and 1975, LEEP grants grew from $6.5 million for 485 funded institutions to $40 million for 1,065 colleges. Thousands of police officers returned to school for college education and degrees in law enforcement programs.[23] For example, in 1972 there were 177,472 persons studying police science; 55 percent were in-service personnel receiving 84 percent of the LEEP funds. The remaining 45 percent were pre-service students who received 16 percent of the money.[24] Before 1970, 80 percent of the federal funds went to law enforcement. After 1970, that share went to 60 percent as the concept of "criminal justice" began to take a firmer hold and more money was allocated to corrections.[25]

As the federal largess began in the late 1960s to pour down into the institutions of higher learning one issue stood out: Just what kind of education did the police really need? The answer depended upon what one thought the police really did. Clearly, the turbulent 1960s highlighted two police problems. On one hand there was crime: its prevention and detection. Intentionally or not, the Vollmerites had been addressing this problem for a generation. The solution was technical training, something the community colleges and state colleges had been doing for thirty years. University criminologists might help a bit with theories on criminal behavior. Vollmerites might help too by providing better administered and controlled police departments.

On the other hand, the 1960s exposed deeper problems of order maintenance, dealing with an ethnically diverse society in which public hostility was closely connected to police insensitivity and brutality. One does not easily learn empathy and sensitivity in a crime lab or through organizational flow charts. Part of learning that was the concept "criminal justice" itself, in other words, seeing oneself as a police officer in something much larger than policing. This was a viewpoint not commonly held by personnel in policing, the legal system, or corrections. Practitioners as well as the public needed to be converted to such a notion. Many argued that the best type of education to accomplish this socially worthy task was liberal arts, an orientation already in place in the colleges and universities of America. However, most in-service people did not want sociology, political science, history, or literature; they wanted relevant and familiar stuff. Consequently, much money went to the creation and expansion of new and existing criminology and law enforcement programs. Federal money breathed new life into the field and created new problems for the professionalizers.

It is against this societal and political backdrop of the 1960s that one must examine further developments and challenges to the Vollmerian tradition.

INTERNATIONAL ASSOCIATION OF POLICE PROFESSORS

The larger issues of higher education and the place of the Vollmerian model in it took on greater significance as the decade wore on, but initially there were more immediate issues confronting the IAPP. Yet one issue was put to rest for the time being: the place of criminology as increasingly defined by the American Society of Criminology. The IAPP was a police educators' organization going back to the orientation of the late 1940s and early 1950s. Throughout the 1960s, these police professors were conscientious in making and maintaining the distinctions. LEAA and LEEP provided political affirmation of the police professors in the IAPP. The issue had become more than one of semantics; society seemed to agree that great consideration should be given to the agencies and personnel fighting crime.

Now the most immediate concern for the police professors and their new organization was twofold: the place of the junior college program in the police education movement, and the control of the growing number of four-year programs. Both problems related to the issue of quality control.

The Community College Issue

More than in any other academic field, the presence of law enforcement programs in junior college proved the uniqueness of police education and provided an important Achilles heel in the professionalization process. It became one of the more heated political issues in law enforcement education. When the IAPP's constitution was written in 1963, junior college faculty were forbidden membership. Prior experience in the 1950s had taught many police professors that no matter what you called it—criminology or police science—there was a real difference between the two- and four-year institutions. Indeed, when the first president of the IAPP, Donald McCall, gave his keynote address, most of his message focused on the problems of transferring student credit hours between two-year and four-year schools.[26]

But the junior college issue would not go away. Law enforcement programs increased at a rapid rate throughout this period. For example, California (the state with the greatest number of two-year institutions) had 36 police programs in the community colleges by 1962. That number increased to 56 in 1965, 68 in 1967, and 74 by 1970.[27] Similar patterns of growth occurred outside California as well. The police professors now became caught in between two extremes. On one hand, was what they perceived to be the more elitist academics who had taken over "their" organization, the American Society of Criminology, and continued to hold them up to ridicule for not being sufficiently academic. On the other hand, were the highly vocational junior college programs that proved the point of those critics.

Certainly more than for other disciplines, law enforcement programs in junior colleges did pose a problem for the four-year institutions. The "mission" of the community college—besides offering courses that might be transferred and acceptable at a four-year institution—was to offer unique and usable knowledge for residents who might not want to go on to college. For example, a community college in one area might offer dental hygiene technology. Another might offer electronics repair. Since police education was so new and rare in traditional universities and colleges *and* so vocational, it was seen as fitting the more occupational mission of the community colleges.

The year Felix Fabian became the second president of the organization, he finished his doctorate at the University of Idaho. His dissertation, a study of pre-service law enforcement education, surveyed 18 colleges and 51 community colleges offering police science programs. He compared the curricula of both types of institutions and arranged them according to frequency. The similarities between junior college and four-year offerings were remarkable. Criminal investigation, for example, topped the list for all programs. In fact, only the slightest variations distinguished the two categories. So course differences were not the problem, except that four-year colleges were evidently as vocational as the two-year ones.

In addition, most community colleges at the time used the "upside-down curricula" made popular by William Wiltberger thirty years earlier. This meant that community college graduates took too much law enforcement too early at the expense of general education courses. A transferring student might arrive at a four-year institution and find very little in the major that had not already been taken. Law enforcement programs in four-year institutions, therefore, were robbed of their clientele.

Even more troublesome was the way in which the similar courses were taught. The university and college systems—with the exception of the professional school—were supposed to liberally educate the undergraduate and give the graduate scholarly training. Of course, how well they fulfilled that mission depended upon where they fell on the continuum from Ivy League to state college. The community college's vocational lean did not affect history, sociology, foreign languages, and chemistry. But it had a profound impact on law enforcement, forcing Fabian to distinguish between the "how-to" orientation of the community college and the "why" orientation of the four-year college.[28] Consequently, a transfer student from a two-year institution might arrive at a four-year one having taken all the prescribed courses but having had a much different educational experience.

The junior colleges, however, did not lack spokesmen. James D. Stinchcomb constantly reminded the police professors of the importance of the community college. When the U.S. Department of Health, Education, and Welfare listed police science in its 1969 publication "Twenty-five Technical Careers You Can Learn in Two Years or Less," Stinchcomb took that as proof that the two-year college played a vital role in police education.[29] It also verified the worries of the police professors in four-year institutions. Such a report was a problem for the police professors. It went contrary to what they were trying to do: create a profession wherein education rather than training was essential.

Edward Farris became one of the more important defenders of the junior college programs. In 1964 he wrote a master's thesis at the University of California's School of Criminology; it was called "The Role of the Junior College in Police Education in California." The junior college had a very important role to play, he felt. It screened out students who might not achieve the minimal standards in a police department. It gave pre-employment preparation for students interested in policing. It provided in-service education for practitioners. Finally, it offered general and adult education for the community it served. Thus far, he contended, the major problem of police education was a failure of practitioners and educators to communicate. This was particularly true in many colleges and universities. "The failure to understand what the other is attempting to accomplish," Farris maintained, "has been perhaps the greatest drawback to progress in the field."[30] It was at the junior college level that this communication was most likely to occur.

Although there was concern over the community college issue throughout this period and into the next, the 1965 meetings at East Lansing, Michigan, inspired some change.[31] Donald Riddle was attending his first meeting at that time and argued effectively that no organization could have much of a future if it was exclusionary. The best way to control and change the community college police programs was to let them in and then educate them, he reasoned.[32] Apparently Riddle was persuasive, because constitutional revisions were made and in the next year they were formally admitted. This move may have been merely political, however, because in the next year considerable opposition resurfaced over whether junior colleges should get a share of the federal moneys that were beginning to appear from OLEA.[33] A lot of this was moot, however. Skimpy travel allowances for community college instructors meant that unless meetings were held in California there would be scant participation anyway. That became an issue as well. Here was a large educational group disconnected to an organization, according to Riddle, that should be bringing it along to more closely resemble the four-year institutions. Symbolic gestures were in order. In 1966 Richard Hankey, who had spent ten years as a junior college teacher before moving to Los Angeles State College, was elected president. More blatant was the election of B. Earl Lewis in 1968.

Lewis was a product of the San Jose State police program. In addition, he had spent considerable time as a police officer before starting a teaching career in the community colleges of California. In fact one of those colleges, DeAnza College at Cuperchino, was a regional police academy. Furthermore, in 1968 Lewis was president of the California Police Educators Association, a group made up entirely of community college and police academy people. Gordon Misner, a graduate of the University of California School of Criminology and now professor at San Jose State, was a close friend and mentor to Lewis; Misner was also in charge of the IAPP program arrangements at the San

Francisco meetings. Although Lewis was not even a member of the IAPP, he gave a speech and—more surprising—was elected president. Some charged that it was rank personal politics by Misner, clearly something he enjoyed. There is some evidence for this contention. Apparently, Misner was opposed to a major candidate for president, William Hewitt, and looked to Lewis as an attractive alternative. Others felt it was an attempt of the "San Jose crowd" to capture the organization.[34] In light of what would happen to San Jose State during the following year when the IAPP was flirting with quality control of four-year programs, the latter explanation had some credence. Nevertheless, Lewis's election—shaky and contrived as it was—seemed to suggest that the IAPP was willing to play politics and provide token support of the community college police professor.

As time went by, however, such second-hand treatment of the community college law enforcement programs rankled some individuals. James Stinchcomb had tolerated the situation for much of the decade, but he felt increasingly alienated and his speeches to the membership took on the tone of a person in a hostile camp. Finally, by the end of the decade he all but left the organization to devote more time and energy to the IACP.[35] Many junior college instructors, whose attendance had been sparse anyway, simply stopped coming to IAPP meetings; a dual world of police education was developing in spite of the work done by some academic politicians. By that time the IAPP had moved on to a more pressing and profound issue that further alienated the community college instructors.

Accreditation and Quality Control

A major issue—discernible early but gaining urgency as the decade wore on—was the increasing number of four-year programs. Of course, the great flood of four-year "criminal justice" programs occur during the 1970s. But there were enough older programs and enough new ones springing up in the 1960s to warrant concern over issues of quality. Perhaps the junior college could be excused because of its peculiar place in higher education, but variations in quality in four-year programs might suggest the lack of consensus on the nature of police education. Fabian's research suggested that the differences between two- and four-year programs were not all that great. The IAPP founders had agreed in 1963 that there was a need for a "substantially increased degree of uniformity in curriculum organization and content." Felix Fabian, looking beyond course listings to college missions, felt at the time that the educational situation in four-year colleges and universities was "one of considerable contrasts in terms of philosophy and objectives."[36] At the second meeting of the organization, President McCall once again raised the issue because the Ford Foundation had given the International Association of Chiefs of Police $400,000 to study the nationwide development of police education. They were to establish standards, evaluate police programs, and stimulate the expansion of academic degree programs.[37] Clearly, IAPP members were friendlier to the IACP than academic criminologists. Nevertheless, any profession needs to monopolize its own activities and become judge of its own quality. To give that responsibility to the police chiefs and their organization would have finished the IAPP. Professors, not police chiefs, would have to be in control of issues of education.

Felix Fabian, then president of the IAPP, went to the IACP meetings to argue that he and his organization should be in charge of quality control. To be on the safe side he took along his old friend O. W. Wilson, now chief of the Chicago police department, to bolster his credibility. Fortunately, the president of the American Society of Criminology, Walter Reckless, was attending one of the meetings. Much as Fabian was thinking, Reckless argued against any police involvement in setting standards in education. Then Reckless astonished everyone by questioning the idea of educating the police at all. Members of the IACP sat in stunned silence as Reckless and Fabian squared off. Fabian carried the day because he was closer to the police establishment in background and orientation, and he argued a point that the chiefs had already accepted. The Reckless-Fabian debate was more symbolic than substantive, showing the gap between the ASC and the IAPP. It did, however, convince many that if accreditation of police education were to occur, it would best be done by Fabian and his organization.[38]

Accreditation is a quality control process by which consumers are assured that members of an occupation, or an institution that trains the practitioners of that vocation, has met commonly accepted standards. Although it is a "progressive" idea with roots in the Progressive era's craze for regulation, government has generally not been involved because the process can be easily interpreted as a form of dictation. Most often a special accreditation agency representing a profession establishes standards of quality and judges practitioners accordingly. Consequently, this peer group activity has become an important ingredient in the professionalization process.[39]

Accreditation may take one of two forms, which highlight a basic issue in the police education movement. One form, commonly referred to as "general accreditation," is the judging of an entire institution such as a university or college. Any specific programs within that college are judged and accepted along with the overall institution. A weak program might be carried by the strength of the entire college, a camouflage that was not overlooked in the early days of program development. From 1914 to 1948 the Association of American Universities performed this activity. From 1950 onward, six regional accrediting agencies routinely examined colleges and universities within their regions. Another form of professional control, which might be called "special accreditation," has to do with professional schools. Many professional schools, though loosely connected to a university, have considerable autonomy and are not part of the general evaluation process. Instead, they are evaluated by some mechanism connected to their professional organization. The American Medical Association followed this procedure to drive out substandard medical schools in the first decade of the twentieth century. By 1940 dentistry, engineering, and pharmacy—to name just a few—had set up their own accrediting bodies to control growth, insure the expertise of the practitioner, and generally upgrade the status of the profession. Police professors, still reeling from being displaced by academic criminologists, found the accreditation idea tantalizing in the 1960s. It also pointed up the divergence of opinion within the IAPP on the basic educational nature of police education.

An "accreditation panel" was appointed by President Felix Fabian as early as 1964. It advocated special accreditation. Some did not understand accreditation, and words such as "fundamentals," "standards," and "guidelines" appeared. A committee on standards for police education issued two reports: "Return to Fundamentals" (1965) and "Fundamentals Revisited" (1966). Shortly after the Committee to Establish Guidelines for the Development of Law Enforcement Programs made its report in 1966, the impact of OLEA made quality control all the more urgent.[40] Finally, President Robert Scheehan suggested that the organization look into the issue more deeply and it became the main theme of the Atlanta meetings in 1969.[41]

In the politics of accreditation at Atlanta there were two small groups with their minds set. On one hand, were those in favor of special accreditation. They generally had professional backgrounds in law schools, business schools, or the School of Criminology at Berkeley. They wanted the IAPP to provide accrediting services. On the other hand were those who were against accreditation altogether. Junior college people felt that such a process would rob them of their unique offerings and make them become more similar to the four-year programs.[42] Donald Riddle and Richard Myren, who were setting up new programs at John Jay and State University of New York at Albany (SUNY), were against any accreditation that took them out of mainstream academic circles.[43] The majority needed to be educated, however, and the information coming out of the Atlanta meeting was not encouraging.

Several representatives of the general accreditation method dominated the presentations. Charles B. Vail, dean at Georgia State University, found accreditation a good idea but felt the IAPP should not get involved.[44] Jerry W. Miller was an associate director for the National Commission of Accrediting, one of the coordinating bodies for the regional accrediting agencies. A profession needed to be well-established before it got involved in the accrediting business, he warned. Perhaps not realizing his own perceptiveness, Miller touched upon an important point at the core of the motives behind the accreditation issue among the police professors:

> There is great temptation, I think, to view accreditation as a quick means of developing professional characteristics and requirements which have public significance. It is viewed as the quick and easy route to public recognition, but this is not the considered view. Standards on which there is little consensus will command little support as will the organization or agency which tries to apply them.[45]

A concrete example of the dangers of accreditation was presented at the Atlanta meeting. An evaluation report had been made earlier that inspired heart-wrenching moments and rehearsed for the membership some of the possible repercussions of quality control. Donald Riddle and Richard Myren had been asked as private consultants by the San Jose State College to evaluate its police school, which was headed by a Wiltberger disciple Melvin Miller. Riddle and Myren, as program builders and administrators in the East, were emerging as powerful figures in the new "criminal justice" movement. San Jose State's police school, going back in an almost unbroken chain to William Wiltberger's work in the 1930s, remained an important manifestation of the more conservative wing of police education in four-year institutions. Riddle and Myren represented some profound changes occurring at the end of the decade. The upshot of their report was very negative. Miller's "harness bull" (Miller's own designation) program was found to be inappropriate and out of step. It was too vocational, doing many things more appropriate for a police academy than for an institution of higher learning. Miller was forced to step down as chair of the school, and his faculty and sympathizers in the IAPP were stunned. "We don't need a kick in the teeth or a kick in the pants," lamented Miller in Atlanta.[46] Many agreed and even shared the Wiltberger-Miller approach; and the last discussions and votes at the Atlanta meeting constituted a repudiation of accreditation.[47]

Academic Politics of Professional Associations

More than previous meetings, the Atlanta conference drew the political lines signaling significant changes in the organization and in police education. On one side were the conservatives who were very close to the junior college people. Melvin Miller, the sacrificial lamb to accreditation, was representative. Miller had degrees in education from the University of South Dakota (1938) and Stanford University (1955). He had worked with the Border Patrol of the Immigration Department from 1941 to 1953. He started teaching at San Jose State in 1953, heading the school from 1963 to 1969. Under his administration, Miller felt, San Jose had become the best "harness bull" program in the country. This was not a pejorative term; in fact, Miller coined it to mean a highly vocational police program. It was in keeping with the Wiltbergerian tradition, and Wiltberger himself was frequently a guest speaker at the school. A liberal education was fine, Miller believed, but law enforcement in America demanded that the employee start at the bottom and work up the professional ladder no matter how many or what kind of college degrees the employee had. Therefore, fundamentals or police basics (i.e., vocational courses) needed to take priority. Miller was not alone in such thinking. Richard Hankey, William Melincoe, and Felix Fabian—to name a few—shared his outlook. However, more outspoken than any was Edward Farris.[48]

Although Farris was not strictly speaking a V-man, his respect of and constant reference to that time and those characters made him an unofficial historian of the police education movement.[49] He had received an undergraduate degree in policing at the University of California in 1949 and became a member of the Berkeley police department shortly thereafter. He had taught at Visalia junior college for five years before moving to

New Mexico State College to establish its program in 1963. He then returned to the University of California to get his master's degree in 1964. As discussed earlier, the School of Criminology had changed direction by that time; and in his alienation Farris became even more adamant in the espousing of the traditional Vollmer-Wiltberger ideals.[50]

The focus of police education should be the patrol officer, Farris believed. The education of police administrators and scholars was important, but not as crucial as "the man on the beat." This could be done with a proper balance between vocational and academic courses similar to those offered in the early days by Vollmer and Wiltberger. Farris's clarion call seemed to be summed up in a series of reports demanding a "return to fundamentals."[51] The founding of the IAPP, Farris believed, was a return to Vollmerian principles. Squabbles between the Wiltberger and Vollmer-Leonard mindsets were healthy as long as the Vollmerian ideals provided the backdrop. The School of Criminology had moved away from those ideals. That is why it was all the more important for the IAPP to hold strongly to these historic principles. But by the decade's end Farris seemed increasingly anachronistic ("an antique," in his own words) and an embarrassing reminder of an earlier time.[52]

Throughout most of the 1960s the philosophical distribution was not widely scattered; the distance from mainstream to the most conservative points in the IAPP was a matter of degree. The middle ground, personified by Arthur Brandstatter and Robert Borkenstein, developed very early and held firm. To these men the IAPP was to make police science an academic discipline. As in medicine and law (their favorite analogies), the police professor had to forge a healthy interrelationship between practitioner and educator, between skills and theory.[53] They wanted a professional school as the academic model. Representatives from the University of California School of Criminology were largely absent from the IAPP; the School was making significant shifts toward corrections or penology and therefore was less interested in the police issues. Of course, there was enough activity from the School and its graduates to become a part of the centrist position. Its historic influence and present power provided a backdrop to the IAPP deliberations. The police professors were hungry for leadership from the more prestigious universities, and although it was not forthcoming from Berkeley, people cast their eyes expectantly westward. Those less friendly to Berkeley, as Farris had become, misinterpreted the Lewis election in San Francisco as a takeover attempt by the "Lohman crowd" at Berkeley or by the "San Jose State group."[54] One key person in the centrist group at this time was Gordon Misner, whose academic and political career will be discussed at length later.

Slightly left of center some people were rethinking police education altogether, placing it in larger contexts. As early as 1964, William H. Hewitt of Kent State University presented a paper at the IAPP meetings ("The Objectives of a Formal Police Education") that best indicated the left-of-center position. According to Hewitt, although no college degree is a union card and no college education is a guarantee of success, such experience should indicate that the student has learned discriminating thought, critical independence, and moral responsibility, characteristics that seem to be universally accepted as "professional." Hewitt did not point out the dangers of being a critical, reflective thinker in a bureaucratic environment, however. The best way for police personnel to achieve this would be one in which the liberal arts and vocational skills were held at a ratio of 4 to 1. For every hour of law enforcement training there should be four hours of traditional liberal arts education, Hewitt declared. There needed to be "a well-balanced liberal arts program so that the graduate will not only be knowledgeable and informed, but also to exercise authority wisely and maintain an absolute integrity of character in keeping with the goal of professionalized police service."[55] No one to that point had gone beyond the academic versus vocational issue and placed liberal arts education in the forefront. This principle became a standard for a new generation of thinkers in the next decade.

Hewitt was slightly left of center, but nonetheless he kept the focus on police and policing. At least two members were poised to take the organization and the movement even more leftward, pushing police education toward academic criminal justice. Donald Riddle and Richard Myren were able to do this in part because of the prestigious positions they held in New York. Riddle became president of the IAPP in 1970. Shortly thereafter, the organization was renamed the Academy of Criminal Justice Sciences, ushering in a new era of defining the field. Once again, the West Coast Vollmerites were challenged.[56] This came at a time when changes of seismic proportions were occurring at the School of Criminology at the University of California.

CONCLUSION

Just when the academic attack on police education was most successful, societal conditions throughout the 1960s and 1970s aroused the public and politicians to the need for more efficient and humane systems of justice. The IAPP, created in protest to developments in the American Society of Criminology, benefitted from the rise of government attention and money that inspired numerous new programs of law enforcement. But such benefits quickly turned to challenges as the perplexing problem of vocationalism—in both the community colleges and the state colleges—threatened to undo the efforts of police professors who were trying to create a new academic discipline. Academic politicians from other disciplines resented the popularity and un-intellectual forces around law enforcement education. Furthermore, the rapid growth of law enforcement programs due to sudden federal funding made issues of quality control important. Such growth showed the internal contradictions and dilemmas most vividly and highlighted academic politics within professional associations.

Chapter 6

The Fall of the School of Criminology at Berkeley, 1960–1975

Concerns over crime in the 1960s inspired the proliferation and popularity of police education as never before. As in the 1920s and 1930s, the professionalization of the police, officers on the streets and leaders in headquarters, became panacea. Police programs in four-year institutions went from 65 in 1965 to 700 ten years later.[1] Even though it had already changed its name to the Academy of Criminal Justice Sciences in the early 1970s, the IAPP remained a symbol of the persistence of August Vollmer's dreams. The School of Criminology at the University of California, though not as active in the IAPP as might have been expected, continued to be a model for most police educators. As we shall see later, two other universities emerged to challenge the School of Criminology, but neither one had the stature of the University of California. Berkeley remained alone as one of the finest universities in the country having a school dedicated to the study of crime and the training of upper-level practitioners in the field. It was a standard by which many marked the progress and acceptability of their own academic professionalization.

On the other hand, the growing number of police programs and the increasing vitality of the IAPP gave rise to questions over the place of this curriculum in the hierarchy of America's colleges and universities. The issue spoke broadly to the pecking order of these institutions of higher learning and, in turn, their definitions and tolerances of a field still unsure of itself as a professional or academic discipline. The acceptance and stability of police education in the community colleges and state colleges seemed assured by the late 1960s and early 1970s. Such a development may have been an excuse for the more prestigious universities to overlook police education. With rare exception universities of excellence, the so-called Ivy League and flagship institutions of state university systems, were quick to abandon earlier commitments or slow to develop new ones. Some mainstream universities allowed police education (or criminal justice, as it was slowly beginning to be called) to be part of their "urban mission" in satellite city extensions. Hence, places like the University of Illinois at Chicago Circle created a police program (largely owing to the prodding of Superintendent of Police O. W. Wilson), but the more established and traditional downstate campus did not.[2] This had occurred in slightly different ways earlier in Michigan.[3] It was true also in Wisconsin, Nebraska, Kansas, Missouri, Alabama, and North Carolina. Once again, the School of Criminology at the University of California offers an agonizing example of this sorting out of police education from first-tier to second- and third-tier places of higher education. It became a testament not only to police education but to the evolving nature and diversification of America's higher educational system. It is also an example of academic politics.

THE LOHMAN ERA

Joseph Lohman—his background and career—accurately personified the School of Criminology throughout the 1960s. After receiving a master's degree in sociology from the University of Wisconsin in 1932, he served as research criminologist for the Behavior Research Fund and then the Institute of Juvenile Research for the State of Illinois from 1933 to 1939. For the next twenty years, when political and professional duties permitted, he was on the faculty of sociology at the University of Chicago. Once again—as Vollmer's and Wilson's careers had shown—practical experience was seen to be as valuable as any doctoral degree. In addition, Lohman was chairman of the Division of Corrections for Illinois from 1952 to 1953. Then he was elected sheriff of Cook County (Chicago), serving in that capacity until 1958 when he was elected treasurer of the state. That term of office was running out when he was selected to be dean of the School of Criminology. In short, he brought considerable political and professional savvy to his new post as dean.[4]

After the departure of O. W. Wilson, the School of Criminology made stronger commitments to research, an important political decision. Although it was not a Ph.D. (the research degree commonly equated with academic scholarship) a doctorate of criminology was in place by 1963-64. Such a degree seemed more appropriate and maintained the School's distinction as a professional school. By 1966 there appeared to be a distinct research component, an area created by Lohman that was determined to be essential for any kind of respectability across the campus. Fifteen people were named as researchers. Some were full-time scholars working on various grants such as the Prison College Project and the Food and Drug Administration Training Center Program. Several researchers—be they full-time or part-time—had linkages to Lohman while he was at the University of Chicago. One of them, Herbert Blumer, had been at the University of Chicago for over twenty years before he came to Berkeley to head the sociology department. Blumer, a preeminent sociologist and former professional football player for the Chicago Bears, was undoubtedly an important political ally for the School in any cross-campus academic battles. Three-fourths of the research personnel had interests that were mainly in the area of corrections, thus showing the drift of the School under Lohman away from policing. However, many of the researchers were ill-prepared graduate students who were listed only because they were working on a degree that had obtained some funding or were involved with one of the projects as an assistant.[5] Obviously, much of this roster-padding was a political move to impress.

In spite of such seemingly scholarly developments, the School remained committed to educating practitioners. For example, a survey done in 1968 showed that 72 percent of the people earning degrees after Lohman took over were working in criminal justice agencies. A total of 141 (38 percent of the total 729 degrees) were in law enforcement, 120 (32 percent) were in corrections, 45 (12 percent) were in law, and 34 (9 percent) were in criminalistics. Only 34 (or 9 percent) were in teaching and research, an area of high importance at the University of California.[6] Indeed, the teaching faculty of the School was just as sparse and haphazard. There were twenty faculty members, fifteen of whom had been hired after Lohman's arrival. Over 70 percent of these were part-timers, being shared with another academic unit or operational agency. Many were graduate students—such as Robert Fisher, Gordon Misner, and Richard Korn—finishing their own degrees and doing some teaching.[7] The School certainly did not resemble a traditional academic department.

This situation remained tolerable because after all,

any professional school (even in law and medicine) needed to train practitioners. Furthermore, professional schools were not ordinary academic departments. It should be noted in all fairness that professional schools in general and law schools in particular have never been models of scholarly productivity. One study of 138 accredited law schools in the 1980s, when research and publication was a popular component of the definition of higher education, found that 44 percent of the senior faculty had no publications whatsoever.[8] However, this generalization misses an important point about professional schools in American universities; that is, the standing and mission of a professional school cannot be seen as distinct from the reputation and stature of the university with which it is connected. One may teach law as a practical art, not doing much more than preparing a student to pass local bar examinations. Or it may teach law as an academic discipline, emphasizing legal research and reasoning. On the spectrum of law schools, those of less stature emphasize the former and those of higher quality emphasize the latter.[9]

Consequently, some individuals in the law school and Center for the Study of Law and Society at Berkeley began to regard the School of Criminology with disdain. Caleb Foote, a law professor at Berkeley who began his association with the School of Criminology in 1965, was perhaps the most outspoken. Later Foote had vivid recollections

> of Dean Lohman's frenzied attempts to maintain a balance between professional and academic goals. To meet the requirements of professional training he admitted large numbers of "professionals" and preprofessionals as graduate students, whose intellectual mediocrity and narrow vision hung like a deadly pall over the school's intellectual climate. Two things about Criminology's student body in that era stand out in my memory: the undergraduate students, though far from the cream of Berkeley's undergraduate community, were markedly superior in intellectual potential to its graduate students; and, with rare exception, the graduate students I encountered compared unfavorably with the lowest quintile of my Boalt Hall (law school) classes.[10]

Regarding the scholarship of the School of Criminology and the field, Foote believed that Lohman had overloaded the place with

> ill-conceived "evaluative" or agency-action "research projects" for which he had to hire staff of sufficiently limited vision to be willing to devote themselves to such trivia. As these researchers tended to drift into the teaching program whenever a course vacancy needed to be filled, the level of the faculty tended towards the same mediocrity which characterized the graduate student body.

> This, in turn, inhibited Lohman's efforts to recruit and retain able scholars.[11]

Then in April 1968 Joseph Lohman died, ushering in a crisis from which the School of Criminology would never recover.

FROM PROFESSIONAL SCHOOL TO ACADEMIC DISCIPLINE

The period between 1968 and 1971 was one of critical change for the School of Criminology. Fundamental to this shift was the split among faculty members within the School on the issue of academic versus professional education. Again, Caleb Foote was one of the more articulate. The professional school concept was inappropriate for criminology, he felt. Criminology was not a "profession" in the sense of law or medicine.

> We do not expect the newly graduated lawyer or doctor to work his way up from the bottom of his field by starting out as bailiff or orderly. In criminology, however, lateral entry onto the professional ladder is the rare exception and seniority is a virtual prerequisite for leadership. High status, ample economic rewards, and intellectual rigor assured the high quality of student and faculty in law and medicine. No such rewards existed in criminology.

Forgetting the history of his own profession and remaining ignorant of other professions such as education and social work, Foote believed that the quest for professionalism in criminology was no more than an attempt to upgrade the salary and social standing of underpaid, low-level occupational categories. Several across the campus and even within the School agreed with his analysis.[12]

Leslie T. Wilkins became the acting dean in 1968. At this time the university was in turmoil with student demonstrations. Wilkins alienated old political allies in the administration, even earning the nickname the "dissident dean" for his support of the students. Already the School began to shift its curricular emphasis from "fields of possible employment" to "fields of academic endeavor." There was even talk of changing the doctorate degree from the Dr. of Criminology to the more prestigious Ph.D.[13] But this was not unique to criminology. All professional schools had to find the right mix of basic research and applied training. However, Lewis Mayhew of the Teachers College of Columbia University warned that

> Several of the best known professional schools—education at Columbia, engineering at Stanford, business at Harvard—gained their influence through direct and continuous concern with the practical problems of the field and through preparing the next generation of highly qualified practitioners. But as these schools turned their efforts toward more and more basic research, contacts with the field waned and the possibility emerged that their overall influence on the professions would ultimately decline.[14]

Bernard Diamond became acting dean in 1969, to be followed the next year by Sheldon Messinger. In the meantime, a search committee was formed to find a permanent dean of the School. As had occurred earlier with the appointments of Wilson and Lohman, these times of transition were seen as opportune for change. By 1971 the search was finally narrowed to two candidates. But now the candidates represented the professional school versus academic discipline as approaches for the School. The candidates were Norval Morris and Sheldon Messinger.[15]

Norval Morris had had an illustrious career in law and legal education. After receiving a law degree from the University of Melbourne and a Ph.D. in criminology from the London School of Economics, Morris had an international career in teaching before settling down as a law professor and director of the Center of Studies in Criminal Justice at the University of Chicago in 1964. He authored *The Habitual Criminal* (1951), a *Report of the Commission of Inquiry on Capital Punishment* (1959), *Cases in Torts* (1962), *Studies in Criminal Law* (1964), and *The Honest Politician's Guide to Crime Control* (1970), among others. The more liberal element (some would say radical element) of the School disliked Morris's law-and-order style. Caleb Foote, Anthony Platt, Herman Schwendinger, Jerome Skolnick, and Paul Takagi thought Morris's research and perspective were outdated. Some were increasingly connected with another approach to criminological education called "law and society." In that context, they hoped to minimize both the administrative approach of the police educator and the criminological perspective of the sociologist and replace them with law at the center. In a sense they remained true to the professional school model, keeping such studies more closely tied to the law school. Of course, for them the disappearance of the School of Criminology was no academic tragedy that could not be compensated for by the law school or the Center for the Study of Law and Society. Others, such as Platt and Schwendinger were Marxist and considered Morris's mainstream liberalism as inappropriate. The Criminology Students Association, a student organization for the School, agreed and demonstrated when Morris gave a candidate's lecture. Students petitioned the chancellor as well, and Morris quietly withdrew his candidacy.[16]

Sheldon Messinger had received his doctorate in sociology from the University of California at Los Angeles in 1969. Prior to that he had established an active scholarly life. Throughout the 1960s he had been a research sociologist for the Center for the Study of Law and Society at Berkeley and taught part-time for the School of Criminology. He authored or edited *Civil Justice and the Poor:Issues for Sociological Research* (1966), *C-Unit: Search for Community in Prison* (1968) and *The State of the University: Authority and Change* (1970). In the latter work he demonstrated a remarkable grasp of the changing nature of higher education in general and the problems at Berkeley in particular.[17]

For that book he co-authored an article, "Unequal Peers: The Situation of Researchers at Berkeley," that shed some light on the present plight and ultimate outcome of the School of Criminology. Research and researchers had become increasingly important at Berkeley since World War II. Indeed, Lohman's research component in the School was a reflection of that trend. In fact, full-time researchers as a percentage of the total faculty had increased steadily and well in advance of national norms. For example, in 1940 only 7 percent of the total faculty were full-time researchers. In 1960 that number had grown to 31 percent; four years later it was 33 percent. Although there was no national data for 1940, in 1960 the national average for university researchers to faculty was 21 percent; four years later it was 29 percent.[18] Now, with Messinger, the School of Criminology had a real academic who not only understood classic theory and research in criminology but was intellectually sensitive to the university system. Messinger became dean in 1971 and presided over its demise. After its closing he moved to Boalt Hall to become a professor of law and society. In fact, Messinger was also a founding member of a new and competing perspective in criminal justice studies: the law and society movement.

Interest in the sociology of law goes back to nineteenth-century thinkers such as Max Weber. However, such developments, either in sociology departments or law schools, remained slow and sporadic in American higher education. During the 1950s the Ford Foundation gave money to the University of Chicago Law School for research in law and behavioral sciences, but lawyers and law schools were never great centers of research. In 1959 the Russell Sage Foundation began financing the creation of centers of interdisciplinary work in law and social science. Between 1961 and 1974 the Foundation spent $3 million on such centers. The first money went to the University of California in 1960, and shortly thereafter the Center for the Study of Law and Society was established. The University of Wisconsin set up a center in 1962; Northwestern did so two years later. The University of Denver and Yale University soon followed.[19]

Enough scholars, particularly sociologists, were committed to this perspective that attempts at organizing occurred in 1964. Harry Ball, of the University of Wisconsin, called a meeting of like-minded people in conjunction with the annual meetings of the American Sociological Association in 1964. Two founding members of the new Law and Society Association were Sheldon Messinger and Jerome Skolnick, both from the University of California. The new organization was to study and explain legal phenomena in social and economic terms. Some studies in policing occurred but the courts and the law became central. Actually an academic triumvirate was sorting itself out during the 1960s. The IAPP was police-oriented. The American Society of Criminology looked to corrections. And now the Law and Society people concentrated on the law. Rather than coming together in any integrated whole, studies of crime and the agencies and processes dealing with crime were going their own ways. The Law and Society Association became interdisciplinary, with economics, history, law, and anthropology squeezing under an umbrella hoisted by sociologists. Two years after organizing, a newsletter called the *Bulletin* was renamed *Law & Society Review.* Many of the socio-legal scholars found temporary homes in the School of Criminology. Whether they were true friends or foes remains debatable. Some might charge that they constituted an academic fifth column that was greatly responsible for the closing of the School.

Throughout the late 1960s and early 1970s the School of Criminology remained unchanged within the university administrative structure. However, it did increasingly slough off any pretense of being a professional school in the Vollmer-Wilson-Lohman mold. If anything of the old days remained, it was in corrections; but certainly Vollmerian police education was diminishing rapidly. Although most faculty—both within the School and across the campus—applauded such developments, the university administration was less than enthusiastic. It could understand police education within the context of a professional school, even if it bordered on the vocational. Corrections was tolerable in that context as well because models in social work were available. Law and society studies, though new, were comprehensible, especially when connected to law schools or specialized research centers. But when the professional school model ceased to be anything but a facade for the School of Criminology new questions arose.

THE DEMISE OF THE SCHOOL

Between 1971 and 1973 forces outside the university gathered to place the future of the School in jeopardy. First, Governor Ronald Reagan's campaign in 1966 had promised a constituency tired of student radicals and demonstrators that there would be a cleaning up of "the mess in Berkeley." Edwin Meese, governor Ronald Reagen's legal affairs secretary, was appointed to the School's advisory council. General economic measures, which became a part of the future Reagan Revolution on the national stage, made rapid reductions to education. No new resources were forthcoming, and in this "steady state" any growth in one program was to be at the expense of others. The smaller or unpopular or exotic academic units were threatened. For example, at UCLA the speech department was eliminated in 1971, and the School of Journalism followed in the next year. At Berkeley the departments of design and demography were abolished in 1972. Indicating a bleak future, no promotions or tenure were granted to the School of Criminology after Lohman's death. Eighty percent of the regular faculty, many already having tenure, left by 1972.[20]

Second, the professionals within the School and in the community abandoned the Berkeley model. For example, John Holstrom, a long-time member of the School and chief of police for Berkeley, severed all connections in the early 1970s. He felt that the School had "progressively deteriorated in the view of most informed police and correction administrators in California, if not the country."[21] One graduate, who had become a college teacher himself, disliked the growing adversarial stances of the School. Not only was it ceasing to train professionals, but it was increasingly critical of the people and agencies of criminal justice, and "whatever the School may have gained in moral purity for the positions it took, it lost a great deal in usefulness and support."[22] David Fogel, one of the School's more illustrious graduates, remembered with dismay this disengagement from the professional community and thought it was like watching a Greek tragedy. "Those in control were 'winning,'" he felt, " but [they were] just moving to a higher pinnacle so the fall would be greater later."[23] The School's Advisory Council, so critical under Wilson and Lohman, no longer existed. It had continued for a year after Lohman's death and then disbanded. The School never tried to revive it.[24] A wall of silence separated the professionals and the academics that remained in the School.

Third, other adverse dynamics within the university were at work as well. Chancellor Roger Haynes, a close friend of Joseph Lohman, retired in 1971; and his place was taken by Albert Bowker. On the face of it Bowker should have been a good friend of the School. He had come from the City University of New York system and had helped establish the John Jay College of Criminal Justice in the late 1960s. This experience gave him a sense of the appropriate place of criminology or criminal justice in the college setting. For Bowker the School of Criminology was to be a professional school more similar to that of the Wilson and Lohman days. But it had changed so much already that he was bewildered. He quickly called for an external review by people he trusted, such as Donald Riddle, Richard Myren, James Short, and Marvin Wolfgang. Aside from recommending a decrease in the undergraduate program, they reported favorably.[25] A crisis was averted but Bowker remained suspicious, especially as radicals made their positions known across the campus.

Intellectuals by personal nature and academic nurture are critical. However, bureaucratic structures and organizational people are less amenable to criticism. Consequently, any intellectual approach was automatically viewed with hostility by criminal justice agencies. Furthermore, in a professional school context it was difficult to justify the education of people who would go on to become enemies of the organizations for which they were nomenally being trained to work. David Fogel did realize, however, that the School's student recruitment policy systematically excluded any who expressed an interest in doing anything but teaching and research.[26]

This dispute came to a head with the Anthony Platt case. Platt, a Marxist scholar and outspoken critic of the Berkeley police, had received a doctorate from the School in 1966. He was believed to be one of the best students to graduate from the School. A post-doctorate followed at the University of Chicago where he worked with Norval Morris, until they had a falling out. Platt returned to Berkeley and immediately became a favorite teacher among the undergraduates. However, his political activism and subsequent arrests by the police were embarrassing to administrative officials and he was denied tenure. Some thought it was due to his radicalism. Of course, there was no shortage on radicals across campus. However, tolerances in these days of Governor Reagan and President Nixon had been strained. Radical scholars in sociology, political science or history, might be distasteful, but in the name of academic freedom they had to be tolerated. To be an anti-establishment figure in a School founded to train and professionalize a very conservative establishment strained credibility. In particular, Bowker felt that a central issue raised by the case of the young Marxist scholar—and the entire School as well—was the adversarial relationship between town and gown. Any professional school of criminology had to have reasonably good relations with the leaders in law enforcement and corrections, he maintained. After careful study of Platt's scholarship, the chief of which (*The Child Savers*) was a Marxist interpretation of the origins of the juvenile justice movement, Bowker denied Platt tenure.[27] Shortly, another Marxist Herman Schwendinger was fired. The young scholars became something of a cause célèbre but decisions held, not so much showing the power of the administrators over both faculty and student desires, but instead the lack of political energy and fight left in the School.

The inability of the School to save very popular professors such as Platt and Schwendinger suggests deeper internal problems. How was the School going to fit into the police education-criminology-law and society educational paradigm? At first, as a compromise position between the professional and academic tug-of-war aspects of his school, Messinger declared the mission to be to develop and influence national policies for dealing with crime. This "public policy" approach had considerable academic respectability and practical utility, but it never materialized. Instead, two years after he took the deanship, Messinger admitted in a soul searching memo to the faculty that the School of Criminology had been continuously

> displaced by the development of criminal justice programs at other institutions. The vocational program of the first years is now offered by police and other academies. The vocationally-oriented academic program that followed is now offered by the community college. The agency-oriented but more generalized academic program that came later is now the staple of the state colleges—and, if my guess is correct, the state colleges will be moving into the area of management education.[28]

The School, Messinger concluded, met the challenges of the previous decade "with determined vacillation." This memo (some might have called it a suicide note) would be used by critics later as an example of the confusion and malaise existing in the School of Criminology.

The School remained popular among the students, though, and undergraduate enrollment skyrocketed. In fact, such popularity was one of the School's problems. In 1969-70, for example, 68 percent of the students in the School were undergraduates, a figure considered by most to be too high for a professional school. In keeping with the Riddle Report, Messinger tried to hold down such "servicing" of students from other colleges and departments. Nevertheless, as university economics tightened a high body count seemed praiseworthy, and the undergraduate enrollment continued to soar. In 1970-71, 76 percent of the School population was undergraduate, and it rose to 82 percent the next year.[29] Now excessive popularity might suggest a questionable reputation. "Were students flocking to criminology because it was an easy grade?" some Berkeley academics wondered.[30] "Did the School overstrain itself to be relevant and popular?"—a sign of a field unsure of itself without an established core and content. Courses on the "crimes of imperialism, racism, and sexism" appealed to students but not to more conservative faculty and administrators. Nonetheless, critics throughout the university thought the numbers of students were "unusually high by any standard, and especially so for a professional school."[31]

Finally, in spite of the rise of the American Society of Criminology and the International Association of Police Professors (or the Academy of Criminal Justice Sciences, as it was soon renamed), there was no professional collective strong enough to come to the aid of the School. In part that was the fault of the School and its faculty. Since the 1950s the School had been conspicuously absent in the leadership of those organizations. After Lohman's death the School had moved even further away. Professional schools—such as education, engineering, law, and medicine—have professional associations with accreditation power that inform universities of the strengths and weaknesses of their professional schools. Prior debates over accreditation in the IAPP had ended in the educators moving away from such a process. The American Society of Criminology, with a stronger dedication to traditional academic disciplines, was even more timid when it came to accreditation work. "Unfortunately, criminology does not have a recognized professional society with a recognized professional accrediting program," wrote Chancellor Bowker. "Thus," he added ominously, "our definitions are handled wholly within the institution."[32]

Bowker asked for an academic review of the School in December 1972. The Sindler Committee correctly found an abandonment of the School's original mission, and "a professional school without a professional commitment or program, or without effective links to its professional constituencies is, of course, a contradiction in terms."[33] Ironically, as many police educators in the Academy of Criminal Justice Sciences were critical of police programs for being too professional at the expense of academic scholarship, the School of Criminology at one of the greatest universities in America was being criticized for not being professional enough. Thus, on the horns of that dilemma hung much of the criminal justice education movement.

In June 1973 the Sindler Committee recommended the School's disestablishment. No new majors were accepted after 1973, and the School officially closed its doors three years later. Forty years after Vollmer's arrival on campus the Vollmerian experiment was expelled; it was just too remedial for Berkeley. For such a historically significant event there was remarkably little resistance or fanfare. In fact, many students later remembered with pride that they "had closed down the School." It was like a Hollywood production with lifeboats of sailors cheering as they witnessed their wounded ship go to the bottom. Why such a lack of fight? As the history of the School suggests, a good fight goes a long way in university circles. Indeed, as we shall see in the next chapter, successful resistance saved the John Jay College of Criminal Justice.

Several factors seemed to be at work in the easy death of the School. First, high-level university officials so crucial in previous battles were either quiet or themselves in opposition to the School. Abandonment of the more practical professional school in every way except in name alienated educational administrators who once had been key political allies. Second, the faculty—both across the campus and within the School—seemed to have already accepted a new "law and society" definition of crime-related studies. Many considered criminology education as it existed in the School as a "cheap" degree. Third, the School seemed too radical for many administrators. Classes were canceled for long periods of time as professors got involved with campus political demonstrations. When classes met, they resulted in endless tirades against the criminal justice establishment. Fourth, although Berkeley students had a recent history of activism, many in the School were drawn from the more compliant, authority-respecting student body. They looked to the faculty for leadership but found none. Those being serviced, taking criminology as an easy elective, had little commitment. In fact, on the face of it the School represented aspects of society—policing, courts, and prisons—with which opposition rather than support was trendy for large numbers of the studentbody. Instead, in a sort of scapegoating process disgruntled students and faculty were convinced that an administrative conspiracy was afoot. The tenure decisions regarding Platt and Schwendinger seemed to justify this opinion, making them martyrs and deflecting concerns from real issues.

Fifth, and more important, the School of Criminology was clearly out of step with developments in criminal justice education. Already it had largely abrogated its leadership role in the professional associations that were forming and gaining strength. On one level, the School was an embarrassing memento of an earlier day when criminal justice education was defined as vocational police training. Its own history was its undoing. On the other hand, it had taken on a new orientation, law and society, not widely accepted by current criminal justice educators—one that already had an institutional home in the Center for the Study of Law and Society.

CONCLUSION

Certainly, the University of California remained a preeminent place of higher education, but in the sorting out of criminal justice education more compatible homes were being found in second tier-schools. An academic segregation was occurring, and criminal justice was relegated to the back of the bus. The only steadfast monopoly the police educators emerged with was the new academic designation: criminal justice. It was more general and respectable than police science. It differentiated them from the sociological criminologists who had displaced them in the American Society of Criminology. And it brought them closer to the lawyers, who in all likelihood had coined the phrase in the first place, but allowed a little distance for academic uniqueness and growth. Therefore, even the name of the School of Criminology had become anachronistic. It is more than coincidental that the two schools in New York that had been slowly displacing Berkeley as the central models of education in this new field would use "criminal justice" on their letterhead. They are the John Jay College of Criminal Justice and the School of Criminal Justice at State University of New York at Albany. Just as in the professional associations where there had been a drift from West to East, the focus of criminal justice education went from the West Coast to the eastern seaboard.

Chapter 7

A Tale of Two Campuses: Criminal Justice Education in New York, 1965–1980

Owing largely to federal funds, criminal justice education in America underwent considerable growth and change between 1965 and 1980. Particularly in the 1970s criminal justice programs sprung up everywhere. The number of degree-offering programs went from under 500 to over 1,000 in the same period. Ironically, this "golden age" of program development occurred at the time when the School of Criminology at the University of California was being successfully attacked and eliminated. Now the focus of political leadership in the criminal justice education movement turned to two other places. One was the Academy of Criminal Justice Sciences, the offspring of the American Society of Criminology renamed from the International Association of Police Professors. More discussion of this organization will occur later. The other source of leadership, and the topic of this chapter, came from two schools established in New York.

One of the models, the John Jay College of Police Science in New York City, came closest to the Vollmerian ideals being relinquished at the University of California. Although it remained mostly concerned with undergraduate education, it had a small number of very "professional" graduate degrees. The other model at SUNY-Albany sought another very important approach, that of preparing the scholar-academic. Simply put, the popularity of the field was greater than the number of adequately trained professors to teach and do research in it. Many argued that practical experience in the "real world" was the best preparation for being an academic in criminal justice. Indeed, students generally were more interested in the career experiences of their teachers than the number of degrees they possessed. Still, there was an academic bias against such people and their pedagogical technique of "war stories." Besides, no academic profession would succeed unless it found ways to reproduce its own educators.

The history of both these schools and their independent contributions to the field of higher learning show the prospects and problems inherent in the criminal justice education movement of the time. A host of political battles in both places needed to be engaged as well. Periods of exhilarating growth and challenge occurred at the same time.

JOHN JAY COLLEGE OF CRIMINAL JUSTICE

As early as the mid-1950s police education was being undertaken in New York City. A joint effort between the city's Police Academy and the Bernard M. Baruch School of Business and Public Administration within the city college system offered a police science concentration within the public administration department. There were 700 undergraduates studying law enforcement in the fall of 1955; within two years that number grew to 1,100 and remained there for several years to come. However, for many officers going to school to enhance their careers the faculty seemed too academic. Complaints could be heard that the curriculum was aimed too directly toward business administration.[1] Unfortunately, there were few alternatives for ambitious police officers until the baby boomers, that post-World War II population bulge coming of college age in the 1960s, inspired educational change. In 1964, responding to student population growth, the Board of Higher Education for New York City restructured the urban college system. Hunter, Queens, Brooklyn colleges and the City College were brought together to form the City University of New York system (CUNY). Along with these other units, a new one was established in Manhattan called the John Jay College of Police Science.

John Jay officially began classes in the fall of 1965. The name, reflecting semantic currents in the field at the time, changed to the College of Criminal Justice during the next year. Several people played important roles in its early days. Obviously, the police department, particularly the leadership ranks, became ardent supporters. So did the chancellor of the CUNY system, a man by the name of Albert Bowker (who, as noted, moved to Berkeley to preside over the closing of the School of Criminology). One of Bowker's first acts was the selection of Leonard Reisman as president of the college. Reisman had been trained in the law and had gained experience as a special prosecutor investigating corruption in New York's construction industry before he was made Deputy Commissioner of Police. Reisman set the mission of the college in May 1967.

> Police administrators are beginning to recognize that as the general level of education rises throughout the country, the level of education of its police service must keep pace and, indeed, move ahead. It is John Jay's purpose to strengthen this recognition by graduating more and more police administrators who themselves have had the advantages of higher education.[2]

Such statements put Reisman and John Jay in the mainstream of the police professionalization movement begun by August Vollmer forty years earlier. It was the police leader who was to bring the change; and, in a "trickle-down" fashion, all police persons would be affected if reform occurred at the top. Unfortunately, Reisman died unexpectedly in 1967. Fortunately, the dean of students from 1965 to 1967, Donald Riddle, was ready to step in and guide the college for the next decade. He would put a different spin on Reisman's comments and philosophy. In addition, he would help revolutionize the field.

Donald Riddle's impact upon John Jay—and the entire criminal justice education movement, for that matter—is so important that a word about his career development and ideas is necessary. After World War II, during which time he served in the army air force, Riddle took advantage of the G. I. Bill and studied political science at Princeton University. There was a year of teaching at Hamilton College and another year working for Paul Douglas, U.S. senator from Illinois, before Riddle finally joined the Eagleton Institute of Politics at Rutgers University. From 1958 to 1964 he worked on developing teaching materials for social studies classes in secondary schools. Unknown to Riddle, an old friend and colleague had recommended him for the position of dean at John Jay. Although he knew nothing of police education, an ignorance he readily admitted, he was offered the job. Another friend at the Ford Foundation encouraged Riddle to take it and even offered him a little money to educate himself in this new academic field of study. Within a week of his hire Riddle was indeed traveling, talking, and networking. He met with O. W. Wilson, William Parker, James Osterburg, and Robert Borkenstein, to name a few, in his quest to understand this relatively new academic endeavor. He even attended some of the early meetings of the

International Association of Police Professors.[3] Along the way his ideas began to slowly take shape.

Although Riddle eventually joined a chorus of those demanding more scholarship in the field, his initial contribution was in the area of undergraduate education. In a speech officially opening the College in September 1965, Riddle addressed the question on most people's minds: How do you educate policemen? The answer was twofold and showed the philosophical disposition of Riddle and the eventual direction of the College.

First, you taught the practices and techniques of policing because "sending a young man of twenty-one years into the street armed with his high school diploma, a gun and a club, a few weeks of instruction in rules and regulations, some instruction in the use of the gun, and a few lectures on police-community relations, [was] an act of public irresponsibility unmatched by any other major western nation."[4] In expressing this opinion Riddle was not out of line with many police professors of the time. Unabashedly, he went on to advocate a strong mix of technical and liberal arts education. Liberal arts was not a label one applied to one field and not to another, he believed. Instead, it was an approach to instruction, a way of handling materials. "A course in traffic can be vocational in orientation, relatively sterile in terms of development of the student's capacity to think," he lectured his fellow educators, "or it can be liberal and liberating and raise the kinds of questions which induce thought and reflection and speculation and may lead to the thoughtful consideration of change."[5] In fact, the distinction between vocational and liberal arts courses was moot because, as he was fond of quoting Alfred North Whitehead,

> There can be no adequate technical education which is not liberal, and no liberal education which is not technical; that is, no education which does not impart both technique and intellectual vision. In simpler language, education should turn out the pupil with something he knows well and something he can do well. This intimate union of practice and theory aids both.[6]

Furthermore, it was necessary to continue to teach police matters because "the traditional method of developing fields of study into academic disciplines is through the process of teaching them."[7]

Riddle's second answer to the question of educating the police was: "like anyone else!" In other words, John Jay should be like most any other college with a full spectrum of curricula ranging from anthropology to zoology. On one hand, he was against any attempt, currently growing in popularity in New York at the time, of creating a West Point of Law Enforcement. Leon Radzinowicz, the leading criminologist of England, had convinced many in New York that such a school as found in Bramshill, England, was the logical next step in law enforcement higher education. That school was an officer training center for future officials in the English police forces. Similar training for correctional officers occurred at Wakefield. Eliot Lumbard, the special assistant council to Governor Nelson Rockefeller and head of New York City's Municipal Police Training Council, and the local bar association, supported Radzinowicz's idea. Riddle and Richard Myren of Albany did not, and they fought successfully to keep the police education movement from following such military models.[8] For them, police or criminal justice education needed to remain within the traditional American system of higher education. To create a specialized officer training academy as found at West Point or Annapolis might jeopardize the development and legitimacy of the academic nature of the field. On the other hand, John Jay in the early days was as close to an officer's candidate school as possible without actually joining the corps.

When the College began its first year it had 35 faculty members, one-third of whom were in classical academic disciplines. Ten years later there were 307 full-time professors and 125 part-timers. Of the total faculty 182 were females. From 1965 to 1968, five programs existed: police science, forensics, behavioral science, social science, and criminal justice. In the next three years five more were added: American studies, arts and languages, Black studies, history, and social services. Departments of chemistry, economics, English, government, mathematics, psychology, and sociology, to name a few, found a place in the 1970s.

Although over 75 percent of the courses were of a classic liberal arts orientation, they were geared to the particular needs of law enforcement personnel. On one hand, this meant that the departments, at first, could not expect to attract traditional majors. They were in place to supplement law enforcement studies. This caused many to do some creative thinking about their discipline and how it might contribute to the fundamental skills needed by police officers. For example, some believed that in police work a person must be able to express themselves clearly and be understood. They must also have the capacity to understand exactly what it is someone is saying. Hence, for all students, communication skills are developed by a variety of courses: English, Speech, Literature, Music, Philosophy,

Religion, and Foreign Languages. Although none of these directly relates to Police Science, a man will function more effectively as a police officer after becoming more proficient in them.[9]

Richard Ward, a senior at John Jay in 1967 and a patrolman in the detective division of the city police, thought that the drama classes were useful because they taught him "to perform in front of an audience—that's something policemen are called on to do all the time. When a policeman has to control a crowd or handle an accident he may be as frightened as the next guy, but he can't show it. You may be scared, but you've got to know how to take command of the situation."[10]

Another important skill, implicit in any college education, was critical analysis. Students may want to consume information, but professors ultimately want them to process it. In the classroom, Riddle maintained, "no aspect of the policies and practices of the police departments anywhere are sacrosanct."[11] Since many current or future work environments were suspicious of intellectuals, critical analysis can lead to controversy, as the Jack Shaw incident illustrates.

In 1970 Jack Shaw, a 37-year old-former marine captain with a seven-year unblemished record as an FBI agent, enrolled at John Jay. For one class he did a study of the FBI and its involvement in the civil rights movement. Although his paper was a general defense of the practices of the agency, Shaw did acknowledge that a "cult of personality" was encouraged to develop around the director, J. Edgar Hoover. Foolishly, Shaw submitted his paper to the agency typing pool and he was reported to the leadership. Shortly thereafter, he was reprimanded and suspended for "atrocious judgment" and transferred to Butte, Montana. Since his wife was ill, Shaw resigned from the agency and with the help of the American Civil Liberties Union successfully sued the government. However, in the meantime the remaining fifteen FBI agents taking courses at John Jay submitted to pressure and quietly withdrew from the College.[12]

Although it is difficult to prove, Riddle began to feel that there was a personal vendetta from the FBI against John Jay. For example, shortly after the Shaw affair LEEP gave heads of criminal justice agencies the power to certify those courses eligible for government money. Such courses must have direct bearing on the officer's future role as a law enforcement agent or criminal justice representative, according to the new policy. Many people at John Jay, where the liberal arts courses did not always seem to have such direct impact, felt that the national government had caved in to Hoover, who remained piqued over the Shaw affair.[13]

Writing to Attorney General John Mitchell, Riddle thought "it was Shaw's objectivity that got him into trouble." Should not education liberate the mind rather than enslave it, Riddle asked? Jack Shaw, and indeed every educated person, "has learned that although a worshipful attitude may be appropriate for a man to take to his God, it is not an appropriate attitude to take towards other men and towards human institutions." Senator George McGovern had the letter read into the Congressional Record.[14] In many ways, Riddle was drawing sharper lines between criminal justice education and training. But in another way he got caught on the horns of one of the field's dilemmas. That is, how can a critical thinker exist in an environment unfriendly to such an activity? Does not a good education prepare a person for failure in this highly bureaucratic environment bordering on the military? Conditions would not allow reflection on that point as another crisis hit.

From 1955 to 1970 student enrollment went from 1,089 to 3,700. Most students were white (75 percent), going to school part-time (66 percent). John Jay was predominately a "cop's college" with a clear and distinct mission. There were no traditional academic divisions. Such class designations as freshman, sophomore, junior, and senior made no sense in an academic environment where the typical student might take eight rather than four years to graduate. Because students had varied and fluid work schedules, the college operated almost around the clock. In the tradition of Wiltberger and the California police professors, courses were to be duplicated and synchronized in such a way that an officer might easily change work shifts and still find the appropriate course operating in tandem with the one taken earlier.[15] Most important, there were to be no selective admissions standards. Riddle (himself a product of the G.I. Bill, which allowed older people to attend college regardless of the extent of their academic preparation) felt "that the motivated student, almost irrespective of his preparation, can make it—to his benefit and that of the whole society."[16] Such a philosophy, combined with the tailoring and tinkering with the curriculum, led many to think of John Jay as a "college of remedials," a four-year junior college. Short as it was, such a history made John Jay a likely candidate and casualty to the new "open admissions" policy.

In 1970, the New York City Board of Higher Education instituted an open admissions policy. This meant that any young person in the New York City metropolitan area—regardless of preparation and inclination—could get into the CUNY system. An allocation schedule was established to insure an equitable distribution among all the colleges. However, because of John Jay's "unique mission" and past levels of student quality, it received a disproportionate number of open admissions students.[17] A flood ensued, and by 1973 the student body had grown to 10,000, many of them minorities.[18]

As early as January 1971 police students began to feel that it was they who were minority. Lou Cappore, a police lieutenant and president of the John Jay student council, pointed the following:

> There's a great feeling on the part of police officers that the school is going away from its intended purpose. For example, police science has become one of many things, whereas before it was the only thing. A lot of students feel that if we don't retain our police orientation, it'll be just another liberal arts school.[19]

Riddle was aware of this alienation but thought that in the name of a truly liberal arts education the police needed to think less of John Jay as their particular professional school. Open admissions, Riddle felt, made

> our classrooms a better reflection of what goes on in the city than they used to be, even though there have been frictions between the kids from the ghetto and the cops. Probably the most negative result of open admissions has been a slight alienation of those cops who had proprietary interest that this was "their" college.[20]

The number of police officers studying at John Jay steadily dropped until they formed only 20 percent of the student body by 1979.[21]

Almost overnight the demographics and atmosphere of John Jay had changed. Not only was the college overwhelmed, but in many ways the institution and the faculty were set up for frustration and failure as well. For example, 87 percent of the first open admissions students were poorly prepared for higher education. By 1975, John Jay succeeded in graduating only 6.8 percent of its students. The other CUNY institutions had a graduation rate of 21.8 percent. On one level, that was not particularly alarming because John Jay had a history of part-time long-term students. It was the dropout rate that was disturbing. Fully 63 percent of John Jay's students dropped out and never returned. A 43 percent dropout rate characterized other colleges in the CUNY system.[22] In other words, John Jay lost most of its original clientele and in return received a large number of poorly prepared people who lacked the motivation and skills to graduate in spite of attempts to give them remedial education. The result was a general dilution of quality of courses and the disorientation and frustration of the faculty. Margaret Tabb, of the English department, lamented that "at a school like John Jay, where most of the teaching is necessarily geared to a very elementary level—particularly in departments such as English—there is a disparity between what we teach and what we must think and write about."[23]

An evaluation team for the Commission on Higher Education of the Middle States Association, an accreditation agency, visited John Jay in 1975. The college was well aware of its problems, particularly in the overabundance of remedial classes, and dreaded the visitation.[24] As expected, the report of the Commission was unsettling. The evaluation team reaffirmed and commended the uniqueness of John Jay's original mission, that of providing education for in-service criminal justice personnel. But, the report noted, at mid-decade the college was "confused over its mission," having trouble adjusting its curriculum and pedagogy to the vast majority of students who were so poorly prepared and motivated. The team called for a hard look at the present curriculum with an eye to its reform.[25] At that critical juncture, Donald Riddle resigned as president to become chancellor of the University of Illinois, Chicago Circle. And then the next crisis hit.

On February 23, 1976, the *New York Times* broke a story that CUNY chancellor Robert Kibbee was about to propose the closing of John Jay; much of its faculty, course work, and students were to be assimilated with Baruch, claimed the report. Kibbee believed that the City University of New York, buffeted by a devastating financial crisis, stood at a crossroads. In just one year there had been a 20 percent reduction of spending on higher education in the city. Under Kibbee's cost-cutting scheme all colleges would have a strong liberal arts education plus a particular professional thrust. For example, Hunter would emphasize social work and health sciences. Queens College would specialize in training teachers for secondary education. Baruch College would concern itself with administrative studies, including criminal justice. Besides the elimination of John Jay and Richmond colleges, several others would be merged or downgraded to junior college status. The CUNY system had grown rapidly during the 1960s and early 1970s, but by mid-decade the economic situation of the city required reconsideration, declared the chancellor.[26] At best, based upon a last-ditch survival effort by the new president, Gerald Lynch, the liberal arts courses might be taken from John Jay, leaving the police science and criminal justice offerings intact. But since the liberal arts courses had been so much a part of the ideological and bureaucratic fat of the institution, such surgery would probably devastatingly emasculate the school.[27]

Students were thunderstruck and faculty in panic. When one officer-student, who had just lost his police partner for budgetary reasons, heard of the closing, he said: "First they take my partner. Then they take my school." Andy Dantschisch, a police sergeant in the city police Narcotics Division working on his master's degree, thought it was "very sad that they pick on the least militant college in the City University [system] to close."[28] Gerald Lynch, the president who replaced Donald Riddle, became field general and, later in more reflective times, admitted that "the college bucked too many traditions in higher education. It combined liberal arts and career-oriented majors and thus wasn't pure. It offered majors in criminal justice, which again wasn't a pure discipline and thus [was] suspect."[29]

Next to Lynch in importance was Richard Ward (the police officer who had liked drama classes earlier), who had returned to his alma mater after doing graduate work at the University of California's School of Criminology and now was a dean at John Jay. One of Ward's personal friends was a veteran media consultant, Tony Schwartz, famous for his media campaigns for President Lyndon Johnson in 1964. Ward and Schwartz were in the forefront of the "save the school" crusade.[30]

The campaign followed two basic strategies. First, a rationale was created for keeping the College. Overlooked by most academics, but certainly not by the politically astute Ward and Schwartz, was the necessity of proving its uniqueness and essential nature. To do this several points were stressed. First, John Jay was a unique educational experiment. It was midway between traditional college education and the Radzinowicz idea of a "West Point of Law Enforcement," providing a practical source of agency personnel for New York City's criminal justice agencies. When the New York City police commissioner, Robert McGuire, took office in 1978, for example, eleven of his thirteen top-level appointees held one or more degrees from John Jay. A public opinion survey was conducted in the metropolitan area and found that 75 percent of those polled opposed any closing of any CUNY colleges. Second, since the Board of Education made so much over the tight economic times, John Jay's cost effectiveness was stressed. The transferring and consolidating of faculty and facilities would simply be too expensive. In addition, over $1.5 million in federal grants obtained by the school would be jeopardized. Third, John Jay had become a major gateway for minorities. By 1976 26 percent of the student body were black and thirteen percent were Latino. In 1973, the school had become one of the first in America to create a department of Puerto Rican studies.[31]

Ideas without some sort of action are doomed to failure. After all, politicians respond to pressures coming from the streets more readily than from those coming from the classroom. So the second major strategy was more basic and active. A rally of over 2,000 students initiated the campaign.[32] Support from Congressman Mario Biaggi and State Assemblyman Herbert Miller was obtained. Advertisements in *New York* magazine and the *New York Times* spelled out the position of the defenders of the school. Buttons were made and distributed to supporters, and a dirigible blimp hovered over the skyline urging citizens to "save John Jay." Statements and testimonials from across the country, as well as from local leaders, reached the Board of Education. The Academy of Criminal Justice Sciences came out with a letter of support. Rallies and marches occurred with regularity across Manhattan in which as many police officers were in the demonstrations as were guarding them. Though less dramatic, similar activities occurred for the other threatened schools as well.

Such a showing was irresistible, to be sure; and on April 7 the Board voted to keep the college as it was, though there was to be a 14 percent cut in operating funds. By sheer political will, John Jay was saved to grow to be the only major institution of higher education whose main mission was the teaching of criminal justice. As some sort of reward for his efforts Richard Ward followed Donald Riddle and went to the University of Illinois at Chicago Circle to become a vice chancellor. But there was one more crisis (though not aimed directly at John Jay) that besmirched the entire criminal justice education movement and reflected unfavorably on the school in New York City.

In the summer of 1976 the Police Foundation set up a National Advisory Commission on Higher Education for Police Officers. Under the guidance of Warren Bennis, the 1978 Commission report, nearly three hundred pages in length, severely criticized the police education movement. Certainly criminal justice education had not grown naturally. Some sort of artificial insemination had occurred on the federal level, with millions of dollars flowing from LEEP. Much self-serving greed and opportunism characterized the period. The Commission quoted the now infamous statement by Gordon Misner while he was president of the Academy of Criminal Justice Sciences:

> The infusion of LEEP money has brought into being the greatest number of harlots the world has probably ever seen. An awful lot of hustlers, and some college presidents serving as pimps, are all looking for the LEEP dollar. In fact, I think what is going on now in criminal justice higher education is perhaps the most scandalous thing in the history of our education.[33]

Of course, greedy, opportunistic educators were not new to the history of higher education. Of great concern was the doubt over the quality of faculty and courses. Too much reliance upon part-time faculty led many to fear that "the nature of the higher education experience offered to police officers has very often been little different from that offered in police training academies."[34] The report went on to declare:

> Whatever the potential value of higher education for changing the police, police education is now falling short of that potential. Much police education today is intellectually shallow, conceptually narrow and provided by faculty that is far from scholarly. Rather than helping to change the police, police education appears to support the status quo, teaching what the police do now instead of inquiring what they could do differently.[35]

Bennis was quoted in an article in the *New York Times*, ominously called "Ripping Off the Police," that most criminal justice programs did not deserve to be in colleges. Although John Jay was not singled out, the report attacked the general premise upon which the College was founded. Other colleges and universities might buffer a weak program, but police education and the philosophy that it could make a difference in police performance formed the bedrock upon which John Jay had been built. One point was taken to heart: the importance of scholarship. Police educators not only had to teach prospective policemen but also had to create themselves. John Jay would establish a doctorate program in 1979. In the meantime, the main production of criminal justice scholars was going on at SUNY-Albany.

SCHOOL OF CRIMINAL JUSTICE AT THE STATE UNIVERSITY OF NEW YORK-ALBANY

Historically, it was the private colleges that dominated state education in New York, essentially stunting the development of the public colleges. In fact, the lion's share of the Morrell Land Grant money in the nineteenth century went to private college—most notably Cornell University, which was established in 1867. By the early 1940s New York ranked 47th of the 48 states in gross support of public higher education. Returning veterans crowded existing institutions after World War II, and in response the State University of New York system (SUNY) was created in 1949. Originally, there were eleven teachers colleges, seven professional schools, and eleven junior colleges. Gains were modest throughout the 1950s, and the colleges of choice remained the private institutions in New York. In the meantime, SUNY became overly crowded and undistinguished in quality.[36]

The 1960s became the great period of growth for public higher education mainly due to the work of Governor Nelson Rockefeller (1959-73). Public higher education was one of his pet projects until he resigned to become Gerald Ford's vice president. Although he was a product of private schools himself (Dartmouth), Rockefeller felt that they were incapable alone of handling the large number of students reaching college age. Consequently, he began a huge expansion of the flagging SUNY system, hoping to make it the "Berkeley of the East." Of course, there was some resistance—particularly from the private schools, who succeeded in getting a "gentleman's agreement" that SUNY would not be a major competitor and threat to their mission of providing high-quality undergraduate liberal arts education. Therefore, from the beginning, there was an attempt to keep SUNY as a medium of mediocrity.

In addition, political support for SUNY throughout the state could only be obtained after promises were made that no New Yorker would live farther than 50 miles from a public institution of higher learning. This meant that SUNY, soon to be the largest state public education system in the world, was also to become notorious for its decentralization. It was a symbol of democracy at its best and at its worst.

The new SUNY system under Rockefeller was made up of thirteen liberal arts schools, most of which were former teachers colleges, and nearly fifty junior colleges. But the flagship was to be the university, in this case four universities or "research centers." They were Binghamton, Buffalo, Stony Brook, and Albany. The oldest was Albany, which had been founded as a teachers college in 1844. Although it had come into the SUNY system earlier, it did not become a comprehensive university until 1963. Because of its location in the state capital, its supposed specialty was to be public policy and administrative studies, a natural home for criminal justice.[37]

Thanks to the support of Governor Rockefeller, money and students flowed into the SUNY system. For example, in 1959 SUNY had a total of 7,482 employees and 142,081 students. By 1973 there were 34,342 employees (a 358 percent increase) and 515,536 students (a 264 percent increase).[38] It was in this context of a rapidly growing SUNY and a vigorously committed governor that Eliot Lumbard created the School of Criminal Justice at Albany.

Although he was trained in the law, Lumbard had a profound interest in criminology and criminal justice. Courses under Thorsten Sellin at the University of Pennsylvania and Herbert Wexler at Columbia University's law school gave direction to his career. In the late 1950s he joined the newly formed New York State Commission of Investigation, where he coordinated investigations into organized crime including the famous "Apalachin Meeting," that event in which numerous leaders from the crime families of New York had gathered. From 1961 to 1967 he was an advisor on crime control in Governor Rockefeller's legal staff. In that capacity he was chairman of the Oyster Bay Conferences on organized crime (1965-67), liaison on behalf of the state to the President's National Crime Commission (1965-67), and developer of the New York State Information and Intelligence System (NYSIIS), the first computer-based criminal justice records system in the United States. He also established the School of Criminal Justice at SUNY-Albany.[39]

Governor Nelson Rockefeller, a no-nonsense pragmatist, asked his advisors a basic question in the early 1960s: "How much does crime and the agencies dealing with crime cost the state?" In trying to find the answer to that question, Lumbard was shocked over the lack of criminal justice information existing in New York. Furthermore, what little information existed was guarded by local politicians and bureaucrats who feared it might be used against them by vigorous leaders in the state capital. "I've always found that reform in the criminal justice system is opposed not by the public but by the people in the system," observed Lumbard. Better trained and less politicized personnel were needed at both the state and local levels of criminal justice, he concluded. More systematic and skillful collection of data and its understanding at higher theoretical levels was needed as well. In short, New York in general and the state capital in particular needed a clearinghouse, a think tank, a college of criminal justice.[40] Both Lloyd Ohlin, a prominent sociologist, and Frank Remington, the law professor from the University of Wisconsin who was so important in the Law and Society movement, were called to Albany to act as consultants in the creation of the School of Criminal Justice.[41]

The process of establishing the School was surprisingly long and laborious, taking nearly seven years. One reason for the drag of time was that the Rockefeller and Lumbard forces kept the state government's role in the background. Lumbard was to plant the seeds and nurture them, but the academics were to be mainly in control. Of course, this opened the door for academic politics, which stalled development for some time. The lessons learned at Albany would not be forgotten, and Lumbard would use an entirely different strategy at the end of the decade when he helped set up a similar program at Rutgers University.[42]

One of the earliest, and very telling, problems was nomenclature. What was this new educational creature to be called? "Criminology" was a tried and tested phrase that most sociologists (including Ohlin) favored. But at this time, in the mid-1960s, the memories of O. W. Wilson's School of Criminology at the University of California and its troubles were still fresh. Perhaps such notoriety had tainted the word. In addition, in Albany, a state capital filled with administrators, there was considerable bias against sociologists and criminologists. As Eliot Lumbard recalled

> The word criminology was political anathema and this school could not be created if it had such a tag nor could it be seen as another label for sociology; that if it was to be interdisciplinary it had to be that in fact and it couldn't be confined to sociologists.[43]

Ohlin had favored sociology as the disciplinary approach and the word "criminology" as the identifier. Remington favored a more administrative approach; based upon his years with the American Bar Foundation and the Law and Society movement, he liked the title "criminal justice." No doubt because he was a lawyer too, Lumbard agreed with Remington.[44]

But the words "criminal justice" gave rise almost immediately to another revealing problem, this time from the state Civil Service Commission. Simply put, but more difficult to overcome, there was no job title or classification in state government for someone trained in criminal justice. Going back several decades one might find a position called "state criminologist," but nowhere could the phrase "criminal justician" be found. The obvious solution was to ignore such concerns, or perhaps create a new job title. Of course, that is not so easy for a state bureaucrat; and the commissioner, in his naiveté, asked Lumbard a profound question: "What will these people do? What does a Ph.D. in criminal justice do?" It would have been flippant to say that like any other Ph.D., they would teach. Any informed educator in the late 1960s knew that only 45 percent of all Ph.Ds in the previous fifteen years had gone into college teaching.[45] It may or may not be easier to answer the commissioner's conundrum today, but it was a perplexity of the time left to the academics to solve.

In addition, not everyone felt that the School of Criminal Justice should be at Albany. For example, the state lieutenant governor, who had been educated at Buffalo, threatened that "it goes to Buffalo or nowhere." Cornell University, with a strong claim to the land-grant status for the state and a well-developed series of programs dealing with social problems, felt it should have the new school. Syracuse University also lay some claims to the new program.[46] True to its history, criminal justice inspired academic politics and the highest levels.

There were academic disciplinary tugs of war as well. Eliot Lumbard, like his friend Frank Remington, was committed to criminal justice as an interdisciplinary study. Such an approach had been most successful in professional schools like law, medicine, and divinity. But not so in traditional universities, where intellectual and methodological lines had been drawn by the disciplines. Like warrior-kings in new nation-states, defenders guarded these academic boundaries ferociously and jealously. The sociology department at SUNY-Albany would have nothing to do with an interdisciplinary approach and went so far as to claim that "no respecting sociologist would join it." To a limited degree the psychology department agreed.[47] On the other hand, the dean of the college of public administration liked the idea and felt that criminal justice should be part of his responsibility. Anything in the area of public service should automatically fall under public administration, he advised. These battles were substantive and symbolic, taking up enormous amounts of energy and time.[48] All the while, Nelson Rockefeller and Eliot Lumbard were in the background prodding and pressuring, and more than bewildered over the academic politics involved. Once the School was set up, however, the focus of power shifted to its new dean, Richard Myren.

Myren had been raised and educated in Madison, Wisconsin. Although his college career at the University of Wisconsin had been interrupted by World War II, he was able to return and obtain a degree in chemistry. After a year as a research scientist he went to Harvard Law School. Upon graduation in 1952, Myren took a position with the Institute of Government at the University of North Carolina, where he conducted studies on the state police and the coroner system. Four years later he went to the department of police science at Indiana University, where he remained for a decade. Somewhat dismayed over the general intellectual environment of police education, Myren planned to return to the University of Wisconsin and work as a scholar-in-residence under Frank Remington. However, before he had made that move, the new position of dean of the School of Criminal Justice at Albany became known. He applied and got the job, starting in the summer of 1966.[49]

Along with Donald Riddle, Myren became one of the thought-leaders in criminal justice education during this period. For Myren the next step in the historical development of the field was scholarship. Police science had never really succeeded in the academic world, he felt. "Existing largely in state-supported institutions, they have never been held to the academic standards of other programs in higher education," he maintained. Second-career faculty and second-rate students had been attracted to police education over the years, thereby tainting its development. Unimaginative curricula and shoddy teaching became characteristic; the result was perpetuation of the agency practices of the past without any new insights from scholars for the future. Police professors generally were politically conservative whereas their academic colleagues were liberal, making the crime-related faculty "a right-of-center island in a left-of-center sea."

> Because the programs were essentially non-academic although housed in an academic setting, because their faculty members as second careerists did not share academic traditions, and because the programs took from the college but gave nothing in return, an isolation from general college life developed that was almost universal.[50]

The major problem was the parochial nature of police education. As an intellectual descendant of Frank Remington and the Law and Society movement, Myren felt that for too long police professors had ignored the entire system.

> One of the difficulties with the present situation is that we have got an awful lot of people who are walking around with blinders on, aware only of their own little areas and their own problems with little consideration of the problem of the system as a system.[51]

Myren became a proponent, therefore, of "systems analysis," or the notion that what happens in policing has an impact on the courts and on corrections, and vice versa. America needed a "criminal justice career system," he proclaimed. The current system was fragmented and insular, with very few people going from one branch to another. He wanted to create through education a body of people—"careerists," he called them—who were wide-ranging generalists. They would go from one area of criminal justice to another before finally settling down in one as a leader. Although such models did exist in Europe, America's crime-fighting apparatus did not allow for such a career development. Consequently, leadership for such a newly defined professional practitioner had to come from the educators.[52] But expanding the field meant more to Myren than providing better education for the practitioner.

Myren wanted to open up the field to scholarship. If John Jay had historical ties to Wiltberger, SUNY-Albany had them to V. A. Leonard. For Myren, undergraduate education was a "way station along the route to the doctorate." Graduate education as practiced in the past, indeed, was appropriate for the reflective bureaucrat, but Myren wanted to create criminal justice scholars. Of course he remained concerned with the professionalization of the practitioner, but more than any other before he was advocating the professionalization of the professor. To that end the broader conceptualization of the field away from police science to criminal justice became all the more important.

> If we move to the criminal justice system as the target area, we will get an area where we have intellectual challenge, where we have intellectual content, where we have developed literature which can move us to a point where we do have academic viability.[53]

The center of these activities, translated from the general principles to specific curricula, was SUNY-Albany.

Myren operationalized his philosophy in two ways at Albany. First, criminal justice may interconnect policing, law and courts, and corrections, but it must be done in an interdisciplinary way. In that respect, there was little difference between Myren and Donald Riddle at John Jay. Of course, in this context not all disciplines were necessarily equal. In spite of Myren's undergraduate education and the earlier history of police education at Berkeley, the physical sciences were not present. The humanities—with understandably relevant courses like philosophy, literature, and anthropology—were underrepresented as well. Although history was taught as an afterthought, Myren quickly warned students away from writing historical dissertations. In the last analysis, the interdisciplinary approach was to be limited to social science.

Second, it was to be a research-oriented graduate degree. Albany was to turn out graduates who were outstanding researchers, people who could move with ease between the disparate divisions of criminal justice. "Give them three months to immerse themselves in the literature of any social problem and they would be able to design research to explore the ramifications of the problem."[54] This interdisciplinary approach was to be tied together by the common thread of social science research methodology.

One of Myren's first tasks, therefore, was to recruit top-flight scholars. In the exhilaration of growth going on across campus, turf battles subsided and Myren was able to develop the School undisturbed by further academic politics. In fact, he had an essentially a blank check allowing him to hire whomever he thought to be the brightest and the best. William Brown (from public administration), Donald Newman (sociology and social work), and Hans Toch (psychology) were the three earliest hires. In terms of the faculty, the school grew rapidly in its first three or four years and then leveled off during the 1970s. From the first three members in 1966-67 the School grew to thirteen by 1970-71. Vincent O'Leary joined in 1968; Fred Cohen, Gilbert Geis, and Leslie Wilkins followed in the next year. Throughout the 1970s a few prominent regulars and illustrious visitors were added, but by 1980 the faculty's numerical strength was where it had been ten years earlier.[55] That was largely due to the general fiscal crisis hitting the state in the early 1970s. But also there were not many qualified academics willing to leave positions in a traditional department to align themselves with this new program. A few, out of a sense of academic noblesse oblige or personal professional crisis, did make the move to give Albany a surprisingly strong intellectual base. Of course, Albany had to be chary when hiring its own. Being products of an interdisciplinary program, they became something different—criminal justicians, as Myren would call them. With the exception of a social science methodology, they had only a dilution of the traditional disciplines themselves.

Another related task was the recruitment of excellent graduate students. Undergraduate education would not be added until 1982. Myren remembers that very early he wrote to 1,200 Woodrow Wilson fellowship designates (and 1,200 alternates, as well) to convince them to come to SUNY-Albany. He got one student! The next year he did it again and got a few more. Myren did that every year until "we had more Woodrow Wilsons in our small School than any other entire campus in the whole state system, including Columbia." He went on to say that "when you get students like that there is no way you can fail. Regardless of what you do to them they are going to make you look good. And that was frankly our strategy."[56] The first class of students, in 1968-69, had fourteen. In the next three years the number grew to 36 (1969), 50 (1970), and 110 in 1971. Throughout the 1970s there was a steady growth, peaking at 167 in 1977-78, before years of slight decline and leveling off occurred.[57]

These earliest students partook of interdisciplinary education in its purest form. The thirteen faculty represented a variety of academic fields such as sociology, psychology, law, political science, and public administration. Interdisciplinary education can be fragmented and uneven unless there is a core of knowledge expected of all. The "Albany model" had four substantive areas: criminology, justice administration, law, and planned change. To this core was added a heavy requirement of research methodology and data analysis.

In addition, there was to be a two-track system. A master's degree program designed to produce generalists who were to become planners and administrators of criminal justice agencies was in place. Arrangements were made with both the New York City and the State Police to allow gifted officers time off for a year so that they might pursue a graduate degree. Some of the top leaders in the State Police became Albany graduates. But the jewel in the crown was the doctoral program, whose graduates were expected to become researchers, teachers, and scholars.[58]

As would be expected, however, the master's program seemed more relevant, practicable, and marketable to career-oriented students. It tended to support the doctoral program. For example, using the earliest reliable data, the following chart may be constructed.[59]

GRADUATES	1972	1973	1974	1975	1976	1977	1978	1979	1980
Master's	37	57	68	55	50	45	32	55	24
Ph.Ds	1	0	5	7	4	9	10	4	7

Of course, such ratios are common to any doctoral program. In this case, over the time period an average of 9 masters to 1 doctorate is not out of line with the national ratio.[60] Essentially, master's and doctoral students took the same program, though it is not clear that such an academic experience was equally applicable. There is some evidence to suggest that those interested only in the master's degree did not feel well served having to take a program geared as preparation for the doctorate experience. Even the most friendly thought the two-track system to be "schizophrenic."[61]

No matter, because for Myren and his immediate successors it was the doctorate that was the capstone of the Albany program; the small number of Albany scholars were carrying the criminal justice movement one step further, to the creating of a truly criminal justice professoriate. Trained by representatives of the mainstream disciplines, they would go out as something new and unique: not as sociologists, political scientists, or even criminologists. They would be, as Myren liked to say, criminal justicians. These young scholars would influence other colleges such as the universities of Maryland, Wisconsin-Milwaukee, Nebraska-Omaha, Arizona State, Florida, Cincinnati, Northeastern, and Temple, to name a few. When Richard Myren left Albany in the mid-1970s, he went to set up and direct the program at American University in Washington, D.C. More importantly, the graduates of SUNY-Albany began to have influence through research.

One of the earliest textbooks on criminal justice was prepared by Donald Newman, a long-time professor at Albany. Several of his students would eventually write their own textbooks, helping to further shape the way the field was delivered to students. At first blush, textbook writing does not seem monumental; it is the synthesis of existing materials, a summary of information commonly accepted by a discipline as an essential or core understanding of the field. It is here that the clearest boundaries of a discipline are drawn for a wide public: the lay student. If there is no discipline—and most in criminal justice agreed that there was no discipline as yet—then these pioneering textbooks had a grave responsibility. They drew the dimensions of the field. Previous textbooks in criminology and police science were derivative from sociology and public administration. However, a new construction of knowledge was necessary for a field redefining itself as criminal justice. At first the lines were sketchy, becoming sharper as the period wore on. In no small measure the Albany model was responsible for the kind of criminal justice education made available to students making decisions on their majors. There might be small points of differing emphasis, but the essentials were well established by 1980. They were (1) crime: its type, extent and measurement; (2) criminology; (3) criminal law; (4) processing of the defendant; (5) police: organization and behavior; (6) courts: structure and personnel; (7) sentencing; (8) probation; (9) institutionalization; and

(10) parole. By 1980, when studies on the productivity and prestige of criminology and criminal justice faculty and graduate programs became known, SUNY-Albany was ranked number two across the nation. John Jay College of Criminal Justice was in first place.[62]

CONCLUSION

To be highly ranked in the field of criminal justice, however, did not mean that the field had yet achieved widespread academic respectability. By 1980 John Jay remained too vocational, still struggling with lower-quality students. It may have achieved local prominence in criminal justice circles, but it remained on the periphery in the wider world of higher education. Furthermore, the open admissions policy had undermined the earlier unique mission of the school. In addition, by 1980 the SUNY system was the weaker sister in higher education in the state, and Albany was a weaker component in that system. Of the four university centers in SUNY, only the Buffalo campus (at 36th place) was ranked in the top fifty schools in America with real research facilities. Stony Brook was ranked at 75th and Albany trailed at 84th place.[63] Critics charged that the SUNY system, some thirty years after its founding, had not yet found its place in higher education. "Few, if any, individual departments [had] moved into the top ranks of their fields," it was charged in 1981.[64] Such comments suggest that the media and wider public either disparaged criminal justice or, more likely, simply overlooked it as a solid disciplinary representative in higher education. The place and significance of John Jay and SUNY-Albany, and the ideological positions of Donald Riddle and Richard Myren, therefore, needed another platform: that was to be the Academy of Criminal Justice Sciences.

Chapter 8

Academy of Criminal Justice Sciences and the Hard Labor Creek Group, 1970–1980

Changing the name of the International Association of Police Professors to the Academy of Criminal Justice Sciences in 1970 was an important event, both ideologically and politically. It indicated the rise and power of a small number of thought-leaders who came to dominate positions of power in the Academy for the next decade. I refer to them as the Hard Labor Creek group. The less charitable would call them the "ole boy clique" or simply "the Machine."

William Mathias, who had come to head the newly established law enforcement program at Georgia State University two years earlier, was in charge of the IAPP convention in Atlanta in 1969. At that time he also hosted a retreat at Hard Labor Creek State Park just outside of Atlanta, an informal weekend affair for the more outspoken and concerned people attending the conference. The purpose was brainstorming—to discuss issues such as the appropriate place of criminal justice programs in the university, the future of criminal justice as an academic field, the proper content of criminal justice curricula, and the correct interface between academics and practitioners. In short, they wanted to address, if not resolve, fundamental issues in the definition and development of the field. A consensus developed, generally around the ideas of Riddle and Myren, whose academic administrative positions at John Jay and SUNY-Albany had given them enormous influence.

Criminal justice was to be an interdisciplinary field bridging police science, criminology, legal studies, and corrections. It should achieve independent academic status, eschewing subordinate and dependent positions within a sociology or political science department. Academic professionalism, with scholarship and research being important, was an article of faith. Individual programs in colleges and universities should be developed freely but not without an eye to the reputation and future of the entire field. The Academy of Criminal Justice Sciences should be the medium by which these principles would be rationalized and proselytized to the growing numbers of teachers and professors in the field. In addition, that professional association should be the chief agency of change and control of criminal justice higher education.[1]

Meetings of the Hard Labor Creek group were held for much of the decade. Meeting sites changed, though the name of the group remained the same, as professional positions shifted. Attendance changed a little as well, but the core regulars remained: Donald Riddle, Richard Myren, Gordon Misner, Richard Ward, George Felkenes, and William Mathias.[2] Besides being a networking group, it became a solid block of power and persuasion. Richard Ward remembered the Hard Labor Creek get-together as a time when issues were discussed and consensus achieved. It was a place where aspiring academic politicians could articulate their views and form agendas, platforms, and support for future positions of power.[3] Seven of the next eight presidents of the Academy of Criminal Justice Sciences were charter members of this group. Several other presidents became latter-day converts. Their ideology and politics dominated the next decade of developments in this academic profession.

The views of Donald Riddle and Richard Myren brought the Hard Labor Creek group together originally. But they always remained on the cutting edge, the more radical and intellectually flirtatious of the group. It was left to others, with the moral force of Riddle and Myren in the background, to actually implement ideas into actions. The ideologists needed the pragmatists to carry the day, to moderate and compromise positions that otherwise might not be palpable to an organization still filled largely with police professors. There were at least three broad concerns of the Hard Labor Creek coalition: making the Academy as effective and powerful as possible, giving an academic tone to the field of criminal justice education, and enhancing their own academic careers. None was more important in this than Gordon Misner. Two of the group, Richard Ward and George Felkenes, had been his students at the University of California's School of Criminology. In many respects he verged upon being the political boss of the Hard Labor Creek group.

Born in Colorado but educated in California, Misner began his career as a newspaperman in San Francisco. An earlier stint in the merchant marine whetted his appetite for the Far East, and he began studying comparative political science. He took degrees from Marin County Junior College, San Francisco State College, and the University of California. In the meantime he also worked in a local sheriff's department, eventually running unsuccessfully for election to be sheriff. In his intellectual trek, he moved from journalism to political science to criminology. His first teaching was done at San Jose State College, where he spent ten years in Melvin Miller's police school while at the same time working on a doctorate of criminology at Berkeley. In the late 1960s and early 1970s while teaching at the School of Criminology, he became a close friend and admirer of Joseph Lohman. When the International Association of Police Professors met in San Francisco in 1968, Misner was in charge of local arrangements. He badgered his students—Richard Ward and George Felkenes were two of them—to join the IAPP. At that time, also, Misner first played academic politics, getting an old friend and junior college teacher, Earl Lewis, elected president. Indeed, Misner was a curious member of the Hard Labor Creek group. On one hand, he was devoted to the ideals of Riddle and Myren. On the other hand, harking back to his own roots, he was best friend to the junior colleges and the practitioner police professors in the entire Hard Labor Creek coalition. Also, he was a consummate politician. After he finalized his degree, Misner moved to head the new criminal justice program at the University of Missouri at St. Louis, where he remained during most of this period under consideration, the mid- and late-1970s.[4]

THE ORGANIZATION MEN

Perhaps the greatest contribution of the Hard Labor Creek group was in the managerial revolution of the Academy of Criminal Justice Sciences. Gordon Misner, during his first term as president (1971-72), was preoccupied with setting a tone. He felt that the organization previously had acted like a "beer and chowder" society and now needed to pattern itself after other learned societies.[5] Consequently, at Misner's convention meeting in Boston, prestigious scholars completely unconnected to the Academy were asked to speak. The presence of scholars from Yale University and the Harvard Law School made it clear that an intellectual and scholarly shift was occurring.[6]

Misner was the managerial innovator throughout the decade, but other Hard Labor Creek members followed his lead. For example, Richard Myren, president in 1972-73, created the office of historian. Depending on one's definitions, the organization was in the midst of a short history, but the Hard Labor Creek people were proud and vain enough to want their place and accomplishments to be properly recorded. They were magnanimous and confident enough, as well, to select an archenemy, Edward Farris, to be the official historian. However, Farris was not a real historian and little was done with the office. Later they tried again, perhaps realizing that those in control of writing history ultimately are making it.

In addition, an awards structure was begun in 1973 to recognize outstanding persons in the field of operational and academic criminal justice. The implication was that any organization giving prestigious awards to established persons must be noteworthy itself. Misner, during his second presidency in 1976, expanded the awards structure. The Bruce Smith, Jr., award was established going to Sir Leon Radzinowicz and Thorsten Sellin in 1976, and to Ralph Turner, Leslie Wilkins, and James Q. Wilson in subsequent years. The Founders Award went to V. A. Leonard in 1976. Arthur Brandstatter, George Felkenes, Donald Riddle, Gordon Misner, and Richard Myren became recipients shortly thereafter.

In other ways the Hard Labor Creek group—with Gordon Misner assuming major responsibility in his two presidential terms (1971-72, 1976-77)—made the Academy increasingly complex and rational. By 1977 there were twenty standing committees and several ad hoc groups.[7] The Affirmative Action Committee, first chaired by a Black and later by a succession of females, was concerned with issues in criminal justice pertaining to minorities. At the 1978 meeting in New Orleans 25 women delivered papers, the highest thus far in the history of the Academy. The next year, at Cincinnati, 75 women were on the program. The 1980 meeting marked a 455 percent increase of minority and female participation over the decade.[8] A Journal Committee was to survey membership attitudes toward the *Journal of Criminal Justice*, a scholarly publication set up for the dissemination of the research of the membership. The History of the Field Committee was to interview Academy leaders and write contemporary histories of the organization. An Ethics Committee was to study the several "sham academic operations" existing under the guise of criminal justice programs. The problem of giving college credit for police academy training and life experience was scrutinized by the Life Experiences Evaluation

Committee.

William Mathias, with degrees in business administration, was instrumental in the managerial revolution of the Academy as well. He had been secretary-treasurer under presidents Riddle and Misner. When he took over the books at the Chicago meetings in 1971, the Academy had $100. Two years later it had $9,000.[9] The programs of the annual meetings had been thin; frequently a three- or four-page fold-out brochure outlined the events. Mathias started printing conference programs, and according to Richard Ward the organization now had left the "mimeograph era."[10] Donald Riddle, reminiscing over his presidency, felt that Mathias was the person "who really straightened out the secretary's office and turned it into a going operation."[11] Before Mathias became secretary-treasurer the office had been fairly insignificant, but after his work it became a springboard to the presidency.

Another cherished idea of Mathias and the Hard Labor Creek politicians was a national secretariat. Previously, the secretary-treasurer merely exploited his or her own college or university for printing, mailing, and secretarial services. But this practice seemed flawed because of the short-term nature of the office and the variable generosity of the host campuses. Ultimately, the leaders wanted a national office in Washington, D.C. However, for the time being they settled for a more permanent, three- to five-year, secretariat. Since so many of the Hard Labor Creek group were on the more prestigious campuses, the secretariat idea was seen by many police professors as oligarchical and so was shelved for a time.

REGIONALISM

Gordon Misner was the father of regionalism as well. Most professional organizations eventually have to come to terms with grassroots membership and establish regional affiliates.[12] The Hard Labor Creek people had some good reasons to do so. First, Misner understood that many people could not travel to national meetings and, therefore, did not join the Academy. Some sort of regional structure within the national organization would encourage local and regional meetings, allowing for participation and debate for those unable to travel across the country.[13] He was convinced that the regional affiliates would even recruit members for the national body. "Once they get their feet wet," he told Felkenes, "total immersion" in the Academy would follow.[14]

Second, the regions might be safety-valves, places

were battles might be fought and energies spent. It was clear that the national leadership was preaching criminal justice but that many college programs were practicing police science. It was on the regional level, for example, that William Mathias and Richter Moore fought to "eliminate the highly technical Handcuffs I and Billy Club II type of programs" in the South.[15] Californians, such as Misner and Felkenes, remembered that many important confrontations between junior colleges and state college criminal justice programs occurred on the state association level.[16] Misner had been instrumental in allowing the more practitioner type into the organization and bridled at the growing academic elitism. The regions would give the practitioners some voice in the Academy, he wrote to Robert Culbertson in 1978.

> You know I feel strongly about giving regions and junior college people representation in Academy affairs. (Some would accuse me of going too far in this regard.) In my opinion, no single factor would be more destructive to the Academy's future than a feeling by j.c. people that they had been excluded from the activities and the recognition of the Academy—even if it professes to be a learned society. I am sure that many of our status-starved Ph.D.s would like to limit active membership to holders of research doctorates! Don't ever take it to a vote, that sort of mentality is disastrous.[17]

Third, since there was little consensus on the appropriate type of criminal justice education, the regions became places where Hard Labor Creek members converted people from police science to criminal justice. Troubleshooters, most often Gordon Misner himself, went to the grassroots and promoted the Hard Labor Creek ideology. Finally, regionalism (especially in the South) was already occurring without advice and consent from the national organization. Misner simply needed to take hold of a movement already in progress and insure that the national organization had an important place in that development.

Fortunately, there were Hard Labor Creek people involved in the regional development in the South. William Mathias was key in the founding of the Georgia Association of Criminal Justice Educators in 1967.[18] Richter Moore was the first president of the North Carolina Association of Criminal Justice Educators in 1970.[19] A Southern Association of Criminal Justice began in 1968 but soon died. It was revived in 1972 with Mathias and Moore as founding fathers. Donald Riddle, Richard Myren, and James Curran came from the North to gauge and support this new regional organization.[20] The Southern Association grew rapidly, and Richter Moore felt that in the early 1970s it was a stronger force in criminal justice than the Academy.[21] Southerners were justifiably proud because their organization came into existence independently of the national one. Probably there was no danger of secession, especially with such nationalists as Mathias and Moore on the scene, but nonetheless the history of the American Society of Criminology did show that strong regional leaders uncontrolled by the national organization could pose a threat. It was essential, therefore, for the Hard Labor Creek group to muffle the thunder and control regional development.

In 1973, Gordon Misner proposed his regionalization plan. State and regional organizations, based roughly on the LEAA regional boundaries, were to be encouraged with a 10 percent rebate of dues to the Academy from members of the local area.[22] That money would go back to help support the regional organization. What the Southern Association would do was critical to Misner's plan. Since it was the only regional group in existence, the entire plan might fail and a splintering of the national group would result if it balked. Thanks to the work of Mathias and Moore, however, the Southern Association petitioned to be the Academy's first recognized region at the very meeting at which Misner proposed his plan.[23] Two years later, largely due to the work of Misner, the Midwest Association of Criminal Justice was organized in St. Louis and accepted by the national.[24] Soon other areas such as the Southwestern (1976), Northeastern (1976), and North Atlantic (1977) would round out the Hard Labor Creek regional effort. Therefore the regional structure was really a plan of the Hard Labor Creek group to make the national organization stronger. But there were challenges coming from the regions as well.

Misner's model region was the Midwest, the one he personally brought into existence. Its sprawling eleven-state geography held 22 percent of the total membership of the Academy. Also, many leaders in the criminal justice education movement—Donald Riddle, Robert Borkenstein, George Felkenes, James Osterburg, Richard Ward, Robert Culbertson, Larry Hoover, and Gordon Misner, to name a few—were members of the Midwest. Preoccupation with activities on the national level, however, forced many leaders to relinquish power in the region to others. In Misner's opinion the Midwest should have been the strongest region, but instead he felt it to be the weakest.[25]

Most problems in the Midwest region were symptomatic of any new organization. Attendance at meetings was sparse. Leaders had to give up office unexpectedly as their careers took them elsewhere.[26] Of course, there were ideological differences as well. For example, when Misner came to explain the Academy's new accreditation guidelines, a "hot and heavy" discussion resulted.[27] In 1976 and 1977 an anti-Academy faction tried to take over the regional organization. The November 1976 meeting, reported Robert Culbertson, took on the air of a "closed shop" with people secretly meeting to plan voting strategies to topple pro-Academy leaders.[28] Misner reprimanded the organization but was met by allegations that the Academy as a "good ole boy" organization was unsympathetic to small schools interested in teaching and training criminal justice personnel. A showdown election occurred, with the anti-Academy forces being narrowly defeated.[29] But another rebellion arose in 1979 to try once more to break the regional and national tie. This was unsuccessful too, but the regions continued to be small battlefields watched carefully by the Hard Labor Creek leadership.

THE FIELD OF CRIMINAL JUSTICE

Clearly, changing the name of the academic field and its organization of educators to "criminal justice" was important, a feat accomplished for the organization during Riddle's presidency. For the rest of the decade there was a largely successful crusade to get the law enforcement and corrections programs and departments to change their names as well. One survey of 177 programs in the mid-1970s found that 106 were labelled as criminal justice. Around 40 remained law enforcement or police science. Others were corrections, forensics, criminology, public safety, or police administration.[30] In spite of the name changes, however, many remained devoted to law enforcement and the training of occupational tasks. Indeed, fully 40 percent of LEEP recipients were attending junior colleges, where vocationalism was at its highest.[31]

Since so much criminal justice education was done at the undergraduate level, the Hard Labor Creek leaders focused on the importance of the liberal arts nature of the curricula. This position was based upon their understanding of the true work environment in a bureaucracy. Functionaries in the system did not always go by the book, many felt. In fact, the more one went down the criminal justice agency ladder, the more prevalent was the use of discretion. One did not need training, therefore, to follow orders so much as to make good moral judgments.[32]

It was left to George Felkenes to make the Hard Labor

Creek point. Actually, Felkenes was a good choice. He had restructured a program at Long Beach State College earlier. Now, he was creating a new one at the University of Alabama at Birmingham. Besides holding a doctorate in criminology from the University of California, he also had a law degree, even setting forth his argument as a legal brief: "The Case of the Proper Balance: Liberal Arts (Plaintiff) with Criminal Justice (Defendant)." Contrary to popular belief, according to Felkenes, job placement should not be the goal of an academic criminal justice program. Intellectual ideas, not vocational techniques, were the essential product of any program. "Attention must be given to a critical analysis of conditions existing in criminal justice so as to impart to the students a broad knowledge of ability to appreciate the complexities of the field." True academic courses, Felkenes felt, were future-oriented; they sought to change and improve existing theories and processes. Vocational or operational offerings, on the other hand, were always status quo-oriented. All "nuts-and-bolts" courses, therefore, needed to be eliminated and replaced with more established liberal arts ones. Especially in the first few years of a student's program, criminal justice courses should be held to a minimum.[33]

Such views were cherished by the Hard Labor Creek group and their growing number of fellow travelers. On the other hand, many old-line police professors balked at the liberal arts approach. It seemed obvious to them that they would have less and less to do in an academic field as described by Felkenes. Many remembered what had happened to them and their organization when sociologists began redefining and renaming the American Society of Criminology. Others in the Academy worried over the implications of the criminal justice-liberal arts nexus. Charles Tenny of Northeastern University, for example, made a disturbing point challenging the Hard Labor Creek ideology. If criminal justice were to be interdisciplinary, and thus so derivative of other established disciplines, why should it have its own departmental standing? Why should not students just float from department to department studying the appropriate courses in their home discipline?[34] Of course, such a logical notion would be suicidal for a young academic profession. Instead, the Hard Labor Creek group supported the Osterburg resolution, which further threatened the old line police professors.

With rare exception, criminal justice programs were loaded with people possessing more practical experience in operational agencies than degrees from academic units. Some rare characters, such as Donald Riddle, had no "real world" experience in criminal justice operations. Others, such as Richard Myren, had marginal nonacademic practical experiences. But they were the exception. Therefore, a tradition or expectation had developed in which the successful criminal justice faculty member had to have some practical experience. But these "second-career" faculties were too vocational and added little to the respectability of the field. Besides, the liberal arts direction of the Hard Labor Creek group demanded a new policy.

In a poorly attended business meeting of the Academy at Omaha, Nebraska, in March 1973, James Osterburg, himself a former police detective from New York City who had studied at John Jay, proposed a resolution that quickly and quietly passed. The Osterburg resolution, in the guise of affirmative action, had the Academy declare that "practical experience in an operating agency no longer be viewed as an essential criterion as a qualification for a collegiate teaching position in the field of criminal justice."[35] Although not everyone followed the Osterburg resolution, it was a revolutionary device that met several practical problems and changed the character of criminal justice faculties. Also, it set the Academy—at least the Hard Labor Creek wing of the organization—further apart from the two-year colleges and the more vocational four-year ones.

First, the resolution allowed the various programs to tap into other pools of professors until a criminal justice professoriate was trained. Second, it was in line with the Hard Labor Creek position on the interdisciplinary nature of the field. Instead of scholarly work on crime-related issues remaining in traditional departments, it could be brought into the new criminal justice programs. Political scientists, sociologists, and psychologists—people who had no operational experience in the field but who had a research interest in criminal justice—could be hired by the Hard Labor Creek program builders. Some flush departments, such as the one headed by James Osterburg at the University of Illinois at Chicago Circle, even had an engineer, economist, and historian on staff.[36] Third, these traditionally trained academics now residing in a criminal justice department could act as liaison with their home disciplines on campus. A network, useful in university politics, might be built to ward off designing deans. After all, how could a department filled with mainstream academics be accused any longer of being too vocational? Finally, such new faculty recruits—with research degrees and scholarly agenda in hand—would become role models for existing criminal justice faculty members. As their careers developed, it was believed, the academic respectability of the individual departments and the entire field would increase. The Osterburg resolution, with the full backing and encouragement of the Hard Labor Creek group, had the potential for revolutionizing the field of criminal justice. But revolutions do not come that easily. The mixing of "insiders"(those with practical experience) and "outsiders" (those without such agency experience) took on a marbling appearance. One study found that 74 percent of the junior colleges and 47 percent of the four year institutions still felt that practical experience was a necessity by mid-decade.[37]

Fundamental to academic respectability, for the Hard Labor Creek group, was research. The scholarly thunder of the criminal justice educator for too long had been stolen by people in the traditional disciplines. People like Marvin Wolfgang, Albert Reiss, Norval Morris, and James Q. Wilson (rather than people in the Academy) were the experts on the crime problems of America. During Misner's presidency Richard Ward and James Curran were called upon to articulate a "Statement of Philosophy of Criminal Justice Degree Programs in the Area of Research" for the Hard Labor Creek group. Although program development and administration were important activities encouraged by LEEP and the Hard Labor Creek group, Ward and Curran predicted that the future of criminal justice education was tied to scholarship. However, the current research and scholarly literature was inadequate. Vigorous social science methodology needed to displace the old evaluative studies characteristic of the field going back to Vollmer. Furthermore, agency-specific studies should give way—just as the field was to give way—to total systems research showing the interrelationships of the various agencies. Finally, the Academy of Criminal Justice should have a means to publish research through a professional journal.[38]

Both segments of the criminal justice professorate—the older group, ill-trained in research, and the post-Osterburg resolution group of younger scholars—found difficulty publishing in mainstream sociology, psychology, and political science journals. The American Society of Criminology had a journal, but most police professors found *Criminology* equally difficult in which to publish. Consequently, very high on the Hard Labor Creek agenda was the establishment of a scholarly journal. Coincidentally and independently, Kent B. Joscelyn, director of the Institute for Research in Public Safety at Indiana University, established the *Journal of Criminal Justice* in 1973 "for the sharing of research and practical experience." The Hard Labor Creek interest was obvious, and Richard Myren was on the editorial advisory board when the first issue appeared. President William Mathias began negotiations with Joscelyn at the Omaha meetings of the Academy in 1973.[39] Agreement was reached readily, and the first issue announcing the affiliation came out one year later. Thus began an eight-year relationship in which the Academy of Criminal Justice Sciences (ACJS) could claim it had an academic journal for the dissemination of research.

Another issue connected to research was graduate education in criminal justice. Clearly, SUNY-Albany and John Jay could not supply the need for criminal justice doctorates. One could borrow from the traditional disciplines only for a limited time before getting a reputation of a nondiscipline. As early as 1971 LEEP administrators saw the need for developing more graduate programs in criminal justice.[40] An "Educational Development" grant of $3 million was given to five universities (later the number was increased to seven) in 1973. They were Northeastern University in Boston, University of Maryland, Eastern Kentucky University, University of Nebraska at Omaha, Portland State University, Arizona State University, and Michigan State University. Independently for their own regions of the country, and as a national consortium, they were to develop research identifying the educational needs for careers in criminal justice education and practice. Specifically, they were to (1) clarify the role of their college or university in developing scholars and teachers, (2) establish the type of education needed on the graduate level for people working in criminal justice agencies, (3) define the common denominators between training and education, (4) and devise counseling systems to better advise the pre-service and the in-service students. By 1976, the seven universities had graduate programs at least on the master's level.[41]

For most Hard Labor Creek people, academic legitimacy might be enhanced for criminal justicians if they merged with the more respected criminologists in the American Society of Criminology. In 1977 a Liaison Committee was set up to discuss the possibility of a merger. It was estimated that 30 percent of the memberships of both organizations actually belonged to both the ASC and ACJS. Presidents and past presidents of both organizations made up this committee. The ASC was represented by President William Amos as well as by Harry Allen, Simon Dinitz, C. Ray Jeffery, Donal MacNamara, Charles Newman, Walter Reckless, and Joseph Scott. The Academy was represented by president-elect Richard Ward, George Felkenes, William Mathias, Gordon Misner, Richard Myren, and Richter Moore. The Hard Labor

Creek position was that both groups had similar goals and purposes; they both were interested in research and teaching of crime-related topics. The merger of the two would create a larger and more influential organization that could impact on crime policies in Washington, D.C. Quality control, such as accreditation, would be easier with both organizations as one, they argued.[42] There was opposition almost immediately from two sources.

Several members of the Liaison Committee, particularly from the American Society of Criminology, were against the idea. C. Ray Jeffery felt the two organizations to be too different in makeup and outlook for a compatible blend. Sixty percent of the Society were sociologists and criminologists who were more academic and research oriented than the Academy. On the other hand, the Academy was filled with department builders and administrators, police professionals, and junior college teachers. Merging the two organizations would drive away substantial numbers from both and cause frictions and factions among those who stayed.[43] Rank-and-file members of both organizations were opposed as well. Barbara Raffel Price, of the ASC, maintained that any merger would weaken the reputation of the Society.[44] A few ACJS people, especially those remembering their displacement some fifteen years earlier, did not want to be gobbled up again by the "elitist academics" in the ASC. However, more fundamentally the younger and ambitious members of both organizations were fearful of losing leadership opportunities. Representative of this group in the Academy was Robert Culbertson, a secretary-treasurer who wanted to be president of the ACJS. For Culbertson the Academy presented "an opportunity for a significant number of other young people in the field who probably at the time couldn't even get on the program of ASC, who if they wanted to get into this organization [ACJS] and really hustle and work could get elected to an office and assume leadership positions."[45] So the Hard Labor Creek group wanted one organization for the good of the field, but the membership wanted two for the good of their careers. The merger issue was voted down in 1978, but the Hard Labor Creek group kept the issue alive in other ways. For example, representatives from ASC were invited to be on the ACJS Accreditation Council (they declined) and on the Joint Commission, both topics to be discussed shortly. And as late as 1979 president Richter Moore considered reopening the merger option anew.[46] In the meantime, another Hard Labor Creek drive became all consuming.

ACCREDITATION

No other movement within the Academy, and the field as a whole, better characterizes the Hard Labor Creek group's attempt to control quality of criminal justice education than accreditation. With the exception of Riddle, most of the Hard Labor Creek group was unanimous concerning its importance. It was a natural reaction to the previous decade of rapid growth; there was a desire to control growth and quality. The Hard Labor Creek group, many having professional school backgrounds, chose specialized accreditation. This seemed a contradiction to other principles in the Hard Labor Creek agenda because, as the National Commission on Accreditation put it, such accreditation was to focus on practice-oriented degree programs concerned with occupational competence.[47] But of course those were exactly the programs that were growing out of control. Earlier, Riddle had dissuaded Misner and the Academy from specialized accreditation, but the first five years of the 1970s proved that institutional accreditation was insufficient. Too many substandard programs had arisen to "jeopardize the field and tarbrush the entire criminal justice in higher education field."[48] As early as 1972 Richard Myren abandoned Riddle with a speech declaring that "Accreditation Rides Again." Then Gordon Misner, after being told that both the IACP and the American Society of Criminology were planning accreditation efforts, rekindled interest with a speech at the Atlanta meetings advocating accreditation as a top priority for the Academy.

In 1974 President Felix Fabian had asked one of his former students, Larry Bassi, to head a work group studying standards in criminal justice education.[49] This committee was filled with Hard Labor Creek people such as George Felkenes, Gordon Misner, and William Mathias. Gilbert Bruns and Ben Menke had been cultivated and converted over the years by Misner. Arthur Brandstatter and Felix Fabian were to be a sop to the police professors. Larry Bassi, who was teaching at Niagara Community College at the time, was a good choice because of his capacity for hard work and his ostensible connection to the practitioner-oriented police professors.[50]

Throughout the spring and summer of 1975 the committee established guidelines remarkably similar to the original principles of the Hard Labor Creek group. Like any cultural commandments, these should be read not only as future goals to be achieved but as present problems to be resolved. They are as follows:

Program Objectives: Each criminal justice program

should have clearly defined purposes consistent with higher education.

Administrative Identity: Although freestanding departmental status was desirable, it did not matter as long as criminal justice was treated like all other academic units. However, it should not be run out of "the hip pocket" of some designing dean.

Curriculum: Courses should reflect the multidisciplinary nature of the field.

Students: Students in criminal justice should have the same facilities as other students on campus.

Faculty: People teaching at the junior college level should have a master's degree. Although a law degree or master's degree may be acceptable at the baccalaureate level, a majority of the faculty should have the doctorate. However, at the graduate level the doctorate was necessary. Over reliance on part-timers should be avoided. No more than 50 percent of the annual credit hour production should be taught by part-timers at the community college level. In a baccalaureate program no more than 30 percent, and in a graduate program no more than 25 percent, of the annual credit hours should be offered by part-time professors.

Learning Resources: Criminal justice units should have all the teaching resources that other academic departments have.

Supportive Resources: Criminal justice programs should have all the space, supplies, equipment, and staff that others have to run a quality operation.

Financial Resources: Money should be available for the maintaining of a quality program. Funds should not be limited to external sources; in fact, institutions should be prepared to fully fund their own criminal justice programs within three years of their establishment without reliance on outside sources. Clearly, the demise of LEEP was on the minds of the potential accreditors.[51] In short, it was felt that criminal justice should be on a par with other academic departments on campus, certainly a sign of the legitimacy the Hard Labor Creek group wanted to achieve.

Criticisms arose immediately. Some felt the Academy was not truly representative of the variety of existing programs and had no right to evaluate them.[52] Others felt it was another example of the Hard Labor Creek elite trying to monopolize the field.[53] But it was the practitioner-trainer group who felt most offended. To them the requirement of a master's degree as a minimum teaching credential was unrealistic. Such a requirement would destroy many community college programs, they complained. Besides, they argued, any number of practitioners with only baccalaureate degrees were far superior teachers than those with graduate degrees and no practical experience.[54] They saw little evidence of the practitioner's influence on the guidelines document. In the opinion of Edward Small, president of the New Jersey Council of Educational Institutions for Law Enforcement, the complete absence in the faculty guidelines (particularly in terms of associate degree programs)

> of the desirability of professional experience for those teaching law enforcement courses clearly indicates which faction has emerged victorious in the lengthy struggle within ACJS between the theoretical academics and the practitioner-educators.[55]

Since this trainer element was underrepresented and largely voiceless in the Academy, the accreditation program passed, further driving a wedge—in spite of Misner's attempts to the contrary—between the trainers and the Hard Labor Creek educators.

Three things had to be done before the Academy of Criminal Justice Sciences won approval from the Council on Post Secondary Accreditation (COPA) to become an accrediting agent. First, throughout 1976 and 1977 Larry Bassi and Gordon Misner set up a series of accreditation workshops to train a pool of program evaluators. In addition, Misner felt that holding workshops throughout the country was a way to convert many to the Hard Labor Creek position and "dispel much misinformation about our hidden agenda."[56] Second, a body independent of the Academy had to be set up to actually administer the accreditation. An Accreditation Council, heavily loaded with Hard Labor Creek people, was shortly in place.[57] Third, several "pilot" accreditations needed to be carried out to show COPA that the Council was capable for the task. Two colleges were quickly assessed. Ball State University at Munice, Indiana, was accredited. However, McKendree College at Lebanon, Illinois, was denied accreditation. Another half dozen were to be visited shortly.

Forces were at work, however, to undermine the Academy's accreditation effort. First, there was no widespread agreement, even within the Academy, on the Hard Labor Creek position on appropriate criminal justice education. Perhaps Donald Riddle was correct when he reminisced that his philosophy "seemed to be in the head but not the heart" of the criminal justice educators at the end of the decade.[58] Second, an even more fundamental question arose with regard to the pilot accredtitations. What real advantage was there to gaining Academy accreditation? Was a certificate on the wall important enough? More important, what disadvantage was there to not being accredited? The Academy had no sanctions.[59] Third, COPA remained hesitant to recognize another specialized accrediting body. There were already over fifty specialized accrediting bodies in the United States by the mid-1970s.[60] Fourth, college and university administrators disliked specialized accreditation. General or regional accreditation seemed adequate enough, to them. Fifth, accreditation was costly, with many colleges refusing to pay for the service. Even within the Academy, as internal politics began to shift, allocations to the accreditation effort began to dwindle. Robert Culbertson, a man working his way up in the various positions of leadership, felt that the entire accreditation process "was another activity that ACJS had stuck its neck out on, and without any planning or predicting, and man we were going to suck the well dry!"[61] When Gilbert Bruns was asked to evaluate the accreditation effort in 1980 he reported that there was no way it could pay for itself.[62] Sixth, some resented the Hard Labor Creek domination of the process. Again, Robert Culbertson felt the Accreditation Council was just another example of the "closed club" nature of the Hard Labor Creek group.[63]

But for many accreditation was the Academy's finest attempt to control and guide the development of criminal justice education. George Felkenes had become president of the Accreditation Council in its last days. He and others remained staunch supporters for years to come. Felkenes felt "it was the best effort we had because it was something which kept us together, and it was an attempt to improve criminal justice education."[64] Perhaps the problem had been an overabundance of enthusiasm without a clear understanding of what standards should apply in evaluating criminal justice education. The Hard Labor Creek group now turned to that issue.

JOINT COMMISSION ON CRIMINOLOGY AND CRIMINAL JUSTICE EDUCATION AND STANDARDS

Another program central to the Hard Labor Creek agenda was a national office located in Washington, D.C. Many major professional associations, be they vocational or educational, had such a "Washington presence," it was argued. Accreditation, a national movement itself, might have had more credibility emanating from such a place. Attacks on LEEP could have been better controlled from Washington. A staff in an established office could ferret out federal resources for funding in a more professional manner. In the past, the secretary-treasurer's office floated to the college of the person holding office. Therefore, there was an expectation of institutional support that went along with the candidacy of any new secretary-treasurer. But that was spotty and unreliable, especially as money became more scarce at decade's end.[65] Consequently, grant drafts were written first by George Felkenes, then by Gordon Misner, and then by Richard Ward for federal money to help set up a national office.

Price Foster of LEAA was reluctant to favor the Academy, especially since the American Society of Criminology had an even more historic and legitimate claim for such funds for a national office. The Society had settled on a secretariat office at Ohio State University. Instead, in March 1977 William Mathias and Richard Ward met with the Office of Criminal Justice Education and Training and were persuaded to drop the national office idea for the time being, and, instead, accept funds to conduct a massive study on the quality of criminal justice education. It was suggested that such money might be "seed" money for a national office anyway, and Ward himself felt that a national office would be open by fall of 1977.[66]

Money was granted to establish a Joint Commission on Criminology and Criminal Justice Education and Standards, a body much like the famous Flexner Commission some 60 years earlier that had studied medical education. It would be made up of representatives interested and involved in education on crime-related studies. There would be four representatives from the Academy, four from the Society, and one each from the American Sociological Association, the American Psychological Association, the American Society for Public Administration, and the Association of Doctoral Programs in Criminal Justice.[67]

Actually, such an enterprise was not new to criminal justice. As mentioned earlier, the National Advisory Commission on Higher Education for Police Officers was conducting its own project at the same time, and its report (*The Quality of Police Education*, or the Sherman report) was published in 1978. The John Jay College of Criminal Justice in cooperation with the Academy had done some studies too. Finally, a short-lived ACJS research center at Youngstown State University, under the directorship of Richard Bennett, specialized in research on criminal justice education. Thus, in some respects the Joint Commission was redundant—but at least it brought together representatives from the Society and the Academy, showing the wisdom of the membership in turning down any plans of merger. In fact, the representatives of the two organizations could not agree on anything except a series of monographs exploring the nature and differences of criminology and criminal justice as intellectual and academic pursuits.[68]

The grant was awarded to the Academy with Richard Ward, who was president at the time, as project director. During its first year of operation (it had a life span from 1977 to 1980) the Joint Commission, with its principal investigator Julius Debro, was based in Washington. For a time the Joint Commission project allowed the fiction of a national presence in Washington to continue. Debro conducted secondary and bibliographic studies. After the first year it moved to Chicago, where Ward had gone to be Riddle's assistant at the University of Illinois at Chicago Circle. That one university had now Donald Riddle, Richard Ward, Gordon Misner (who had just moved there from St. Louis), and James Osterburg. Vincent Webb, from the University of Nebraska at Omaha, was called in to take over for Debro. A more vigorous sociological research methodology resulted as Webb surveyed criminal justice and criminology programs and faculties across the country to determine the "state of the field." Familiar issues and categories (i.e., administration, curriculum, faculty, and students) emerged from the data. Over forty standards, most of them remarkably similar to the guidelines established by Larry Bassi's Accreditation Committee three years earlier, were set forth as minimum criteria in this "Quest For Quality."[69] Many of the Hard Labor Creek group felt they had a controversial document. However, Webb carefully distinguished between standards and standardization, thereby diffusing much criticism. In fact, when the report, *Quest For Quality*, was ready for public debate, the main criticism was "so what!"[70]

Uncharacteristic of most Hard Labor Creek activities in the past, the drama of the Webb report was over its conventionality. According to Richard Ward, the field had grown so rapidly and so many of the Joint Commission's future recommendations had already been adopted by the time the report was made public that little debate resulted.[71] In short, the *Quest For Quality* was less a call to future action than a benchmark on the successes of the Hard Labor Creek agenda at decade's end. This was due in part to the vision of the Hard Labor Creek group. They had seen what had to be done to legitimize the field and set out to do it. But it was due to their academic politics as well.

ACADEMIC POLITICS

Clearly, one of the consequences of the activity of the Hard Labor Creek group was an enhanced politicization of the Academy of Criminal Justice Sciences. Of course, there had been politics before. But now most became aware that professional activity in the Academy had become, as Misner liked to say, like "playing hard ball."[72]

One event stood out as indicative of the political environment. The Riddle, Misner, Myren, and Mathias presidencies had led some to think of the Hard Labor Creek group as a political machine. For many, particularly from the ranks of the old-line police professors, an election to high office became critical. In 1973 Edward Farris, the perennial representative of the Vollmerian tradition, called for reform. To placate the police professors and assure the membership at large that the members of the Hard Labor Creek group were democratic, a new nomination system was introduced. A nominations committee was to be elected, making sure each geographical area had equal representation. This committee would solicit nominations for office from the membership. The chairperson of the committee would submit to the secretary-treasurer the two names for each office that came up most often. It was from this grassroots revolution that Felix Fabian was elected president in 1974. George Felkenes, in his run for president, narrowly beat out a candidate from the police professors.

Also, in the grand style of machine politics, there appeared to be some corruption. For example, in the election during Fabian's term many ballots went to the secretary-treasurer rather than to the nominations committee. The secretary-treasurer, an ambitious man from East Tennessee State College, delivered several opened ballots to the committee. When the situation came to light at the Atlanta meeting in 1975, President Felix Fabian was called to accounts. It appeared that the election had been fixed. As Fabian remembers it,

> I had to stand there before the entire membership present trying to explain what happened. To top it off my secretary-treasurer doesn't even show up at the meeting. He is there, but he doesn't show. In fact I sent runners all over the hotel trying to find him. They couldn't find him.[73]

The election was invalidated and another one quickly held by those in attendance at the meeting, about one-third of the total membership. Of course, George Felkenes was already president-elect for the next term, so this "rump election" was for his successor. The errant secretary-treasurer was soundly defeated in his bid for the presidency and Gordon Misner was elected for the second time.

The tainted election with its apparent ballot stuffing and the "smoked-filled room" atmosphere of Misner's election weighed heavily on George Felkenes during his tenure as president. Caught between two disillusioning, events Felkenes wanted to maintain an air of progressivism and professionalism. Early on, he had to assure everyone that he was above the growing number of factions in the Academy and that he would work to rid the organization of its "growing divisiveness."[74] In addition he promised the police professors, who generally were more concerned with LEEP, that he would be an activist in Washington warding off any attacks on government funding of criminal justice education.[75] Indeed, two months later Felkenes went before a congressional committee when President Gerald Ford threatened a 50 percent cut in educational funding in LEAA.[76] But all this was stalled when another disaster struck.

Shortly after the Atlanta meeting, President Felkenes asked his secretary-treasurer, Richter Moore, to obtain all the necessary accounts and books from the retiring officer, the man from East Tennessee State who was under suspicion for the election debacle. No progress was made until Moore did some investigative work himself and discovered that the previous secretary-treasurer had actually embezzled nearly all the Academy's funds. The embezzler was expelled from the Academy and prosecuted. However, the affair became a cause célèbre for the membership. Many police professors felt the entire affair had been staged, in some sort of professorial entrapment, to embarrass Fabian and the membership he represented.[77] Several accused Felkenes of being too aggressive and punitive.[78] The future of the Academy, now nearly bankrupt, was in question. Most of Felkenes's presidency would be spent in reforming the bookkeeping and finances of the Academy, and convincing friend and foe alike that the organization was still legitimate and viable. He and Richter Moore were remarkably successful, with membership attendance going from 125 in Atlanta in 1975 to over 500 at Dallas the next year.[79] But just at that point another political embarrassment occurred.

Gordon Misner headed the Administration of Justice program at the University of Missouri at St. Louis (UMSL) beginning in 1970. Under his direction the department grew to 500 majors by mid-decade. In the same year that he was elected to head the Academy for the second time, Misner set out to control the growth and quality of criminal justice education in Missouri.

His actions represented the Hard Labor Creek ideology at the local level and how it would fare in the "hard ball" game of university politics. Besides the main campus at Columbia, the University of Missouri system had campuses at St. Louis, Kansas City, and Rolla. Due to the developments of the previous five years, all the campuses wanted to have their own criminal justice programs. Misner felt such growth would be too expensive and ultimately produce substandard offerings.[80] Already it was known that college administrators might take federal funds for criminal justice education and "divert" them elsewhere.[81] Beginning in the summer of 1975 Misner began pushing for inter-campus cooperation. His department at UMSL would offer all criminal justice offerings, or at least coordinate all others on the other campuses, and in exchange other campuses would get some curricular monopolies. Of course, this brought Misner into politics with other campuses and other disciplines. Besides empire building, which it clearly was, this Intra University Department approach summed up Misner's views on program control. When the Intra University Department's initials (IUD) lent themselves to ribald suggestions of contraceptives, Misner acknowledged that "this endeavor does have something to do with both birth control and protection of the species."[82] University of Missouri officials did not agree, and after months of squabbling they scrapped Misner's plans and forced his resignation.[83] Fearful that this would embarrass the Academy, Misner offered to Felkenes to step down as president-elect. The Hard Labor Creek group convinced him to stay as president and then found him a succession of jobs until he finally moved to the University of Illinois at Chicago Circle, where Riddle and Ward already resided.

Many of those won over by Felkenes viewed Misner's second presidency and its avowed accreditation agenda as a disaster. Edward Farris feared more factions would arise.[84] Indeed, Gordon Misner appeared to many as a political boss trying to perpetuate an academic machine. For example, he was always interested in cultivating and developing leaders for the Academy. All those who showed any energetic interest in the managing of the Academy, even if they did not completely share his ideas, found their way onto his numerous lists of "potential talent."[85] Correctly or not, they were viewed as "Misner's people." In the name of leadership development he was able to make some changes on the executive board. By 1976 the executive board consisted of the immediate past president, the president, and the first vice president (who was actually president-elect), the secretary-treasurer, and three trustees-at-large. Regional representatives would soon find positions on the board as well. Hoping to prolong the period of training (and conversion to the Hard Labor Creek positions, if necessary), Misner succeeded in getting the second vice presidential office adopted. The "president-in-waiting" would sit on the board for two years before assuming office as president. With less success, Misner wanted to grant board membership to all past presidents as well, as "a mechanism for capturing and making use of this experience." Of course, many of those were members of the Hard Labor Creek group. However, there was considerable concern over such "front-loading" and "back-loading" of the board in favor of the Hard Labor Creek group, and Misner had to settle for having past presidents sit without voting rights.[86]

In his presidential address at Dallas, Misner had emphasized his determination to reinforce the national rather than the segmented nature of the Academy.[87] But at that same convention there were some "young Turks." Just one year earlier Robert Culbertson and Calvin Swank had been outraged over the "unprofessional" and bungled meetings in Atlanta. They vowed to go to Dallas and "press the flesh" and "work the hotel corridors" as if they were in a nineteenth-century political ward. "It was politics in the raw!" Culbertson crowed. "I won't say anyone was dishonest, but I would say that if you want to see real politics in a professional organization it was in that process," in Dallas in 1976.[88] Culbertson figured prominently during the next decade as the Hard Labor Creek group and their power diminished. Clearly, the tone had been established by academic politicians such as Misner.

CONCLUSION

Academic politicians, like most politicians, are motivated by two things: a vision as to how things ought to be, and by personal ambition. Individual politicians have limited impact. In groups, call them organizations or a machines, they can accomplish a great deal. The Hard Labor Creek group became such a machine and by doing so revolutionized the Academy of Criminal Justice Sciences and the criminal justice education movement. They increased the real or perceived level of politics as well. Like all political machines, however, they gave birth to their own opposition. Forces arose that would displace and replace one set of academic politicians with another. In that process the organization and the field would be further impacted.

Chapter 9

Academy of Criminal Justice Sciences and the Politics of Populism, 1975–1985

From the late 1970s through the early 1980s, the field of criminal justice—and the professional association that tried to represent and guide it—grew rapidly. For example, there were 55 baccalaureate programs in criminal justice in 1970, and ten years later there were 589. At the same time the number of institutions granting master's degrees in the field went from 21 in 1970 to 198 in 1980. Those giving doctorates grew from 7 to 24.[1] Attendance at Academy meetings kept apace, going from 125 participants in 1975 to over 1,000 by 1982. In 1978 there were 1,068 members of the organization; the next year that number had grown to 1,447.[2] Such growth had called into existence the Hard Labor Creek machine and its attempts to give direction and definition to the field. In addition, it excited many other academic politicians in the Academy of Criminal Justice Sciences.

Furthermore, the membership of the field and the Academy diversified throughout this period. Police professors, those who held most dearly to the Vollmer tradition, still existed in large numbers but had a decreasing presence in the Academy. Their greatest influence remained in the community colleges and small state schools. By 1990 there were over 1,042 community college programs alone offering associate degrees in crime related studies.[3] According to the Riddle-Misner strategy, these police professors were to be brought into the Academy and converted to the Hard Labor Creek ideology. The unconverted stayed away in large numbers and went their own way. Any resentments they felt continued to be ideological, with dislike and distrust focusing on the broadening of the field outside of law enforcement. Closest to the grassroots operational agencies, these police professors held more firmly to the vocational trainer aspects of the field and questioned the Hard Labor Creek idea of a liberal arts basis for criminal justice education. Representation of those police professors in the Academy was largely in the regional affiliations; any national presence was symbolic or happenstance. Some regional presidents or representatives with this perspective did find their way on to the Academy board and several were not even official members of the national organization. In 1978, President Richard Ward stirred up a battle when he declared membership in the Academy a prerequisite for voting on the governing board. Ward only carried the day because the vote in the executive board split 6 to 6, thereby (according to the bylaws of the Academy) allowing a presidential resolution to stand.[4] Increasingly, these people felt as if they and their ideas were being pushed out of the Academy, which had occurred at Berkeley and in the American Society of Criminology.

Clearly, another element—the educator administrator group best represented by the Hard Labor Creek political machine—had found significant place in the Academy leadership circles. Issues of program development, quality control, and academic respectability were paramount to them. They differed with the more vocational programs of the police professors because they wanted a more academic and scholarly approach to criminal justice education. Intellectually, their ideas prevailed within the educator wing of the Academy. The "vocationalizers" were no threat here. Politically, however, the place of the Hard Labor Creek group was challenged from another wing of the educator faction, those who were angry over the apparent "boss machine" politics that had existed for about a decade. The success of the "young Turk" movement, as it was called by those in power, rested largely upon the arrival in large numbers of another group in the Academy membership, the researchers.

There had always been some researchers in the criminal justice professional associations, be they the IAPP or ACJS. Of course, the ASC liked to claim that it was scholarship that made it so different from the ACJS. But by the late 1970s and the early 1980s, researchers came into the Academy in larger numbers. This was just another logical step in the professionalization process of this academic field. Furthermore, the new researchers were different from earlier ones. Criminal justice research was changing in two ways, which were evident as the period progressed.

First, there was a shift from the "educational" aspects of the field to the more substantive ones. Although questions on the quality of criminal justice programming and curricular development remained, other topics emerged as important. More work on crime, policing, and corrections began to appear. That is not to say that such research had not been going on elsewhere. In 1975 the International Association of Chiefs of Police started the publication the *Journal of Police Science and Administration.* In addition, the Police Foundation was established in 1970 to sponsor and conduct research on police practices. One of its most famous studies, the Kansas City Patrol Experiment (1972-73), called into question current patrol practices. The RAND Corporation, a California-based think tank, studied detective work in 1973. The Police Executive Research Forum (PERF) began in 1975 to encourage research on criminal justice projects. Thus considerable research was beginning to be done at the outset of this period, but it was generally outside the ranks of the criminal justice professoriate. Perhaps the greatest political competition for establishing the legitimacy of crime related studies came from the criminologists in the American Society of Criminology (ASC).

The American Society of Criminology, through its publication *Criminology* had been adding to the literature throughout the 1970s. Some claimed that the ASC had outdistanced the ACJS as a scholarly organization. On one level, criminology—substantively, symbolically and semantically—was closely related to criminal justice. Before the great name change, for example, police science was criminology. In law enforcement programs one might find classic criminology courses. And in criminology textbooks token chapters on policing might be found as well. In all criminal justice curricula today criminology is offered. But being so close did not make them so similar. There was a Cain and Abel quality to the development of their academic character.[5] One criminologist caught an interesting dichotomy. C. Ray Jeffery saw criminology as dominated by the nineteenth century view of the psychological orientation of human nature. On the other hand, criminal justice was dominated by the eighteenth century view of humans as political creatures.[6] In short, entirely different and profound philosophical concepts separated the two fields. In addition, unlike the growing interdisciplinary nature of criminal justice, sociologists dominated the ASC. For example, twenty-two of the twenty five presidents of the organization between 1965 and 1990 were trained sociologists who for the most part remained in sociology departments. Much like the Academy, the ASC underwent considerable growth throughout the 1970s and 1980s reaching 2,000 members by 1990. Many of its new members were research-oriented criminal justice professors who felt the Society to be more "academic" than the Academy.

Second, an evolution of research had occurred going from simple to complex methodologies. Earlier, as in many academic disciplines, more descriptive and valuative studies predominated. Some historical and comparative methods had been used as well to bolster their credibility. Now, however, participant observation and survey research became more important, with statistical tests of significance giving weight to the word "science" in the Academy's title. This seemed to be the next step in the professionalizing process. Since the 1930s the amount of official statistics had been increasing. Such data, however, was seen as unreliable and self-serving of those agencies that collected it. Its very existence became a reason to carry out self-reporting and victimization surveys. Not only could one discover new information, but one could disprove the government's data as well. Such a "critical attitude" might drive a wedge between criminal justice agencies and academics. Many of these agencies—especially the police—had an "us versus them" attitude. "Them" were any number of representatives of the news media, do-gooder politicians, or academic scholars who might be critical of agency practices. Obtaining permission to do research, then, became as arduous, diplomatic, and political as actually conducting it.

Furthermore, a change in the funding agencies impacted on the nature and quality of research. From the late 1950s, when the Russian satellite Sputnik first orbited the earth, to 1980 the money available for social science research from private sources nearly doubled, going from $21 to $41 million. But government money went from $30 to $424 million. Federal funding through LEAA declined by 1980 and new agencies with greater peer review and social science agendas began to appear: the National Institute of Justice, the National Institute of Corrections, the Bureau of Justice Statistics, and the National Institute for Juvenile Justice and Delinquency Prevention to name a few. The quantity and quality of criminological and criminal justice research changed.

The Academy, therefore, had three political constituencies: (1) A small number of police professors and community college teachers who still clung to the Vollmerian ideas of the past and whose strength was more manifest in the regions. In the name of building a unified academic discipline, efforts were made—by some substantive, by others symbolic—to integrate these people. (2) A strong group of educators who held on to the Hard Labor Creek ideas with varying degrees of commitment and who saw the national organization as a means to bring respectability to the field. To them, the Academy—its growth and stature—became an end in itself. (3) An increasing number of researchers who saw the Academy as a means to further their own academic careers. They might agree with the Hard Labor Creek ideology because it made intellectual sense, but most people were apolitical and preoccupied with their own research agendas. It was the last group to whom the rhetoric of populism was addressed.

ACADEMIC POPULISM

The ascendancy of Robert Culbertson to the secretary-treasurer position in the late 1970s, signaled a historical shift. He was one of the more conspicuous and outspoken figures of a growing number of dissidents. Culbertson's rise occurred during the presidency of Richard Ward—a Hard Labor Creek member whose political style was quite different than that of Culbertson. Ward still clung to a decision-making process following the Riddle-Myren paradigm, with consensus building committee meetings, and networking based upon the Hard Labor Creek coalition. Ward and his friends saw the Academy meetings as a rubber stamp to already agreed upon agendas. Culbertson viewed all of this as elitism. After his training as a sociologist at the University of Cincinnati, Culbertson started an academic trek taking him from Indiana State University (1968-74) to Grand Valley State College (1974-76) and to Illinois State University, where he became chairperson of the department of corrections (a decidedly un-Hard Labor Creek designation for a criminal justice program). Culbertson's first exposure to the Academy was at "the infamous Atlanta meeting" of 1975 when so much corruption and political ineptitude was exposed. Thereafter, due to a professional outrage and embarrassment, his political career began in earnest.[7] Furthermore, his view of the annual meetings was different from the Hard Labor Creek politicians; they were to be "a forum to argue, and to debate, and to challenge, and to fight. And in that process—in that conflict kind of perspective—you move the profession ahead."[8]

Culbertson loved politics and from the beginning

vowed to become an active agent of change. Called a "young Turk" by the Hard Labor Creek group, Culbertson actually thought of himself as a populist.[9] In this context populism could mean two things.

On one hand, it had to do with the greater representation and activity of the membership. This was Culbertson's view of himself. He wanted to "kick open the doors and let in some fresh air!"[10] There was little disagreement over the Hard Labor Creek agenda. In fact, at one time Culbertson's name could be found on Gordon Misner's list of promising young leaders for the future. Populism became a rallying cry, reflecting not so much intellectual issues but a means of opening access to power for a new group of educators feeling left out of the Hard Labor Creek group. In addition, it was an attempt to attract and keep the researchers in the Academy. The American Society of Criminology had established a reputation for being the more intellectually rigorous of the two organizations. Some members of the Academy belonged to both associations, but there was a danger that the researchers might shift allegiances to the Society abandoning the Academy to a reputation of being a low quality "cop shop."

On the other hand, populism must be seen as a politics of personal professorial ambition. Most criminal justice educators came from the less prestigious colleges and universities of America. They had little of the status that comes to established scholars. Consequently, they could achieve all kinds of local glory by being active and prominent in a national organization. More than that, these schools of second- and third-rank, for so long mainly colleges that emphasized teaching over research, began to demand research as part of their mission statements in the 1980s. Professors were being hired even at teachers colleges with the expectation of contributing to the world of scholarship. Therefore, institutional and individual status was increasingly tied to research.

As the Academy population increased rapidly in number and complexity, Culbertson hoped to counterpoise the elitism of the Hard Labor Creek group with the political support of the newcomers. From his base at Illinois State University, Culbertson wrote letters to all the membership—the first time that had been done by someone out of office, he speculated—to express his concerns.[11] He publicly criticized the elitism of the Hard Labor Creek group and advocated greater openness on all issues and freer access to positions of power.

The Hard Labor Creek elites grossly misunderstood Culbertson's personal drive and ambition, and they underestimated his appeal to the ever-increasing new membership. After his surprising victory for the secretary-treasurer position, Culbertson received "fatherly" calls from Gordon Misner reminding him of the proper ministerial role he should play under President Richard Ward. Such advice was contrary to Culbertson's view of academic politics, and it went largely ignored.[12]

As secretary-treasurer Culbertson continued to challenge and campaign against the Hard Labor Creek monopoly on leadership. As he had done earlier to win the secretary-treasury job, Culbertson—using the generous franking privileges at Illinois State University—sent mass mailings to the membership to express his concerns and views.[13] He swept the field for second vice president in 1980, which assured him the presidency two years hence. In addition, his political coattails extended to several friends now elected to the executive board. Calvin Swank, David Burns, Paul McCauley, and John Conley were a few of the "young Turks" who achieved positions at this time, which would guarantee Culbertson a working majority later.

Culbertson was not timid in challenging some of the Hard Labor Creek projects such as the merger with the ASC. Such a joining would curtail opportunities for Academy members to become involved in leadership activities, he felt.[14] The national office in Washington was a particularly hot issue, and "Dick Ward and I went to the wall on that a number of times," he remembered.[15] Admittedly, he was concerned over the funding of a Washington office; the Academy simply could not afford to sustain such an place, he was convinced. Here was just another example of the "old guard" being over zealous and unreasonably ambitious. Later a more modest national office proposal locating the secretariat at a university campus in the Midwest won his support. Significantly, the secretariat was to be located at the University of Nebraska at Omaha, a populist symbol in heartland America far from eastern and West Coast elites.

By 1980 the executive board had a voting block of people who shared many of the Culbertson perspectives. Gordon Misner's unsuccessful move to obtain voting rights for past presidents, most of whom were Hard Labor Creek advocates, was seen as a political attempt to counterbalance the growing presence of young Turks.[16] Consequently, the Hard Labor Creek leaders increasingly felt displaced and unappreciated. Misner summed up a larger feeling some years later, but his sentiments probably reflect his thinking at the time:

> I still have a great affection and respect for the Academy and will do whatever I can to be of help to the Academy, but I really—and I know that some other people feel this way very, very strongly—I've just gotten sick and tired of hearing "well that's another plot of the old boys to get the Old Guard back in" or some damn thing.[17]

Like Misner, several of the Hard Labor Creek group continued to attend meetings, but they were so sensitive about their reputations as political plotters that direct involvement decreased. Donald Riddle graciously stepped forward when any showcasing was needed. Richard Myren and William Mathias, acknowledging that their influence had decreased, largely disappeared from the organization.[18] After his presidency, Richard Ward lapsed to such an extent that he even lost track of who was president of the Academy.[19] Along with Gordon Misner, George Felkenes remained active but resented the scuttling of Accreditation Council by the new executive board.[20] Larry Bassi harbored some anger too over the lack of support for his ideas on the national office.[21] These men became, largely, "loyal opposition."

Although much of the inactivity of the Hard Labor Creek group was due to their displacement, there were other reasons as well. Career development took many of them away. While new blood came into the Academy, these older leaders became busy on other stages, reflecting their placement in the category of educators. For example, Donald Riddle was chancellor of the University of Illinois at Chicago Circle, and Richard Ward was vice chancellor. University governance occupied much of their time. Richard Myren had become dean of the School of Justice at American University, though like Riddle he would retire shortly. William Mathias had a similar position at the University of South Carolina. George Felkenes was head of the criminal justice program at Michigan State and then Dean of Arts and Sciences at California State University at Long Beach. Many of the old political clique simply took their reputations, administrative skills, and educational philosophies to other areas, leaving the Academy to the new populists.

Three of the presidents sandwiched in between Richard Ward (the preeminent Hard Labor Creek politician) and Robert Culbertson (the preeminent populist) may be seen as marking these changes. They were Richter Moore, Larry Bassi, and Harry More.

Richter Moore, a political scientist and lawyer who headed the Appalachian State University criminal justice program, was a Hard Labor Creek advocate who saved the Academy after the embezzlement episode. He had exceptional academic credentials and the type of conciliatory personality that worked well with a variety of others. His personal projection of "just being a country lawyer" disguised considerable political acumen. Nonetheless, his election was largely a reward for putting the Academy back on a firm foundation after the earlier financial scandals.[22]

But it was the next two presidents who indicate dramatically the changes from the Hard Labor Creek machine to populism. Ironically, they also show a "swan song" presence of the police professor tradition. Larry Bassi (president in 1979-80) had been an undergraduate at Washington State University when the IAPP was formed there in 1963. He never obtained a doctorate and spent considerable time teaching at the community college level. He remained a voice for law enforcement studies and the Vollmerian educational perspectives. Given that, he became something of a fellow traveler in the Hard Labor Creek group owing less to ideology and more to attachments to people like Misner. He gained considerable status and stature for his work on accreditation, and his presidency must be seen as a political recognition for his past work for the Academy.[23]

Harry More (1980-81) had been at Washington State for the founding of the IAPP also. In fact, he was first secretary-treasurer of that organization and helped to write its constitution. More was not a Hard Labor Creek advocate at all. In fact, he did not even like the phrase "criminal justice." For him "criminology" was broader and more appropriate.[24] Both these men—transition-like figures, to be sure—achieved position in an organization in which old academic politics and politicians were giving way to new ones.

But it was Robert Culbertson, with his personal energy and commitment, who set the tone of the period. Culbertson felt that the Academy had two major services to offer the membership: providing of a good annual conference meeting and the creation of a truly scholarly journal.

Culbertson wanted to provide an annual meeting for which the organization might be proud. Such mundane things as hotel accommodations, cocktail hours, banquets, and award ceremonies were critical services.[25] If the scholars were to be attracted and kept in the Academy they would need a professional and exciting showplace for their skills and ideas. Awards continued to be given to famous people both in and outside of the organization. Thus the legitimacy of the Academy might be attained and assured.

Most of all, the opportunity to present papers was essential. As early as 1978, with the help of John Conley, Culbertson made the New Orleans meeting a benchmark against which all subsequent gatherings would be judged. Never in the history of the Academy had so many panels and papers been offered. Something of an open-door policy occurred in accepting papers for presentation, a decidedly populist position that guaranteed the membership a place on the program. But it was not just populism; the Hard Labor Creek group had an open door as well. However, now the numbers of potential presenters had increased. There were just more people to walk through that open door. Of course, such democracy threatened to sacrifice meritocracy. In fact, one Academy member felt compelled to educate the membership on the proper and responsible presentation of papers.[26] Quality might not have been guaranteed, but it did give young scholars in a rush to show their deans and department chairpersons signs of professional growth an opportunity to perform. Such activities would tie them more firmly to the Academy, as well.

Naturally, criminal justice and sociology dominated but other disciplines were encouraged too. The Louisville (1982) and San Antonio (1983) meetings had upwards of sixteen different panels devoted to political science, anthropology, history, economics, philosophy, law, and public policy.[27] On one hand, this diversification reflected the earlier Hard Labor Creek position on the interdisciplinary nature of criminal justice and the ever-changing professoriate since the Osterburg resolution. On the other hand, one could think of the annual meetings as an academic "Tower of Babel" with ever so many disciplinary languages being forged. Of course, such cross-fertilization might be invigorating, providing a variety of perspectives around a central concern over crime and criminal justice. But there were dangers that reflected on the historical development of criminal justice education. Pseudo-experts, or those who used a discipline or method when not trained in it, arose. All of a sudden people with no degrees in history appeared as criminal justice historians. Subfields—such as comparative criminal justice—were peopled with many who had little relevant disciplinary or language training. In short, the open nature of the field and this commitment to interdisciplinary studies allowed an image of amateurism to arise, which in many respects reaffirmed the suspicions of traditional academics, especially those in the American Society of Criminology. "Amateur" took on both classical definitions: one who does something for the love of it, and the inexpert.

THE NEW JOURNAL AND NEW POLITICS

Culbertson felt the Academy owed the membership a quality journal. As more and more researchers came into the field and the Academy, the means of publication became most important. There was status in presenting papers at a national convention, to be sure, but the greatest scholarly outlet must be peer-reviewed publication. There was a pecking order for publication, as well. The scientific article in a scholarly journal had the highest standing. And it had a stylistic approach to which all had to adhere. There should be a review of the theory and literature of the problem; a formulation of a testable hypothesis; a discussion of the research design and methodology; a presentation of the findings in words and statistical tables; a statement of significance; and a conclusion suggesting the implications of the study and possibilities for future work. Such a procedure was foreign or distasteful to many of the educators. They were more comfortable with the "learned essay," the second-favored form of publication. Above all, most in the Academy could agree that they had to guard against moving back to any newsletter type of publication that emphasized police science.

Culbertson wanted to provide such a scholarly peer-reviewed journal. This was another essential step in the academic professionalization of criminal justice education. Furthermore, he disliked the elitist editorial policies of the *Journal of Criminal Justice*, the Hard Labor Creek publication. The editorial board had not changed in years, and Academy people had little impact on or control of publication. There was one attempt by Joseph Lentini, president of the North Atlantic region, and Larry Bassi to discontinue the relationship in 1977, but Richter Moore and Gordon Misner had the resolution tabled.[28] Actually, it was an attempt to replace the *Journal* with a more practitioner-oriented newsletter. Lentini and Bassi felt that the journal was too sociological, not giving law enforcement studies enough consideration. As chairman of the Academy's Publications Committee, John Conley fought off for years those "intellectual Neanderthals" who wanted to downgrade the publication to a newsletter.[29] But then Conley and Kent Joscelyn, editor of the *Journal*, entered into a verbal battle that lasted throughout much of 1980.

Actually, the *Journal of Criminal Justice* never belonged to the Academy; it had existed prior to any engagement to the organization. The *Journal* was owned by the Pergamon Press, and Joscelyn was employed by that press. Much of the work on the journal was done by Joscelyn and his staff, who had moved from Indiana University to the Highway Safety Research Institute of Ann Arbor, Michigan. That was a research organization, and although the staff regarded the publication as a secondary concern to be put on the back burner while other research and grantsmanship went on, Joscelyn felt the *Journal* to be his own property and resented interference. At first, Joscelyn had difficulty accepting Conley and the Publications Committee as a necessary line of communication to the Academy. Other channels, largely informal ones, had been established with the Hard Labor Creek group, and information flowed freely and clearly. Conley and Culbertson disagreed with Joscelyn, quickly suggesting instead that the irregular, vague, and incomplete reports coming to the new executive board—which was slowly filling with Culbertson people—were more common.[30]

As early as the March 1980 business meetings of the Academy, Culbertson (by then a second vice president of the organization) raised the issue of the *Journal*. He felt the Academy should have greater editorial control over the publication. Failing that, the Academy should publish its own journal. When the board—still having some leftovers from the Hard Labor Creek group—remained timid, Culbertson stormed out in protest and threatened to resign. Conley counseled that a long-term approach of educating the board was necessary.[31] And for the next two years, in his vice presidential and presidential roles, Culbertson pressed home in a number of speeches, letters, and political tactics the basic problem of the journal. Of course, Joscelyn's uncompromising attitudes, and the diminishing number of active Hard Labor Creek people who might have supported him, helped Culbertson. But in addition, Culbertson's populism joined with a growing number of more research-oriented professors in the Academy who wanted greater control over the publication. By 1982 it was clear that for a new generation of members it was not enough to merely have a scholarly journal; it was necessary to control it as well. Academic professionalization demanded such control. In addition, the editorship would be another choice position for a status-seeking academic politician.

Robert Culbertson presided at the Louisville convention in 1982. At that meeting an ad hoc committee on the feasibility of a new journal was established with Richard Bennett, John Conley, Jack Greene, and Robert Regoli as members. Five months later they recommended that the Academy publish its own journal.[32] This ad hoc committee was transformed into an official committee; and after a formal report was made in March 1983, the Pergamon Press was notified that the Academy would not renew its contract.[33]

The Bennett committee recommended that the new publication be called *Justice Quarterly*. Richard Bennett was from American University, the academic center of Richard Myren and his notions of "justicology." Myren had sought to expand the field and place criminal justice

> as only one justice system within a matrix of justice systems, which range from the formal juvenile, civil, and military systems to the informal justice systems that exist in our homes, schools, and work places.[34]

There was not widespread acceptance of this academic innovation by the field's intellectual gadfly. In spite of Conley's disclaimers, some populists saw the influence of Myren and the Hard Labor Creek group.[35] A new publications committee was formed, which kept the name but modified the scope and mission of the new journal to clearly emphasize criminal justice over generic justice.[36] The new committee also had to publish the first issue and recommend an editor. In September 1983, Rita Simon was suggested to the Executive Board as editor, and she was approved by a narrow margin.[37] This precipitated another political battle, one that brought many populists together with the remnants of the Hard Labor Creek group.

Actually, on the surface Rita Simon was an impressive choice for the editorship. After earning a Ph.D. in sociology from the University of Chicago, she was professor of law, sociology, and communications research at the University of Illinois (Champaign-Urbana) from 1963 to 1983. When Richard Myren retired as dean of the School of Justice at American University in 1983, Simon took his place. Besides her numerous articles, Simon had authored several books including *Transracial Adoption*, *The American Jury*, and *The Criminology of Deviant Women*. In addition, she served as editor of the *American Sociological Review* and as consulting editor of the *Journal of Criminal Law and Criminology*. According to both the Publications Committee and the Executive Board, Simon's experience as editor made her a slight favorite over her nearest competitor, George Felkenes.

Simon's appointment was important for two reasons. It suggested the growing presence and power of the researcher element, or at least those who did not think Academy membership and experience a prerequisite to the editorship. And it brought together the few remaining Hard Labor Creek members and the populist leaders. Much of 1983 was characterized with debate and some intrigue, highlighting the academic politics of professional associations.

Although he no longer held elective position in 1983, everywhere Culbertson turned he saw "crass and clumsy politics." That was probably true, because those involved—the newly arrived researcher types—were largely novices. What was perhaps the most important accomplishment in the recent history of the Academy was "clouded by blatant careerism," he felt. There was a small group, something anathema to him, trying "to dominate the entire ACJS publication process." [38] Those remaining Hard Labor Creek people felt that the Simon appointment over Felkenes was another attempt "to take it away from the old boys." Misner declared the entire selection process as scandalous as the embezzlement episode of the 1970s.[39]

For Robert Culbertson and the like-minded, someone with a long history of activity in the Academy was needed as the journal's first editor. Even before Simon's appointment was announced, Culbertson had warned that Kent Joscelyn's editorship proved the folly of a non-ACJS person editing an Academy journal.[40] When one of his protégés voted for Rita Simon, Culbertson chided that "there are a substantial number of qualities that are important in this process above serving as an editor—like some kind of professional organizational experience—Simon has virtually none."[41] Rita Simon had never been a member of the Academy, and most of her allegiances remained with sociology and criminology organizations, he warned.[42] On the other hand, no one needed to recount the contributions and loyalties of George Felkenes. Editorial experience was not the issue. The question was: Who would better serve the Academy and its journal? For Culbertson the answer was obvious. And even though he sided with Misner and other Hard Labor Creek people, he was consistent. As a populist he resented outsiders, who had not "paid their dues," coming into the organization and usurping opportunity from an insider.

The editorship was not just a political story of insiders versus outsiders in organizational struggles.[43] It spoke as well to the changing nature of the membership. Clearly, the remnants of the Hard Labor Creek group and Robert Culbertson's strong attachment to the organization represented one viewpoint. These and their fellow travelers were academic organizational persons. For all their talk about populism, they resented any segment of the membership that challenged their notions of organizational activity and loyalty. Most likely their professional life was geared to program development and educational issues. Even

Culbertson would soon leave criminal justice at Illinois State University to take up a variety of deanships in Montana and Arkansas. They viewed the role of the Academy in much grander terms.

There were others, however, whom Larry Hoover identified during his presidency (1982-83) as representing "the rise of the researchers."[44] These people, in the name of their definition of academic professionalism, were willing to take the risk and go outside the organization for a scholar-editor. Scholarship rather than allegiance to the organization was more important to them. Of course, lines cannot be drawn that cleanly. Indeed, there were a number of scholars who supported Felkenes. For that matter, Felkenes had a history of research and publication himself. The issue was not scholarship alone; it was the role and importance of the Academy in the grand scheme of things. For the researchers the Academy was a means to an end; for the educators the Academy had become the end. Consequently, even though the issue seemed to be over, the politics was not.

In her political wisdom, Dorothy Bracey had been a friend to both the Hard Labor Creek group and Robert Culbertson. At the time of Simon's selection, Bracey was already first vice president of the Academy, assured of being the first female president of the organization in 1984. She supported Simon and outraged her old friend Culbertson, who announced that he would be of no service during her presidency.[45] He reminded Bracey that many had forgotten that the "ACJS belongs to the membership, not to a small group of individuals who want to control the organization and its publication without the consent of the membership."[46] R. Paul McCauley was second vice president and therefore assured the presidency in 1985. Culbertson let it be known that he was angry over McCauley's voting for Simon. The idea that they had been outmaneuvered on the issue was outrageous to Culbertson.[47] But two people were singled out as archenemies.

Richard Bennett had been an influential member of both committees involved with the journal and its editor selection. Since Bennett was on the faculty of American University, Rita Simon was his boss. This seemed to be a conflict of interest to many populists. "How can a member of the Executive Board maintain membership on an ACJS Board Committee when that committee is deliberating on a decision that affects his/her university and equally important his/her immediate supervisor?" asked Culbertson.[48] He was convinced that a new elite, a group of justicologists headed by Bennett, wanted to step into the place of the old elite he had worked to push from power. He wanted to be the elite. This idea of elites, old or new, offended Culbertson's sense of populism, and he threatened to take the issue to the entire membership. The common sense of the membership would vindicate Felkenes, Culbertson felt, and put an end to such political shenanigans.[49]

Jack Greene, chair of the Publications Committee, was much more vulnerable than Bennett. At least Greene was politically ambitious, taking care to distance himself from Bennett when the furies were released. Nonetheless, there were political blunders in his past that skilled politicians might exploit. For example, in his quest for the second vice presidential nomination Greene tried to obtain an official endorsement from his own Midwest regional organization, a maneuver that was to backfire as an embarrassment. When rumors circulated that Simon had offered Greene a position on the new journal, Culbertson accused him of using the Academy to further his own career.[50] Again writing to Bracey and criticizing her affiliation to Greene, Culbertson charged that, "Unfortunately, you have either lost, or never had, the capacity to differentiate between those who have a vision for the Academy and those who have a vision for themselves in the Academy."[51] Greene's quest for office was stymied.

CONCLUSION

On the surface, populism in academic criminal justice was raw personal ambition mixed with a love of politics. Avenues of leadership had to be opened up to those academic politicians who for personal reasons or out of historic happenstance did not belong to the Hard Labor Creek machine. On another level, it was the continuation of the Hard Labor Creek goal to further legitimize the field. This was to be done by providing an appropriate atmosphere for the growing number of academically trained and rigorous scholars coming into the organization, and assuring their continuous participation and loyalty. It was clear that the Academy of Criminal Justice was to be the organizational expression of academic criminal justice. In the last analysis, the organization and those loyal to it were to direct the future of the field. For example, in 1984 it was learned that law schools discriminated against students with criminal justice majors. "The bias appears to be based on the belief that the criminal justice degree programs are non-academic and fail to provide an analytic, rigorous, and conceptually sound educational experience," reported the Academy's Evaluations and Standards Committee.[52] Shortly after, former president Dorothy Bracey chaired the Professional Development Committee and held a series of seminars in 1984. Interestingly calling them the Hard Labor Creek seminars, this committee sought to be an educational think-tank for the development of criminal justice as an academic discipline.[53]

It might be argued that populism was a healthy vital sign of growth, the next step in the professionalization process. Annual meetings appeared more professional and the *Justice Quarterly* gained a scholarly reputation. Actually to use historical terms, it might be seen more as a "progressive movement" than a "populist" one. More analogous in American history were the progressives, those reformers who arose to break the grip of the urban political machines and to control economic elites at the turn of the twentieth century. While the more agrarian Populists—with some of their demagoguery—might seem to fit, actually this movement in academic criminal justice seems more progressive. But since the prime mover labeled himself as a populist, we shall let that term stand as the standard of the period.

In addition, such a political process—Young Turks v. Old Guard—were just a part of the academic professionalization of the field. Although the literature is skimpy, it can be safely predicted that other disciplines have had similar political infighting.

But, the intoxicating growth of membership that opened up this period and inspired such political movements as described above was short-lived. For example, by 1990—taking all programs labeled criminal justice (now there were 382), criminology (109), and law enforcement and corrections (196) collectively—there were 687 baccalaureate programs available. Master's degree granting institutions dropped to 157.[54] Growth of ACJS membership slowed as well and was at a little over 1,500 by 1990.[55] In other words, a spurt of rapid growth seemed to have ended and leveled off by the mid-1980s leaving all of this politics as something of a tempest in a teapot.

Chapter 10

Epilogue

SIMILARITIES WITH OTHER DISCIPLINES

The history of criminal justice education is similar to that of other disciplines in higher education. It arose a time when the university system was relatively new, and developing under ambitious presidents and department builders. There was a political ideology in place called progressivism touting the importance of useable knowledge and skills for the betterment of society. Academic politicians—at the highest administrative and departmental levels—were building empires and looked to fields of study that would attract students and status. Criminal justice practitioners, for good or ill, became more visible and controversial as the public demanded different roles for the police. In addition, many agencies of criminal justice—particularly the police—under went a professionalization process in the twentieth century. To succeed as a profession three groups need to be converted. In criminal justice those groups are (1) the managers, (2) the rank and file, (3) and the public. Since the managers instigated the police professionalism movement at the turn of the century, they needed to convert the other two groups; this could be done, as with other new professions, by requiring educational attainment as a fundamental aspect of the occupation. Furthermore, as in other disciplines key individuals—such as August Vollmer, O. W. Wilson, Donald Riddle, Richard Myren, Gordon Misner, and Robert Culbertson—provided important paradigm shifts. In addition, issues between the scholarly and the practical aspects of the field were important. Schools of Education, Social Work, Engineering, Law, and Medicine had similar conflicts between the academic and vocational tendencies in their disciplines. Finally, the thesis of this book is that academic politics was key to the historical development of academic criminal justice; it is posited that this is the case of most academic disciplines as well.

DIFFERENCES WITH OTHER DISCIPLINES

On the other hand, academic criminal justice was very different from other academic disciplines. First, very few fields of study have aroused such public interest and concern. Crime and the agencies dealing with it are familiar and compelling to the ordinary newspaper reader and television viewer. For many people, popular culture became the main educational tool; and much of that misinformation had to be undone before real education could take place. Second, although there have been a few general fields (such as science and education, for example) to act as exceptions, most academic disciplines have not received government funding to the degree as criminal justice programs and projects. LEAA and LEEP provided millions of dollars for the creation of programs and financing of students. Third, few fields have been caught on the horns of political ideology—liberalism and conservativism—as criminal justice. Largely the teachers of criminal justice in four-year institutions lean to liberal politics (or operate in an environment in which their colleagues are liberal) while incoming students and outgoing practitioners lean toward the conservative. Fourth, in few fields has the connection to the community college been so important and controversial. And fifth, rarely does an occupational market seem so reluctant to accept the academic product. In spite of over two decades in which various blue ribbon commissions and study groups advocated the requirement of higher education for entry levels in policing most departments on the local level remain content with the completion of secondary school.

CONCLUSION

By 1990 over 1,000 academic criminal justice programs existed in colleges and universities of second- and third-rank. Generally, they were in community colleges, four-year "compass colleges" (Western Illinois University, Eastern Kentucky University, Northern Michigan University, and Southwest Texas State University, to name a few), "urban satellites" of a state's flag ship campus (University of Illinois at Chicago Circle, University of Missouri at St. Louis, University of Wisconsin at Milwaukee, and University of Nebraska at Omaha, for example), and state colleges.

While criminology courses might be found in every department of sociology at all levels of higher education, criminal justice departments remained conspicuously missing from quality research institutions. Any attachment to a flag ship university, with the exception of its urban satellite, was through an institute or other marginal locations. There are many reasons for this academic segregation.

First, the historic connection of criminal justice with police science made it appear too vocational. Furthermore, many aspects of criminal justice could fit into traditional disciplines. For example, police management might just as well belong in public administration programs. Academic politicians who tried to legitimize criminal justice education opted for a liberal arts model instead of a professional school. The history of the School of Criminology at the University of California proved the precarious nature of the professional school model. A few criminal justice programs remained committed to the practical aspects of law enforcement, but most adjusted to the Myren-Riddle ideology. The more scholarly the field became, however, the more irrelevant it seemed to many students and practitioners. For example, in 1988 the Police Executive Research Forum (PERF) reported that only 48.8 percent of the police agencies preferred a criminal justice degree when hiring college graduates.[1] In 1989 PERF declared criminal justice curricula inconsistent with contemporary police needs.[2]

Second, criminal justice borrowed heavily from other disciplines, primarily sociology, psychology, and political science; it never completely formed its own disciplinary identity. While the number of doctorates in criminal justice increased, they never kept up with demand and large numbers of sociologists and political scientists continued to monopolize the field. Furthermore, since the distribution of criminal justice programs in higher education was skimpy, it was not wise for a student to obtain a doctorate in criminal justice. The more practical student would get a Ph.D in a traditional discipline specializing in a criminological topic. That way the new professor might seek positions in departments of the traditional discipline as well as criminal justice. Very few universities of national repute offered a doctorate in criminal justice and left the graduate field to schools of mediocrity.

Divisions between researchers and educators within the Academy remained too. Since the *Justice Quarterly* published criminological and agency research, its standards and interests were such that scholarship and position papers on educational issues had difficulty finding an outlet. Sociologists faced the same situation in the 1970s and resolved it with the creation of a journal, *Teaching Sociology* in 1973. The educator element would remain strong enough in the Academy to start a second journal in 1989 called *JCJE: Journal of Criminal Justice Education*.

Third, academic politics remained a critical factor in the Academy. In 1987 the President of the Academy, a former populist partisan in the war's over the *Justice Quarterly* editorship, got in trouble when Rita Simon applied to be editor of *Criminology*, the journal for the American Society of Criminology. An unsolicited critical assessment of her work for the *Justice Quarterly* went from the president to the American Society of Criminology. Simon was outraged and threatened a law suit. Some members of the ACJS executive board called for a vote to censure the president, but it was voted down. However, the president was forced to apologize for this potential "polarization" of the Academy. [3]

Although this is a history of criminal justice education, it has cast that story against the backdrop of academic politics. It is proposed that other disciplines have had such developments. But it is unlikely that academic politics has played such a role as in the history of criminal justice education.

Appendix A

List of Those Interviewed

Larry Bassi, October 18, 1983.
Arthur Bilek, February 3, 1983.
Robert Borkenstein, April 30, 1982.
Arthur Brandstatter, April 29, 1982.
Gilbert Bruns, March 30, 1984.
John Conley, April 25, 1983.
Robert Corley, March 2, 1983.
Robert Culbertson, October 13, 1983.
Felix Fabian, January 28, 1982.
Edward Farris, March 25, 1983.
George Felkenes, March 25, 1982.
Jack Greene, March 30, 1984.
Larry Hoover, March 29, 1984.
Jack Kenney, February 24, 1983.
Franklin M. Kremil, November 24, 1981.
V. A. Leonard, January 27, 1982.
Earl Lewis, March 25, 1982.
Eliot Lumbard, October 26, 1989.
Donal MacNamara, May 13, 1982.
William Mathias, June 7, 1983.
William Melincoe, March 23, 1983.
Melvin Miller, June 21, 1983.
Gordon Misner, January 18, 1982.
Richter Moore, November 14, 1981.
Harry More, February 2, 1983.
Richard Myren, March 26, 1982.
Charles Newman, January 30, 1982.
James Osterburg, February 10, 1983.
Donald Riddle, March 17, 1983.
James Stinchcomb, June 22, 1983.
Richard Ward, June 3, 1982.

Appendix B

Past Presidents of the International Association of Police Professors and Academy of Criminal Justice Sciences

1963-1964	Donald F. McCall
1964-1965	Felix M. Fabian
1965-1966	Arthur F. Brandstatter
1966-1967	Richard O. Hankey
1967-1968	Robert Sheehan
1968-1969	Robert F. Borkenstein
1969-1970	B. Earl Lewis
1970-1971	Donald H. Riddle
1971-1972	Gordon E. Misner
1972-1973	Richard A. Myren
1973-1974	William J. Mathias
1974-1975	Felix M. Fabian
1975-1976	George T. Felkenes
1976-1977	Gordon Misner
1977-1978	Richard Ward
1978-1979	Richter H. Moore Jr.
1979-1980	Larry Bassi
1980-1981	Harry More Jr.
1981-1982	Robert G. Culbertson
1982-1983	Larry T. Hoover
1983-1984	Gilbert Bruns
1984-1985	Dorothy Bracey
1985-1986	R. Paul McCauley
1986-1987	Robert Regoli
1987-1988	Thomas Barker
1988-1989	Larry Gaines
1989-1990	Edward Latessa
1990-1991	Vincent Webb
1991-1992	Ben Menke
1992-1993	Robert Bohm

Appendix C

Past Presidents of the Society For the Advancement of Criminology and American Society of Criminology

1941-1942	August Vollmer
1942-1949	Orlando W. Wilson
1950-1951	Douglas Kelley
1952-1953	Frank Boolsen
1953-1954	William Dienstein
1955-1956	Richard Simon
1956-1957	Richard Hankey
1957-1959	John Kenney
1959-1960	Marcel Frym
1960-1963	Donal A. J. MacNamara
1964-1966	Walter C. Reckless
1967-1968	Marvin Wolfgang
1968-1969	Gerhard O. W. Mueller
1969-1970	Bruno M. Cormier
1970-1971	Albert Morris
1971-1972	Simon Dinitz
1972-1973	Charles L. Newman
1973-1974	John C. Ball
1974-1975	Edward Sagarin
1975-1976	Nicholas Kittrie
1976-1977	Gilber Geis
1977-1978	Willaim E.Amos
1978-1979	C.Ray Jeffery
1979-1980	Ronald L. Akers
1980-1981	Daniel Glaser
1981-1982	Frank Scarpitti
1982-1983	Harry E. Allen
1983-1984	Travis Hirschi
1984-1985	Albert J. Reiss Jr.
1985-1986	Austin T. Turk

Notes

INTRODUCTION

1. Laurence R. Veysey, *The Emergence of the American University* (Chicago: University of Chicago Press, 1965), pp. 22-56.
2. Ibid., pp. 180-251. Quote is on p. 212.
3. Ibid., pp. 121-179.
4. Ibid., pp. 57-120.
5. Ibid.
6. Ibid., p. 364.
7. George S. Pappas, *To The Point: The United States Military Academy, 1802-1902* (Westport, Ct.: Praeger, 1993), pp. 3-22. Stephen E. Ambrose, *Duty, Honor, Country: A History of West Point* (Baltimore, Md.: The Johns Hopkins Press, 1966), pp.1-23.
8. Quoted in Marcus Cunliffe, *Soldiers and Citizens: The Martial Spirit in America, 1775-1865* (Boston: Little, Brown, 1968), pp.106-108.
9. Ibid., pp. 110, 126-128, 157-158.
10. William R. Johnson, "Education and Professional Life Styles: Law and Medicine in the Nineteenth Century," *History of Education Quarterly* 14 (1974), p. 185.
11 . James C. Mohr, *Abortion in America: The Origins and Evolution of a National Policy* (New York: Oxford University Press, 1978), pp. 147-170. David F. Musto, *The American Disease: Origins of Narcotic Control* (New Haven: Yale University Press, 1973), pp. 1-5, 14-15.
12. Gerald E. Markowitz and David Karl Rosner "Doctors in Crisis: A Study of the Use of Medical Education Reform to Establish Modern Professional Elitism in Medicine," *American Quarterly* 25 (1973), p. 92.
13. Ibid., pp. 95, 106.

14. David Starr Jordan, "Pettifogging Law Schools and an Untrained Bar," *Forum* 19 (1895), pp. 350-355.

15. Jerold S. Auerbach, *Unequal Justice: Lawyers and Social Change in Modern America* (London: Oxford University Press, 1976), pp. 74-99.

16. Ibid.

17. Ibid., pp. 107-118, 228-229.

18. Ibid., pp. 130-136.

19. Nathan Glazer, "The Schools of Minor Professions," *Minerva* 12 (July 1974), p. 346.

20. Ibid., pp. 350-353.

21. Ibid., pp. 354, 356-357, 359.

22. Martin Blumer, "The Chicago School of Sociology: What Made It a 'School'?" *History of Sociology* 5 (Spring, 1985), pp. 63-67.

23. Laurence R. Veysey, "The Plural Organized Worlds of the Humanities," in *The Organization of Knowledge in Modern America, 1860-1920*, eds. Alexander Oleson and John Voss (Baltimore: Johns Hopkins University Press, 1979), pp. 57, 65, 72-74.

24. Barry D. Karl, "The Power of Intellect and the Politics of Ideas," in *Philosophers and Kings: Studies in Leadership*, ed. Dankwart A Rustow (New York: George Braziller, 1970), pp. 431-438. And N. Ray Hiner, "Professions in Process: Changing Relations among Social Scientists, Historians, and Educators, 1880-1920," *History Teacher* 6 (November 1972-August 1973), pp. 201-218.

25. Dorothy Ross, "The Development of the Social Sciences," in *The Organization of Knowledge in Modern America, 1860-1920*, eds. Alexander Oleson and John Voss (Balitmore: Johns Hopkins University Press, 1979), pp. 109-121.

26. John B. Parrish, "Rise of Economics as an Academic Discipline: The Formative Years to 1900," *Southern Economic Journal* 24 (July 1967), pp. 2-6.

27. Thomas M. Camfield, "The Professionalization of American Psychology, 1870-1917," *Journal of the History of the Behavioral Sciences* 9 (January 1973), pp. 66-67.

28. Richard Hofstadter, *Social Darwinism in American Thought* (Boston: Beacon Press, 1963), pp. 31-50.

29. Hamilton Cravens, "The Abandonment of Evolutionary Social Theory in America: The Impact of Academic Professionalization upon American Sociological Theory, 1890-1920," *American Studies* 12 (Fall 1971), pp. 5, 8, 10.

30. Albert Somit and Joseph Tanenhaus, *The Development of American Political Science: From Burgess to Behavioralism* (Boston: Allyn and Bacon, 1967), pp. 16-21.

31. A. W. Coats, "The First Two Decades of the American Economic Association," *The American Economic Review* 50 (September 1960), pp. 555-574.
32. Camfield, "The Professionalization of American Psychology, 1870-1917", pp. 68-69.
33. Somit and Tanenhaus, *The Development of American Political Science*, pp. 22-26.
34. Camfield, "The Professionalization of American Psychology, 1870-1917", pp. 69-70, 73, 75.
35. Somit and Tanenhaus, *The Development of American Political Science*, pp. 27-40.
36. Ibid., pp. 51-61.
37. Ibid., pp.110-112.
38. Barry D. Karl, *Charles E. Merriam and the Study of Politics* (Chicago: University of Chicago Press, 1974), pp. x, 118.
39. Ibid., pp. 140-150.
40. Ibid.
41. Lynton K. Caldwell, "Public Administration and the Universities: A Half Century of Development," *Public Administration Review* 25 (1965), pp. 55-56.
42. Rowland Egger, "The Period of Crisis, 1933 to 1945," in *American Public Administration: Past, Present, Future*, ed. Fredrick C. Mosher (Tuscaloosa, Alabama: The University of Alabama Press, 1975), pp. 65, 73-74.
43. James Carey, *Sociology and Public Affairs: The Chicago School* (Beverly Hills: Sage Publications, 1975), p. 83.
44. Steven J. Diner, "Department and Discipline: The Department of Sociology at the University of Chicago, 1892-1920," *Minerva* 13 (Winter 1975), pp. 515-517.
45. Ibid., pp. 522-553.
46. Anthony Oberschall, "The Institutionalization of American Sociology,"in *The Establishment of Empirical Sociology: Studies in Continuity, Discontinuity and Institutionalization*, ed. Anthony Oberschall (New York: Harper and Row, 1972), pp. 209, 217.
47. Roy Lubove, *The Professional Altruist: The Emergence of Social Work as a Career, 1889-1930* (New York: Atheneum, 1971), pp. 140-141.
48. Steven J. Diner, *A City and Its Universities: Public Policy in Chicago, 1892-1919* (Chapel Hill University of North Carolina Press, 1980), pp. 121-123.
49. Blumer, "The Chicago School of Sociology: What Made It a 'School?' pp. 63, 70-71.

CHAPTER 2

1. A little dated but still very useful works are Eric F. Goldman, *Rendezvous with Destiny* (New York: Vintage Books, 1956), and Samuel P. Hays, *The Response to Industrialism* (Chicago: University of Chicago Press, 1963).

2. George E. Mowry, *The Era of Theodore Roosevelt and the Birth of Modern America, 1900-1912* (New York: Harper Torchbooks, 1958) and Arthur S. Link, *Woodrow Wilson and the Progressive Era, 1890-1920* (New York: Harper Torchbooks, 1954) are older but useful overviews.

3. Samuel Haber, *Efficiency and Uplift: Scientific Management in the Progressive Era, 1890-1912* (Chicago: University of Chicago Press, 1964), p. 105.

4. Ibid., pp. 101, 103, 196.

5. David Rothman, *Conscience and Convenience: The Asylum and Its Alternatives in Progressive America* (Boston: Little, Brown, 1980).

6. Samuel Walker, *A Critical History of Police Reform* (Lexington, MA. Lexington Books, 1977), pp. 40-43.

7. Ibid., pp. 48-49.

8. Lewis Terman and Arthur Otis, "A Trial of Mental and Pedagogical Tests in a Civil Service Examination for Policemen and Firemen," *Journal of Applied Psychology* 1 (1917), p. 21.

9. Read Bain, "The Policeman on the Beat," *Scientific Monthly* 48 (1939), p. 452.

10. Louis L. Thurstone, "The Intelligence of Policemen," *Journal of Personnel Research* 1 (1922), pp. 64-74.

11. Walker, *A Critical History of Police Reform*, pp. 61-67.

12. Gene E. Carte and Elaine H. Carte, *Police Reform in the United States: The Era of August Vollmer, 1905-1932* (Berkeley: University of California Press, 1975), pp. 19-21.

13. For a discussion of California progressivism, see George E. Mowry *The California Progressives* (Chicago: Quadrangle Books, 1963), pp. 86-104.

14. Carte and Carte, *Police Reform in the United States*, pp. 22-23.

15. Ibid.

16. Edward Farris, "The Role of the Junior College in Police Education in California" (Unpublished master's thesis in criminology, University of California, 1965), pp. 25-32.

17. Carte and Carte, *Police Reform in the United States*, pp. 26-27.

18. August Vollmer and Albert Schneider, "The School for Police as Planned at Berkeley," *Journal of the American Institute of Criminal Law and Criminology* 7 (1917), pp. 877-898.

19. Carte and Carte, *Police Reform in the United States*, pp. 56-57, 62.

20. Interview with V. A. Leonard, January 27, 1982.

21. Ibid.

22. Carte and Carte, *Police Reform in the United States*, pp. 58-62.

23. Charles E. Merriam to August Vollmer, September 25, 1932. Vollmer papers, Merriam folder. See *Police "13-13"* 4 (December 1929), pp. 15-16, 90-91 for an outline of Vollmer's course. *Police "13-13"* was the Chicago police department's in-house magazine/newsletter.

24. *Police "13-13"* 7 (July 1932), p. 15.

25. William Wiltberger to August Vollmer, September 25, 1932. Vollmer papers, Wiltberger folder 1.

26. Samuel Walker, *Popular Justice: A History of American Criminal Justice* (New York: Oxford University Press, 1980), pp. 174-175.

27. *Spring 3100* 11 (October 1940), pp. 8, 9, 12, 13. Also see Arthur Niederhoffer, *Behind the Shield: The Police in Urban Society* (New York: Anchor Books, 1969), p. 17.

28. "Proposed Course in Criminology," Vollmer papers, general collection, carton 4. Also A. W. Kidd to Dean Joel Hilderbrand, September 2, 1939. O. W. Wilson papers, box 1.

29. Interview with Thomas Hunter, 1972, for the August Vollmer Historical Project, Oral History Section, Bancroft Library, University of California at Berkeley.

30. The designation "V-Men" was actually created by Vollmer's graduate students at Berkeley between the years 1932-1937. They even had a lapel pin, a many-pointed star with a "V" etched in the center.

31. William J. Bopp, *"O. W.": O. W. Wilson and the Search for a Police Profession* (Port Washington, NY: Kennikat Press, 1977), pp. 14, 16, 21, 28.

32. Ibid., pp. 30-35.

33. Ibid., pp. 40-49.

34. Ibid., p. 56.

35. Ibid., pp. 59-61.

36. "Report of O. W. Wilson, A. M. Kidd, and Paul L. Kirk on Recommendations for the Development of a Criminology Program, November 20, 1939." President's Files: University Archives, Bancroft Library, University of California.

CHAPTER 3

1. O. W. Wilson to August Vollmer, April 22, 1936. O. W. Wilson papers, box 1. Bancroft Library.
2. Felix Fabian, "The Evolution of Pre-Service Law Enforcement Education at the College and University Level" (unpublished Ph.D. dissertation, University of Idaho, 1965), pp. 62, 128.
3. Frank Boolsen to August Vollmer, February 1, 18, and March 26, 1937. Vollmer papers, Boolsen folder. Bancroft Library.
4. Arthur Brandstatter, "The School of Police Administration and Public Safety," *Journal of Criminal Law and Criminology* 48 (January-February 1958), pp. 564-566. And interview with Arthur Brandstatter, April 29, 1982.
5. Wilbur Lewis Rykert, "The School of Criminal Justice at Michigan State University, 1935-1963" (unpublished master's thesis, Michigan State University, 1985), p. 66.
6. Elmo A. Robinson, "The Seven State Colleges of California," *School and Society* 53 (May 24, 1941), pp. 649-650.
7. Ibid., pp. 650-651.
8. Ibib., pp. 651-652.
9. Hugh Ross, "University Influence in the Genesis and Growth of Junior Colleges in California," *History of Education Quarterly* 3 (September 1963), p. 143.
10. Ibid., pp. 144-150.
11. Wilson Compton, "For the Public Institutions," in *Old Times and New Horizons: Addresses Delivered at the Inauguration of Dr. Raymond B. Allen as President of the University of Washington, May 22-24, 1947* (Seattle: University of Washington Press, 1949), p. 44.
12. Robinson, "The Seven State Colleges of California," p. 653.
13. Ibid.
14. Interview with George Brereton, 1972, for the August Vollmer Historical Project, Oral History Section, Bancroft Library, University of California at Berkeley.
15. Ibid.

16. Quoted in John P. Kenney, *The California Police* (Springfield, Il: Charles C. Thomas, 1964), p. 99. And Richard A. Myren, *Education in Criminal Justice* (Washington DC: Coordinating Council for Higher Education, Council Report 70-5, 1970), p. 7.

17. Kenney, *The California Police*, pp. 75, 78-79. See also George H. Brereton, "The California Plan for Peace Officer Training," *Journal of the American Institute of Criminal Law and Criminology* (September-October 1939), pp. 370-378.

18. William Wiltberger to Albert Morris, August 6, 1974. Albert Morris papers, archives of the American Society of Criminology, Ohio State University.

19. Interview with Franklin M. Kremil, November 24, 1981.

20. William Wiltberger to August Vollmer, August 29, 1931. Vollmer papers, Wiltberger folder 1, Bancroft Library.

21. Ibid., September 25, 1932.

22. William Wiltberger to Paul H. Sanders, March 23, 1935. Vollmer papers, Wiltberger folder 1, Bancroft Library.

23. William Wiltberger to August Vollmer, March 30, 1935. Vollmer papers, Wiltberger folder 1, Bancroft Library.

24. William Wiltberger to Paul H. Sanders, March 23, 1935. Vollmer papers, Wiltberger folder 1, Bancroft Library.

25. William Wiltberger, "A Program for Police Training in College" (unpublished master's thesis, University of California, 1937), p. 63.

26. Ibid., p. 118.

27. *San Jose Mercury Herald*, April 2, 1940. Newsclipping in Vollmer papers, Wiltberger folder 2, Bancroft Library.

28. When Wiltberger wrote his thesis in 1937 there were fifteen colleges offering at least one course in law enforcement. They were (1) University of California, (2) University of Texas, (3) University of Hawaii, (4) University of Wichita (Wichita State), (5) University of Washington, (6) University of Louisville, (7) University of Toledo, (8) University of California (Summer School), (9) Indiana University, (10) Northwestern University, (11) Ohio State University, (12) Hobard College, (13) San Jose State, (14) Los Angeles Junior College, and (15) Michigan State College.
Wiltberger, "A Program for Police Training in College," pp. 71, 179.

29. William Wiltberger to August Vollmer, February 10, 1936. Vollmer papers, Wiltberger folder 2, Bancroft Library.

30. William Wiltberger, "A Program for Police Training in College," p. 97.

31. Ibid., pp. 58, 139. T. W. MacQuarrie, "San Jose State College Police School," *Journal of the American Institute of Criminal Law* (July 1935), pp. 255-261. Allen Z. Grammage, *Police Training in the United States* (Springfield, Il: Charles C. Thomas, 1963), p. 65. For a historical investigation of curricular changes, see Jack L. Kuykendall and Armand P. Hernandez, "Understanding Justice System Education and Training at San Jose State University: An historical perspective," *Journal of Criminal Justice* 3 (1975), pp. 110-130.

32. William Wiltberger to August Vollmer, April 8, 1936. Vollmer papers, Wiltberger folder 2, Bancroft Library.

33. Ibid., April 24, 1936.

34. Wiltberger, "A Program for Police Training in College," pp. 94, 95.

35. Ibid., p. 57.

36. Ibid., pp. 139, 171.

37. Ibid., p. 3.

38. Ibid., pp. 62, 138.

39. Ibid., p. 111.

40. MacQuarrie, "San Jose State College Police School," pp. 255-261.

41. Wiltberger, "A Program for Police Training in College," pp. 100-101.

42. William Wiltberger to August Vollmer, April 8, 1936. Vollmer papers, Wiltberger folder 2, Bancroft Library.

43. Minnesota University, *Survey of Police Training: Final Report of the Regents Examining Committee on the Police Training Project* (Minneapolis: University of Minnesota, 1937), pp. 14-15, 19.

44. William Wiltberger to August Vollmer, May 31, 1936. Vollmer papers, Wiltberger folder 2, Bancroft Library.

45. Ibid.

46. Ibid., April 3, 1940, and April 16, 1942. Vollmer papers, Wiltberger folders 2 and 3. William Wiltberger to O. W. Wilson, April 27 and June 26, 1939. Vollmer papers, Wiltberger folder 2, Bancroft Library.

47. V. A. Leonard to August Vollmer, July 10, 1944. Vollmer papers, Leonard folder 10, Bancroft Library.

48. Wiltberger, "A Program for Police Training in College," p. 69.

49. Interview with V. A. Leonard, January 27, 1982.

50. V. A. Leonard to August Vollmer, September 16 and October 16, 1941. Vollmer papers, Leonard folder 7, Bancroft Library.

51. Ibid., April 1, 1944. Vollmer papers, Leonard folder 10, Bancroft Library.
52. Ibid., February 11, 1943. Vollmer papers, Leonard folder 9, Bancroft Library.
53. Ibid., January 29, 1945. Vollmer papers, Leonard folder 11, Bancroft Library.
54. Ibib., January 25, 1946. Vollmer papers, Leonard folder 13, Bancroft Library.
55. Ibid.
56. *San Jose Mercury Herald*, April 2, 1940. Newsclipping in Vollmer papers, Wiltberger folder 2, Bancroft Library.
57. V. A. Leonard to August Vollmer, October 2 and June 5, 1942. Vollmer papers, Leonard folder 8, Bancroft Library.
58. Ibid., February 11, 1943. Vollmer papers, Leonard folder 9, Bancroft Library.
59. Ibid., March 24, 1943. Vollmer papers, Leonard folder 8, Bancroft library.
60. Ibid., September 29, 1943. Vollmer papers, Leonard folder 9, Bancroft Library.
61. William Wiltberger to August Vollmer, July 19, 1943. Vollmer papers, Wiltberger folder 3, Bancroft Library.
62. V. A. Leonard to H. F. Alderfer, April 14, 1944. Vollmer papers, Leonard folder 10, Bancroft Library.
63. Associated Press Newsfeature in typescript, dated Febrary 9, 1945. Vollmer papers, Leonard folder 1, Bancroft Library.
64. V. A. Leonard to August Vollmer, May 27, and June 10, 28, 1944. Vollmer papers, Leonard folder 10, Bancroft Library.
65. Ibid., July 22, 1944.
66. Ibid., November 2 and 11, 1944.
67. Ibid., December 28, 1944.
68. Ibid., August 15, 1947. Vollmer papers, Leonard folder 15, Bancroft Library.
69. Ibid., June 11 and 23, 1946. Vollmer papers, Leonard folder 11, Bancroft Library.
70. Ibid., June 6 and 11, 1945.
71. Ibid., August 20, 1947. Vollmer papers, Leonard folder 15, Bancroft Library.
72. Ibid., March 21, 1952. Vollmer papers, Leonard folder 18, Bancroft Library.
73. Ibid., May 20, 1952.
74. Ibid., December 5, 1951.
75. Ibid., February 20, 1945. Vollmer papers, Leonard folder 11, Bancroft Library.
76. Ibid., September 27 and November 16, 1945. Vollmer papers, Leonard folder 12, Bancroft Library.
77. Ibid., September 27, 1945.

78. V. A. Leonard to Willard Schmidt, January 2, 1946. Vollmer papers, Leonard folder 13; William Beall to August Vollmer, October 4, 1946. Vollmer papers, Willam Beall folder, Bancroft Library.

79. William Beall to August Vollmer, March 5, 1947. Vollmer papers, William Beall folder, Bancroft Library.

80. V. A. Leonard to August Vollmer, July 22, 1951. Vollmer papers, Leonard folder 18, Bancroft Library.

81. Ibid., May 9, 1950. Vollmer papers, Leonard folder 17, Bancroft Library.

82. Ibid., November 13, 1948. Vollmer papers, Leonard folder 16, Bancroft Library.

83. Ibid., November 29, 1949. Vollmer papers, Leonard folder 17, Bancroft Library.

CHAPTER 4

1. Robert Sproul to O. W. Wilson, June 19, 1939. O. W. Wilson papers, box 1, Bancroft Library.

2. V. A. Leonard to Frank Morn, December 8, 1981. In author's possession. Also "Report of First Meeting," Albert Morris papers, Archives of American Society of Criminology.

3. William Wiltberger to Albert Morris, August 6, 1974. Albert Morris papers, Archives of American Society of Criminology.

4. William Wiltberger to V. A. Leonard, January 16, 1942. Vollmer papers, Wiltberger folder 3, Bancroft Library.

5. William Wiltberger to August Vollmer, October 23, 1947. Vollmer papers, Wiltberger folder 3, Bancroft Library. Albert Morris, "The American Society of Criminology: A History, 1941-1973," *Criminology* 13 (August 1975), pp. 124-125.

6. Paul Kirk to Robert Sproul, July 18, 1946. And Monroe Deutsch to Robert Sproul, November 22, 1946. Presidential Files, University of California Archives.

7. George Brereton to Robert Sproul, August 16, 1946. Presidential Files, University of California Archives.

8. Monroe Deutsch to Robert Sproul, November 19, 1946. Presidential Files, University of California Archives.

9. Stuart Daggett, "Report to the Committee on Educational Policy upon Criminology, January 23, 1947." Presidential Files, University of California Archives.

10. Paul Kirk to Colonel O. W.Wilson, May 22, 1947. School of Criminology papers, Office of Chancellor Archives, University of California.

11. Daggett, "Report to the Committee on Educational Policy upon Criminology, January 23, 1947."

12. M. A. Stewart to Percy M. Barr, October 14, 1947. Presidential Files, University of California Archives.

13. Milton Chernin and Edward Rogers, "Statement of Members of Committee Who Support the Appointment of Professor Sellin or Professor Gleuck as Dean of the School of Criminology," Statement II of Appendix B of the Report of the Committee to Advise on the Appointment of the Dean of the School of Criminology, May 23, 1949. Presidential Files, University of California Archives.

14. A. M. Kidd, "Statement I of Appendix B of the Report of the Committee to Advise on the Appointment of the Dean of the School of Criminology, May 23, 1949." Presidential Files, University of California Archives.

15. Ibid.

16. "Further Statement Concerning the Selection of a Dean of the School of Criminology," Statement III of Appendix B of the Report of the Committee to Advise on the Appointment of the Dean of the School of Criminology, May 23, 1949. Presidential Files, University of California.

17. [O. W. Wilson], "Expansion of the Criminology Program at the University of California,"[1948]. Presidential Files, University of California.

18. Russell Barthell to President Sproul on "Current Status, School of Criminology, Berkeley," July 13, 1949. Presidential Files, University of California.

19. Denise Brachnik, "The Rise of the School of Criminology," unpublished paper, pp. 9-10. School of Criminology papers, Office of Chancellor Archives, University of California.

20. Bopp, *"O. W.": O. W. Wilson and the Search for a Police Profession*, pp. 77, 79.

21. "Minutes of the Staff Meeting, School of Criminology," October 15, 1951, and October 20, 1952. Vollmer papers, School of Criminology folder, Bancroft Library.

22. *San Francisco Examiner*, March 24, 1957.

23. "Master's Degrees and Titles of Theses, 1928-1970," prepared by the School of Criminology. School of Criminology papers, Office of Chancellor Archives, University of California.

24. "Statement Made at the November 3, 1959, Meeting of the Educational Policy Committee and Supplementary Comments by O. W. Wilson." School of Criminology papers, Office of Chancellor Archives, University of California.

25. Kenney, *The California Police*, pp. 92, 93.

26. O. W. Wilson to Chancellor Clark Kerr, May 5, 1953. School of Criminology papers. Office of Chancellor Archives, University of California.

27. Memo to Chancellor Seaborg from "Kitty," February 26, 1959, and E. W. Strong to Chancellor Seaborg, June 8, 1959. School of Criminology papers, Office of Chancellor Archives, University of California.

28. Bopp, *"O. W.": O. W. Wilson and the Search for a Police Profession*, pp. 80-81.

29. O. W. Wilson to J. A. Jenkins, February 20, 1958. School of Criminology papers, Office of Chancellor Archives, University of California.

30. *Bulletin of the Society for the Advancement of Criminology* 1, no. 7 (December 6, 1954). See also O. W. Wilson, "A General Philosophy for Criminology Programs in Institutions of Higher Learning," Albert Morris papers, American Society of Criminology Archives.

31. O. W. Wilson to Leon Radzinowicz, August 4, 1959. School of Criminology papers (Goolsby collection), Office of Chancellor Archives, University of California.

32. Leon Radzinowicz to O. W. Wilson, June 30, 1959. School of Criminology papers (Goolsby collection), Office of Chancellor Archives, University of California.

33. Richard McGee to Gordon MacKinney, December 10, 1959. School of Criminology papers, Office of Chancellor Archives, University of California.

34. "Reply by the School of Criminology to the Cline Report Prepared for the Advisory Council of the School of Criminology," August 20, 1959. School of Criminology papers (Goolsby collection), Office of Chancellor Archives, University of California.

35. Ibid. Also "Minutes of the Staff Meeting: School of Criminology," June 10, 1959. School of Criminology papers (Goolsby collection), Office of Chancellor Archives, University of California.

36. O. W. Wilson to Austin MacCormick, July 22, 1959. School of Criminology papers (Goolsby collection), Office of Chancellor Archives, University of California.

37. "Reply by the School of Criminology to the Cline Report Prepared for the Advisory Council of the School of Criminology," August 20, 1959. School of Criminology papers (Goolsby collection), Office of Chancellor Archives, University of California.

38. "Minutes of the Staff Meeting: School of Criminology," September 14, 1959. School of Criminology papers (Goolsby collection), Office of Chancellor Archives, University of California.

39. "Report of the Advisory Council of the School of Criminology to the Chancellor and the Academic Senate Committee on Educational Policy of the University of California," October 16, 1959. School of Criminology papers (Goolsby collection), Office of Chancellor Archives, Univewrsity of California.

40. Bopp, *"O. W.": O. W. Wilson and the Search for a Police Profession*, pp.81-82.

41. G. MacKinney to Glenn T. Seaborg, January 13, 1960; and Glenn T. Seaborg to Howard McDonald, May 9, 1960. School of Criminology papers (Goolsby collection), Office of Chancellor Archives, University of California.

42. *San Francisco Examiner*, February 25, 1960.

43. See Memo to G.T.S. [Glenn T. Seaborg] from E. W. Strong, January 19, 1960. School of Criminology papers, Office of Chancellor Archives, University of California.

44. Memo to Chancellor Seaborg from Milton Chernin, February 25, 1960. School of Criminology papers, Office of Chancellor Archives, University of California.

45. Joseph Lohman to Herbert Blumer, September 9, 1960. And "Report of the Committee on the Reorganization of the Curriculum of the School of Criminology to Chancellor Glenn T. Seaborg," November 11, 1960. School of Criminology (Goolsby collection). Office of Chancellor Archives, University of California.

46. "Minutes of the Meeting of the Advisory Council to the School of Criminology," November 18, 1961. School of Criminology papers (Goolsby collection), Office of Chancellor Archives, University of California.

47. Herbert Blumer to Richard McGee, November 16, 1960. School of Criminology papers, Office of Chancellor Archives, University of California.

48. "Minutes of the Meeting of the Advisory Council to the School of Criminology," October 27, 1964. School of Criminology papers (Goolsby collection), Office of Chancellor Archives, University of California.

49. V. A. Leonard to August Vollmer, October 30, 1941. Vollmer papers, Leonard folder 7, Bancroft Library. Also Willard Schmidt to Albert Morris, August 14, 1974. Albert Morris papers, American Society of Criminology Archives.

50. V. A. Leonard to August Vollmer, February 17, 1942. Vollmer papers, Leonard folder 8, Bancroft Library.

51. Ibid. December 24, 1941. Vollmer papers, Leonard folder 7, Bancroft Library. Albert Morris, "The American Society of Criminology: A History, 1941-1974" *Criminology* 13 (August 1975), pp. 124-125.

52. William Wiltberger to August Vollmer, April 18, 1949. Vollmer papers, Wiltberger folder 1, Bancroft library.

53. Thorsten Sellin, *Culture, Conflict, and Crime* (New York: Social Science Research Council, 1938), pp. 128-129.

54. Morris, "The American Society of Criminology: A History, 1941-1974," pp. 128-129.

55. V. A. Leonard to August Vollmer, December 23, 1948, and January 13, 1949. Vollmer papers, Leonard folders 16 and 17, Bancroft Library.

56. Arthur F. Brandstatter, "The School of Police Administration and Public Safety," *Journal of Criminal Law and Criminology* 48 (January-February, 1958), p. 565. Frank D. Day, "A University Role in the Education of Students for Careers in the Administration of Criminal Justice," *Criminologica* 2 (February 1965), pp.7-8.

57. "MSU: The University on the Make (Or How MSU Helped Arm Madame Nhu)" *Ramparts* 4 (April 1966), pp. 11-22.

58. Felix Fabian, "The Evolution of Pre-Service Law Enforcement Education at the College and University Levels" (unpublished Ph.D. dissertation, University of Idaho, 1965), pp. 77, 140-143.

59. George W. Bemis, Frank M. Boolsen, Earnest A Steiner, and William R. Barker, *A Survey of Law Enforcement Curriculum in California State Colleges* (Sacramento, Ca: Division of State Colleges and Teacher Education, State Department of Education, 1951), p. 1.

60. "Survey of Educational Status of Department," County of Los Angeles Sheriffs Department, July 30, 1959. Richard Hankey papers, John Jay College of Criminal Justice Archives.

61. Kenney, *The California Police*, pp. 97-98. A. C. Germann, "Curriculum Development for Law Enforcement in the State Colleges," *Police Chief* 28 (April 1961), pp. 4, 14.

62. Richard A. Myren, *Education in Criminal Justice*, (Washington DC: Coordinating Council for Higher Education, Council Report 70-5, 1970), p. 3.

63. August Vollmer to Richard Hankey, July 21 and August 11, 1948. Richard Hankey papers, John Jay College of Criminal Justice Archives.

64. Richard Hankey to John Peper, January 17, 1951. Richard Hankey papers, John Jay College of Criminal Justice Archives.

65. Richard Hankey to G. D. Gourley, December 27, 1950. Richard Hankey papers, John Jay College of Criminal Justice Archives.

66. Felix Fabian, "The Evolution of Pre-Service Law Enforcement Education at the College and University Levels," p. 72.

67. Ibid., p. 80.

68. Ibid., p. 84.

69. Ibid., p. 83.

70. David A. McCandless, "Southern Police Institute at the University of Louisville", *Journal of Criminal Law, Criminology and Police Science* 42 (1951-1952), pp. 105-107.

71. G. Douglas Gourley, "In-Service Training of Policemen by Universities and Colleges," *Journal of Criminal Law, Criminology and Police Science* 44 (1953-1954), pp. 229-238. Edward Farris, "The Role of the Junior College in Police Education in California" (unpublished master's of criminology thesis, University of California, 1965), pp. 130-133, 146. Kenney, *The California Police*, pp. 82-85.

72. Quoted in Fabian, "The Evolution of Pre-Service Law Enforcement Education at the College and University Level," p. 88.

73. Douglas Kelley to August Vollmer, November 9, 1951. Vollmer papers, Kelley folder, Bancroft Library.

74. "Bulletin of the Society for the Advancement of Criminology" 1, no. 3 (December 1, 1953). Albert Morris papers, American Society of Criminology Archives.

75. Interview with John Kenney, Februrary 24, 1983.

76. Interview with Donal MacNamara, May 13, 1982.

77. Douglas Kelley to Robert Gualt, August 23, 1950. Vollmer papers, Kelley folder, Bancroft Library.

78. "Minutes of the Meeting of the Executive Committee of the Society for the Advancement of Criminology, April 12, 1953" and "Minutes of the Annual Meeting of the Society for the Advancement of Criminology, December 28, 1954." Albert Morris papers, American Society of Criminology Archives.

79. William Dienstein to David McCandless, November 24, 1953. Albert Morris papers, American Society of Criminology Archives.

80. Arthur Brandstatter to William Dienstein, May 15, 1953, and November 5, 1953. Albert Morris papers, American Society of Criminology Archives.

81. Ibid., April 28, 1954.

82. "Bulletin of the Society for the Advancement of Criminology" 1, no. 5 (May 1, 1954). Albert Morris papers, American Society of Criminology Archives.

83. William Dienstein to David McCandless, November 24, 1954. Albert Morris papers, American Society of Criminology Archives.

84. "Newsnotes of the Society for the Advancement of Criminology, January 1957." Albert Morris papers, American Society of Criminology Archives.

85. John Kenney to William Dienstein, July 18, 1958. Albert Morris papers, American Society of Criminology Archives.

86. Douglas Kelley to August Vollmer, November 9, 1951. Vollmer papers, Kelley folder, Bancroft Library.

87. Frank Boolsen to August Vollmer, April 2, 1953. Vollmer papers, Boolsen folder, Bancroft Library.

88. "Minutes of the General Business Meeting of the Society for the Advancement of Criminology, April 4, 1953." Albert Morris papers, American Society of Criminology Archives.

89. "Minutes of the Executive Committee Meeting of the Society for the Advancement of Criminology, April 12, 1953." Albert Morris papers, American Society of Criminology Archives.

90. Interview with John Kenney, February 24, 1983.

91. William Dienstein to Jack Kenney, July 29, 1957. Albert Morris papers, American Society of Criminology Archives.

92. "A Proposal to Study the Teaching and Research of Criminology in the United States," sponsored by the American Society of Criminology, November 1958. Albert Morris papers, American Society of Criminology Archives.

93. John Kenney to William Dienstein, July 8, 1957. Albert Morris papers, American Society of Criminology Archives.

94. "Proceedings of the Annual Conference of the American Society of Criminology, February 1958." Albert Morris papers, American Society of Criminology Archives.

95. Marcel Frym to William Diensein, May 7, 1959. Albert Morris papers, American Society of Criminology Archives.

96. Interview with Donal MacNamara, May 13, 1982.

97. "Minutes of the Annual Business Meeting of the American Society of Criminology, February 2, 1959." Albert Morris papers, American Society of Criminology Archives.

98. Interview with Donal MacNamara, May 13, 1982.

99. Ibid.

100. Richard Hankey to Gilbert Geis, May 28, 1975. Richard Hankey papers, John Jay College of Criminal Justice Archives.

101. *Criminologica*, 1, no. 1 (1963), pp. 1-5.

102. Morris, " The American Society of Criminology: A History, 1941-1974," pp. 151, 153-156.

CHAPTER 5

1. Albert Morris, "The Amerian Society of Criminology: A History, 1941-1973," *Criminology* 13 (August 1975), pp. 153-156. and Walter Reckless, "American Criminology," *Criminology* 8 (1970), p. 20.

2. Interview with Felix Fabian, January 28, 1982.

3. C. R. Jeffery to G. Thomas Gitchoff, March 12, 1970, and Albert Morris to G. Thomas Gitchoff, March 18, 1970. Albert Morris papers, American Society of Criminology Archives.
4. Interview with William Melincoe, March 23, 1983.
5. Interview with Harry More, February 2, 1983.
6. Interview with Robert Borkenstein, April 30, 1982.
7. Interview with Edward Farris, March 25, 1983.
8. Interview with John Kenney, February 24, 1983.
9. Interview with Robert Borkenstein, April 30, 1982.
10. Interview with John Kenney, February 24, 1983.
11. Interview with William Melincoe, March 23, 1983.
12. Interview with Felix Fabian, January 28, 1982.
13. Interview with Edward Farris, March 25, 1983.
14. See James Richardson, *The New York Police: Colonial Times to 1900* (New York: Oxford University Press, 1970), pp. 51-58; Roger Lane, *Policing the City: Boston 1822-1885* (Cambridge, Ma: Harvard University Press, 1967), pp. 26-38; and John C. Schneider, *Detroit and the Problem of Order, 1830-1880: A Geography of Crime, Riot and Policing* (Lincoln: University of Nebraska Press, 1980), pp. 64-86.
15. Frank Morn, *The Eye That Never Sleeps: A History of the Pinkerton National Detective Agency* (Bloomington: Indiana University Press, 1982), pp. 17-34.
16. Leo J. Coakley, *Jersey Troopers: A Fifty Year History of the New Jersey State Police* (New Brunswick, NJ: Rutgers University Press, 1971), pp. 4, 10-20.
17. Samuel Walker, *Popular Justice: A History of American Criminal Justice* (New York: Oxford University Press, 1980), p. 232.
18. Wilber R. Miller, *Cops and Bobbies: Police Authority in New York and London, 1830-1870* (Chicago: University of Chicago Press, 1977), pp. 8-10, 12-16.
19. William O'Neill, *Coming Apart: An Informal History of America in the 1960s* (Chicago: Quadrangle Books, 1971).
20. Frank Remington, "Development of Criminal Justice as an Academic Field," speech given at The Idea of Criminal Justice: The Development and Future of an Academic Field, a conference celibrating the twentieth anniversary of the School of Criminal Justice, SUNY-Albany, April 13, 1989.
21. "The Way to Cool the Police Rebellion," *Fortune*, 77 (December 1968), p. 150.
22. *Time* 92, no. 14 (October 4, 1968), pp. 21-23.
23. James B. Jacobs and Samuel B. Magdovitz, "At LEEP's End: A Review of the Law Enforcement Education Program," *Journal of Police Science and Administration* 5 (1977), p. 18.

24. Norval Jesperson, "Analysis of Students Majoring in Criminal Justice, July 9, 1973." Velde papers, box 3, National Archives.

25. Ibid.

26. "Curriculum Panel," *IAPP Conference Proceedings, 1964*. (Berkeley, Ca., 1964).

27. Richard A. Myren, *Education in Criminal Justice*,(Washington DC: Coordinating Council for Higher Education, Council Report 70-5, 1970), p. 3.

28. Felix Fabian, "The Evolution of Pre-Service Law Enforcement Education at the College and University Levels," (unpublished Ph.D. dissertation, University of Idaho, 1965), pp. 18-19, 21, 155, 167.

29. Interview with James Stinchcomb, June 22, 1983.

30. Edward A. Farris, "Unoa Passa Alla Volta (One Step at a Time)," *IAPP Conference Proceedings, 1966*. This speech was exerpted from Farris' 1964 thesis. Gordon Misner papers

31. "Additional Minutes for the IAPP Meeting," *IAPP Conference Proceedings, 1965*. Gordon Misner papers.

32. Interview with Donald Riddle, March 17, 1983.

33. "Meeting of Police Science Degree Program Development Advisory Committee for the Office of Law Enforcement Assistance, July 1966." Richard Hankey papers, OLEA folder, John Jay College of Criminal Justice Archives.

34. Interview with Earl Lewis, March 25, 1982, and Interview with Edward Farris, March 25, 1983.

35. Interview with James Stinchcomb, June 22, 1983. Also James D. Stinchcomb, "The Community College and Its Impact," *Police Chief* 33 (August 1966), pp. 29-30; and "Involvement of the Community College with Law Enforcement," *IAPP Conference Proceedings, 1969*. Gordon Misner papers.

36. Fabian, "The Evolution of Pre-Service Law Enforcement Education at the College and University Levels," pp. 148, 149.

37. Memorandum to Joseph D. Lohman from Captain J. A. Lindquist, a summary of the 1964 meeting, dated June 2, 1964. School of Criminology papers (Goolsby collection), Presidential Archives, University of California.

38. Interview with Felix Fabian, January 28, 1982.

39. For a general discussion, see Anthony E. Simpson, *Accreditation and Its Significance for Programs of Higher Education in Criminology and Criminal Justice: A Review of the Literature* (Chicago [University of Illinois at Chicago]: Joint Commission on Criminology and Criminal Justice Education and Standards, 1979).

40. "Fundamentals Revisited," a report of the Committee on Standards for Police Education in *IAPP Conference Proceedings, 1966*. Gordon Misner papers.

41. "Minutes" of the *IAPP Conference Proceedings, 1969*. Gordon Misner papers.

42. Stinchcomb, "Involvement of the Communty College with Law Enforcement," *IAPP Conference Proceedings, 1969*. Gordon Misner papers.

43. Interview with Donald Riddle, March 17, 1983.

44. Charles B. Vail, "An Academic Dean Looks At Accreditation," *IAPP Conference Proceedings, 1969*. Gordon Misner papers.

45. Jerry W. Miller, "Factors in Developing an Accreditation Program," *IAPP Conference Proceedings, 1969*. Gordon Misner papers.

46. "San Jose Case Study-Panel: Mel Miller, Donald Riddle, and Richard Myren," *IAPP Conference Proceedings, 1969*. Gordon Misner papers.

47. C. Robert Guthrie, Richard O.Hankey, and Donald Riddle, "Report of the Committee to Establish Guidelines for the Development of Law Enforcement Programs," *IAPP Conference Proceedings, 1966;* "Membership Discussion on the Accreditation of Law Enforcement Degree Programs, May 3, 1969," *IAPP Conference Proceedings, 1969*. Gordon Misner papers.

48. Interview with Melvin Miller, June 21, 1983.

49. Edward A. Farris, "A History of Criminal Justice Education: Seven Decades (1900-1970)," in *The Report of the Standards Committee of the Academy of Criminal Justice Sciences,* Vol. 1, ed. William Mathias. Gordon Misner papers. In author's possession.

50. Interview with Edward Farris, March 25, 1983.

51. Edward A. Farris, "A Professional Policeman: How Do We Train Him?" *IAPP Conference Proceedings, 1964*. Gordon Misner papers.

52. Interview with Edward Farris, March 25, 1983.

53. See Arthur Brandstatter's presidential message in *IAPP Conference Proceedings, 1966,* Gordon Misner papers. Also Arthur Brandstatter, "A Career Concept for Police," *Journal of Criminal Law, Criminology and Police Science* 61 (September 1970), pp. 438-445.

54. Interview with Edward Farris, March 25, 1983.

55. William H. Hewitt, "The Objectives of a Formal Police Education," *IAPP Conference Proceedings, 1964*. Gordon Misner papers.

56. Interview with Richard Myren, March 26, 1982; and Interview with Donald Riddle, March 17, 1983; also comments by Riddle during discussion on the "San Jose Cas Study-Panel," *IAPP Conference Proceedings, 1969*. Gordon Misner papers.

CHAPTER 6

1. Richard R. Bennett and Ineke Haen Marshall, "Criminal Justice Education in the United States: A Profile," *Journal of Criminal Justice* 7 (1979), p. 148.

2. Interview with Robert Corley, March 2, 1983. And Interview with Arthur Bilek, February 3 and 7, 1983. Also Frank Morn, "Criminal Justice Education in Chicago: The University of Illinois, Chicago Circle Story," unpublished paper delivered at the Midwestern Criminal Justice Association meetings in Chicago, Illinois, October 1988.

3. Arthur F. Brandstatter, "The Genesis and Early History of Criminal Justice Studies at Michigan State University," unpublished paper delivered at the Midwestern Criminal Justice Association meetings in Chicago, Illinois, October 1989.

4. Joseph D. Lohman, "Roster of Faculty and Professional Research Personnel at the School of Criminology, University of California, Berkeley," January 1966. School of Criminology papers (Goolsby collection), Office of Chancellor Archives, University of California.

5. Ibid. Also Joseph Lohman to Herbert Blumer, September 9, 1960. And "Report of the Committee on the Reorganization of the Curriculum of the School of Criminology to Chancellor Glenn T. Seaborg," November 11, 1960. And "Minutes of the Meeting of the Advisory Council to the School of Criminology," November 18, 1961, and October 27, 1964. School of Criminology papers (Goolsby collection), Office of Chancellor Archives, University of California.

6. "Alumni Survey (Preliminary Report) of the School of Criminology, Feburary 2, 1968." School of Criminology papers (Goolsby collection), Office of Chancellor Archives, University of California.

7. Joseph D. Lohman, "Roster of Faculty and Professional Research Personnel," January 1966.

8. Michael I. Swygert and Nathaniel E. Gozansky, "Senior Law Faculty Publication Study: Comparison of Law School Productivity," *Journal of Legal Education* 35 (1985), pp. 221-222.

9. Jerold S. Auerbach, *Unequal Justice: Lawyers and Social Change in Modern America* (New York: Oxford University Press, 1976), pp. 107-118, 228-229.

10. Caleb Foote to Charles Dekkar, June 27, 1973. School of Criminology papers (Goolsby collection), University Archives, The Bancroft Library, University of California.

11. Ibid.

12. Ibid.

13. "Minutes of the Staff Meeting, School of Criminology, October 21, 1968." School of Criminology papers (Goolsby collection), Office of Chancellor Archives, University of California.

14. Geraldine Jonach Clifford and James W. Guthrie, *Ed School: A Brief for Professional Education* (Chicago: University of Chicago Press, 1988), p. 233.

15. Denise Dracknik and Richard Harrison, "The Demise of the School of Criminology," unpublished paper, pp. 1-4. School of Criminology papers, Vol. 1, Office of Chancellor Archives, University of California.

16. Information Newsletter of the Criminology Students Association, March 16, 1971. School of Criminology papers (Goolsby collection), Office of Chancellor Archives, University of California.

17. Carlos E. Kruytbosch and Sheldon Messinger, *The State of the University: Authority and Change* (Beverley Hills: Sage Publishing, 1968).

18. Carlos E. Kruytbosch and Sheldon Messinger, "Unequal Peers: The Situation of Researchers at Berkeley," in *The State of the University*, p. 265.

19. Felice J. Levine, "Goose Bumps and 'The Search for Signs of Intellectual Life' in Sociolegal Studies: After Twenty-Five Years," *Law & Society Review* 24 (1990), pp. 7-33. Also Lawrence M. Friedman, "The Law and Society Movement," *Stanford Law Review* 38 (February 1986), pp. 763-780.

20. Dracknik and Harrison, "The Demise of the School of Criminology," pp. 5, 9.

21. John Holstrom to Albert Morris, July 9, 1974. Albert Morris papers, American Society of Criminology Archives, Ohio State University, Columbus, Ohio.

22. "Report on the School of Criminology (Sindler Committee)," p. 18. School of Criminology papers, Office of Chancellor Archives, University of California.

23. David Fogel to Charles Dekken, September 10, 1973. School of Criminology papers, Office of Chancellor Archives, University of California.

24. Dracknik and Harrison, "The Demise of the School of Criminology," p. 39.

25. Ibid., pp. 13, 40.

26. David Fogel to Charles Dekken, September 19, 1973. School of Criminology papers, Office of Chancellor Archives, University of California.

27. Dracknik and Harrison, "The Demise of the School of Criminology," pp. 30-31.

28. Sheldon Messinger to Criminology Faculty, March 12, 1973. School of Criminology papers (Goolsby collection), University Archives, The Bancroft Library, University of California.

29. Dracknik and Harrison, "The Demise of the School of Criminology," pp. 24-25.
30. "Report on the School of Criminology (Sindler Committee)," p. 10.
31. Ibid., pp. 22-23.
32. Albert A. Bowker to Assemblyman John Vaconcellos, January 30, 1974. School of Criminology papers, Office of Chancellor Archives, University of California.
33. "Report on the School of Crimonology (Sindler Committee)," p. 6.

CHAPTER 7

1. Donald Riddle, "The John Jay College of Criminal Justice: A Case Study in Urban Education," speech given to the annual meeting of the College Entrance Examination Board, October 29, 1968 (John Jay Archives).
2. *New York Times*, December 9, 1967.
3. Interview with Donald Riddle, March 17, 1983.
4. Donald Riddle, "How Do You Educate Police? 'Like Anyone Else'," *University Magazine* (1969), p. 13. This article was actually delivered as a speech in "Report of the Committee to Establish Guidelines for the Development of Law Enforcement Programs," *IAPP Conference Proceedings, 1966*. Gordon Misner papers, in Misner's possession.
5. Comments by Riddle during the discussion on the "San Jose State Case Study Panel," *IAPP Conference Proceedings, 1966*. Gordon Misner papers.
6. Riddle, "How Do You Educate Police?", p. 15.
7. "Report of the Committee to Establish Guidelines for the Development of Law Enforcement Programs," *IAPP Conference Proceedings, 1966*. Gordon Misner papers.
8. Confidential memo from Reisman and Riddle to Eliot Lumbard, September 1965 (John Jay Archives). Also Interview with Richard Myren, March 26, 1982.
9. Quoted in Richard Ward and Vincent Webb, *Quest for Quality* (New York: University Publications, 1984), p. 104.
10. *The Corpus Christi Caller-Times,* July 2, 1967 (John Jay Archives).
11. "Report of the Committee to Establish Guidelines for the Development of Law Enforcement Programs," *IAPP Conference Proceedings, 1966*. Gordon Misner papers.
12. *Houston Chronicle*, October 24, 1970. And *Miami Herald*, January 17, 1971 (John Jay Archives).
13. *Crime Control Digest*, November 6, 1970.
14. *Houston Chronicle*, March 4, 1971 (John Jay Archives).

15. Riddle, "The John Jay College of Criminal Justice: A Case Study in Urban Education."
16. Ibid.
17. "Staff Conference Minutes," October 8, 1969, (John Jay Archives).
18. *New York Times*, November 8, 1973.
19. *Lorain Ohio Journal*, January 31, 1971, (John Jay Archives).
20. *New York Times*, November 8, 1973.
21. Ibid., November 27, 1979.
22. John Jay College of Criminal Justice, "The Advanced Institutional Development Plan; Toward Excellence in Criminal Justice Education, 1976-79: A Period of Appraisal," December 1975, (John Jay Archives).
23. Margaret Tabb to Gerald Lynch, March 2, 1976, (John Jay Archives).
24. John Jay, "Meeting Concerning the Coming of the Middle States Visit," January 9, 1973, (John Jay Archives).
25. Evaluation Team for the Commission on Higher Education of the Middle States Association, "Report to the Faculty, Trustees, Students of John Jay College of Criminal Justice," 1975 (John Jay Archives).
26. Chancellor Robert J. Kibbee, "A Proposal for Restructuring the City University of New York," February 19, 1976 (John Jay Archives).
27. *New York Daily News*, March 5, 1976.
28. *New York Times*, March 4, 1976.
29. Gerald W. Lynch, "The Past Fifteen Years of Criminal Justice Higher Education," paper delivered at the meetings of the Midwestern Criminal Justice Association, Chicago, October 22, 1980.
30. Tony Schwartz, *Media: The Second God* (New York: Random House, 1981), pp. 75-84.
31. Ibid.
32. *New York Daily News*, February 27, 1976.
33. *New York Times*, November 30, 1978.
34. "Minutes of the Advisory Commission," August 30, 1976, (John Jay Archives).
35. *New York Times*, November 30, 1978.
36. Robert H. Connery and Gerald Benjamin, *Rockefeller of New York: Executive Power in the Statehouse* (Ithaca, NY: Cornell University Press, 1979), pp. 295-301.
37. *New York Times*, June 29 and 30, 1981.
38. James E. Underwood and William J. Daniels, *Governor Rockefeller in New York: The Apex of Pragmatic Liberalism in the United States* (Westport, Ct: Greenwood Press, 1982), p. 300.
39. Interview with Eliot Lumbard, October 26, 1989.
40. Ibid.

41. Frank Remington, "Development of Criminal Justice as an Academic Field," a speech given at *The Idea of Criminal Justice: The Development and Future of an Academic Field*, a conference celebrating the twentieth anniversary of the School of Criminal Justice, SUNY-Albany, April 13, 1989.

42. After the School was established, Lumbard left Albany in 1967. Soon he was called to New Jersey to help reform the police there, noted for its politics and corruption. At the time any legislative attempts to deal with local or state police reform were stymied. Everyone wanted to look like reformers but did not really want to tinker with the police. To break through the problem Lumbard convinced several state representatives to support a school of criminal justice. In this way, he argued, the police would be changed slowly and less dramatically as better-educated agency personnel were exposed to more education. But the plan was overlooked or discounted by the enemies of police reform. At the same time, politicians could look every bit the reformers by bringing the police education movement to New Jersey. Although the Rutgers University School of Criminal Justice would be molded after the one in Albany, it would be "state-mandated." It came about overnight, unlike the process in New York, with little or no input from the academics. As Lumbard remembers, "it was probably [the] most successful I have ever been."

Interview with Eliot Lumbard, October 26, 1989.

43. Ibid.

44. Ibid. Also Frank Remington, "Development of Criminal Justice as an Academic Field."

45. Interview with Eliot Lumbard, October 26, 1989. Also Allan M. Cartter (Chancellor of NYU), "The Development of Doctoral Programs by the Small Liberal Arts College," *Proceedings of a Symposium at Bowdoin College, April 21-22, 1967* (Brunswick, ME: Bowdoin College, 1967), pp. 77, 82.

46. Interview with Eliot Lumbard, October 26, 1989.

47. Ibid.

48. Ibid.

49. Interview with Richard Myren, March 26, 1982.

50. Richard Myren, "Building a Criminal Justice Career Tradition," *IAPP Conference Proceedings, 1970*. Gordon Misner papers.

51. Comments made in the "San Jose State Case Panel," *IAPP Conference Proceedings, 1969*. Gordon Misner papers.

52. Richard Myren, "Building a Criminal Justice Career Tradition."

53. Comments made in the "San Jose State Case Panel."

54. Interview with Richard Myren, March 26, 1982.

55. "Facts and Figures, the first 13 years [of development at SUNY-Albany]," David Duffee file, Albany School of Criminal Justice Archives.

56. Interview with Richard Myren, March 26, 1982.

57. "Facts and Figures, the first 13 years."

58. Lawrence F. Travis III, "Criminal Justice Education: An Assessment of the Albany Model," paper given at *The Idea of Criminal Justice: The Development and Future of an Academic Field*, a conference celebrating the twentieth anniversary of the School of Criminal Justice, SUNY-Albany, April 13, 1989.

59. "Facts and Figures, the second ten years [at SUNY-Albany]," David Duffee file, Albany School of Criminal Justice Archives.

60. *American Council on Education: A Fact Book on Higher Education*, vol. 2 (Washington, DC: American Council on Education, 1976), pp. 78-79; vol. 4 (1976), p. 213.

61. Frankie Bailey, "Meeting the Needs of a Diversifying Student Population," paper and report given at *The Idea of Criminal Justice: The Development and Future of an Academic Field* conference.

62. Matthew R. DeZee, *The Productivity of Criminology and Criminal Justice Faculty* (Chicago: Joint Commission on Criminology and Criminal Justice Education and Standards, 1980) pp. 18-20.

63. *New York Times*, June 30, 1981.

64. Ibid. June 29, 1981.

CHAPTER 8

1. Interview with William Mathias, June 7, 1983.

2. Ibid.

3. Interview with Richard Ward, June 3, 1982.

4. Interview with Gordon Misner, January 18, 1982.

5. Ibid.

6. Ibid.

7. Gordon Misner to ACJS Members, January 20, 1977. Larry Bassi papers. In the author's possession.

8. Report of the Affirmative Action Committee, July 3, 1979. Larry Bassi papers. Minutes of the General Business Meeting of ACJS, March 14, 1980. Larry Bassi papers.

9. Interniew with William Mathias, June 7, 1983.

10. Interview with Richard Ward, June 3, 1982.

11. Interview with Donald Riddle, March 17, 1983.

12. For an excellent example, see Bruce Sinclair, *A Centennial History of the American Society of Mechanical Engineers, 1880-1980* (Toronto: University of Toronto Press, 1980), pp. 114-115.

13. Interview with Gordon Misner, January 18, 1982.

14. Gordon Misner to George Felkenes, February 3, 1978. Gordon Misner papers.

15. Interview with Richter Moore, November 14, 1981.

16. Interview with Gordon Misner, January 18, 1982.

17. Gordon Misner to Robert Culbertson, April 25, 1978. Gordon Misner papers.

18. Interview with William Mathias, June 7, 1983.

19. Interview with Richter Moore, November 14, 1981.

20. Interview with William Mathias, June 7, 1983.

21. Interview with Richter Moore, November 14, 1981.

22. Minutes of the 2nd Annual Business Meeting of the ACJS, March 23, 1973. Earl Lewis papers. In possesson of Lewis.

23. Ibid.

24. Gordon Misner to Members of the ACJS, February 16, 1976. Gordon Misner papers.

25. Gordon Misner to James Rumbolz, August 22, 1977. Gordon Misner papers.

26. Ibid., September 2, 1976. Gordon Misner papers.

27. Minutes of the 2nd Annual Conference of the Midwest Association of Criminal Justice Educators, November 1976. Gordon Misner papers.

28. Robert Culbertson to Gordon Misner, March 15, 1977. Gordon Misner papers.

29. Gordon Misner to Robert Culbertson, October 4, 1977. L. E. Synder to Gordon Misner, October 29, 1977. Minutes of the 3rd Annual Conference of the Midwest Association of Criminal Justice Educators, November 1977. Gordon Misner papers.

30. Samuel Sherrid, "A Survey of Life Experience in Criminal Justice Education," for the Committee on Life Experiences in Criminal Justice Education, 1976. Gordon Misner papers.

31. Larry Hoover, *Police Education Characteristics and Curricula*, a monograph for the National Institute of Law Enforcement and Criminal Justice, (Washington, DC: LEAA, 1975), pp. 34-39. Also, Erik Beckman, "Police Education and Training: Where Are We? Where Are We Going?" *Journal of Criminal Justice* 4 (1976), pp. 315-322.

32. Interview with Donald Riddle, March 17, 1983.

33. George Felkenes, "The Case of the Proper Balance: Liberal Arts (Plantiff) with Criminal Justice (Defendant)," in *Report of the Standards Committee*, Vol. 2 (1973), pp. 3, 5. See also Kenneth A. Feldman and Theodore M. Newcomb, *The Impact of College on Students* (San Francisco: Jossey-Bass, 1969).

34. These speeches, delivered in 1970 and 1972, respectively, were reprinted in *Report of the Standards Committee*, Vol. 2 (1973).

35. Minutes of the 2nd Annual Business Meeting of ACJS, March 23, 1973. Earl Lewis papers.
36. Interview with Arthur Bilek, February 3 and 7, 1983. Interview with James Osterburg, February 10, 1983.
37. Dennis E. Hoffman, Joel C. Snell, and Vincent J. Webb, "Insiders and Outsiders in Criminal Justice Education," *Journal of Criminal Justice* 4 (1976), pp. 57-61.
38. Richard Ward and James L. Curran, "Statement of Philosophy of Criminal Justice Degree Programs in the Area of Research," in *Report of the Standards Committee*, Vol. 1 (1972), pp. 1-4.
39. Interview with William Mathias, June 7, 1983.
40. Willam Caldwell to Clarence Coster, March 11, 1971. Velde papers, box 43, National Archives.
41. Norman C. Jesperson to Richard Velde, July 10, 1973. And "Grantees Meeting" at Michigan State University, July 18-19, 1973. Velde papers, boxes 45 and 73, National Archives.
42. Report of the Liaison Committee of ACJS, 1976-77. Gordon Misner papers.
43. Minutes of the ASC-ACJS Meeting, September 16, 1977. Gordon Misner papers.
44. Interview with Robert Culbertson, October 13, 1983.
45. Ibid.
46. Richter Moore to Larry Bassi, February 9, 1979. Also George Felkenes to ACJS Executive Board, August 4, 1979. Also Minutes of the General Business Meeting of ACJS, March 14, 1980. Larry Bassi papers.
47."The Limits of Specialized Accreditation," a statement of the National Commission in Accreditation, 1975. Gordon Misner papers.
48. Gordon Misner, "The Need of Quality Control for Criminal Justice Degree Programs," *Police Chief* 42 (August 1975), pp. 14-15. This is the publication of his Atlanta speech.
49. Interview with Larry Bassi, October 18, 1983.
50. Larry Bassi and Ronald H. Rogers, "The Road to Accredation," *Journal of Criminal Justice* 4 (1976), pp. 250-252.
51. "Academy of Criminal Justice Sciences: News and Notes," *Journal of Criminal Justice* 4 (1976), pp. 261-269.
52. Leo A. Cullo to Ken Joseph, June 1, 1976. Also Leo A. Cullo to Larry Bassi, August 5, 1976. Also Irving Jacks to Larry Bassi, February 12, 1976. Gordon Misner papers.
53. Wynn Weiss to Larry Bassi, May 4, 1977. Gordon Misner papers.

54. Leo A. Cullo to Larry Bassi, August 5, 1976. See also the California Association of Administration of Justice Educators Memo on ACJS accreditation guidelines, February 8, 1976. Gordon Misner papers.
55. Edward S. Small to Larry Bassi, February 10, 1976. Gordon Misner papers.
56. Gordon Misner to Members of Executive Board, June 14, 1977. Gordon Misner papers.
57. Interview with George Felkenes, March 25, 1982. Interview with Larry Bassi, October 18, 1983.
58. Interview with Donald Riddle, March 17, 1983.
59. Interview with George Felkenes, March 25, 1982.
60. Ibid. Also interview with Larry Bassi, October 18, 1983.
61. Interview with Robert Culbertson, October 13, 1983.
62. George Felkenes, "Accreditation: Is It Necessary? Yes!" *Journal of Criminal Justice* 8 (1980), pp. 77-87. Also Minutes of the ACJS, March 10, 1981. Gordon Misner papers.
63. Robert Culbertson, "Criminal Justice Accreditation: Perspectives for the 80's," a paper presented at the annual meeting of the Academy of Criminal Justice Sciences, 1981.
64. Interview with George Felkenes, March 25, 1982.
65. Richard Ward to the Board of Directors, a concept paper on the national office, September 19, 1978. Richard Ward papers. In possession of Ward.
66. Minutes of the Executive Board, June 24, 1977. Larry Bassi papers.
67. Richard Ward to the Executive Board, March 28, 1977. Gordon Misner papers.
68. Interview with Richard Ward, June 3, 1983.
69. Richard Ward and Vincent J.Webb, *Quest for Quality: Report of the Joint Commission on Criminology and Criminal Justice Education and Standards* [a draft copy] (Chicago: Joint Commission, 1981).
70. Interview with Richard Ward, June 3, 1983.
71. Ibid.
72. Interview with Gordon Misner, January 18, 1982.
73. Interview with Felix Fabian, January 28, 1982.
74. Minutes of the Executive Board of ACJS, March 21, 1975. Gordon Misner papers.
75. Ibid., March 22, 1975. Gordon Misner papers.
76. George Felkenes to the Membership of ACJS: a summary of the testimony given, May 1975. Gordon Misner papers.
77. Interview with George Felkenes, March 25, 1982.
78. Ibid.
79. Ibid.

80. Gordon Misner to C. Brise Batchford, June 13, 1975. Gordon Misner papers.

81. Lincoln J. Fry and Jon Miller, "The Organizational Transformation of a Federal Education Program: Refelections on LEEP," *Social Problems* 24 (December 1976), pp. 259-270.

82. Gordon Misner to H. George Frederickson, August 20, 1975. Gordon Misner papers.

83. See Robert Bader to Gordon Misner, October 1, 1975, and Gordon Misner to Robert Bader, October 5, 1975. Also see *St. Louis Post-Dispatch*, December 11, 1975. Gordon Misner papers.

84. Edward Farris to Gordon Misner, February 2, 1976. Gordon Misner papers.

85. Gordon Misner to Executive Board, September 8, 1975. Gordon Misner to Richard Ward, April 19, 1977. Gordon Misner to Richter Moore, January 25, 1978. Gordon Misner papers.

86. Memo to the Members Relative to the Proposed Amendments to the Constitution and By-laws, November 1, 1976. Also Gordon Misner to All Past Presidents, February 23, 1977. Gordon Misner papers.

87. Gordon Misner to Members of ACJS, April 3, 1976. Gordon Misner papers.

88. Interview with Robert Culbertson, October 13, 1983.

CHAPTER 9

1. Robert Culbertson and Adam F. Carr, *Syllabus Design and Construction in Criminal Justice Education*, (Chicago: Joint Commission on Criminology and Criminal Justice Education and Standards, 1981).

2. Academy of Criminal Justice Sciences Secretary-Treasurer's Report, March 13, 1979. Larry Bassi papers. In the author's possession.

3. "Criminal Justice Major Programs of Study in American Colleges and Universities by Type of Program, Level of Degree, and State, 1988-89," *Journal of Criminal Justice Education,* 1 no. 2 (Fall 1990), pp. 261-262.

4. Minutes of the Executive Board of ACJS, March 7, 1978. Larry Bassi papers.

5. Frank T. Morn, *Academic Disciplines and Debates: An Essay on Criminal Justice and Criminology as Professions in Higher Education* (Chicago: Joint Commission on Criminology and Criminal Justice Education and Standards, 1980).

6. C. R. Jeffery, "Criminalogy as an Interdisciplinary Behavioral Science," *Criminology* 16 (1978), p. 151. Also John H. Laub, *Criminology in the Making: An Oral History* (Boston: Northeastern University Press, 1983).
7. Interview with Robert Culbertson, October 13, 1883.
8. Ibid.
9. Ibid. Also interview with Gordon Misner, January 18, 1982.
10. Interview with Robert Culbertson, October 13, 1983.
11. Ibid.
12. Ibid.
13. Ibid.
14. Ibid.
15. Ibid.
16. Minutes of the Executive Board of the ACJS, March 19, 1977, and January 21, 1978. Larry Bassi papers.
17. Interview with Gordon Misner, January 18, 1982.
18. Interview with Donald Riddle, March 17, 1983; with George Felkenes, March 25, 1982; with Richard Myren, March 26, 1982; and with William Mathias, June 7, 1983.
19. Interview with Richard Ward, June 3, 1982.
20. Interview with George Felkenes, March 25, 1982.
21. Interview with Larry Bassi, October 18, 1983.
22. Interview with Richter Moore, November 14, 1981.
23. Interview with Larry Bassi, October 18, 1983.
24. Interview with Harry More, February 2, 1983.
25. Interview with Robert Culbertson, October 13, 1983.
26. David O. Friedrichs, "Paper Sessions and the ACJS Annual Meeting," *ACJS Today* (September 1982), pp. 4-5.
27. *ACJS Today* (May 1983), p. 7.
28. Minutes of the Executive Board Meeting of ACJS, November 16, 1977. Larry Bassi papers.
29. John Conley to Kent Josceyln, February 11, and especially February 18 (two letters on this date), 1980. Edward Latessa papers. In the author's possession.
30. Robert Culbertson to Harry W. More, Jr., March 19, 1980. Edward Latessa papers.
31. Interview with Robert Culbertson, October 13, 1983. Also Robert Culbertson to Dorothy Bracey, March 11, 1984. Edward Latessa papers.
32. Richard Bennett et al. to ACJS Executive Board, August 31, 1982. Edward Latessa papers.
33. Minutes of the Executive Board of ACJS, March 25, 1983. Edward Latessa papers.
34. Richard A Myren, "'Justicology': An Idea Whose Time Has Come," *Justice Reporter* 1 (1980), pp. 1-7.

35. Interview with John Conley, April 25, 1984; with Gilbert Bruns, March 30, 1984; and with Jack Greene, March 30, 1984.
36. Minutes of the General Membership Meeting, March 26, 1983. Minutes of the Executive Board of the ACJS, September 1, 1983.
37. Minutes of the Executive Board of the ACJS, September 1, 1983.
38. Robert Culbertson to Gilbert Bruns, November 1, 1983. Edward Latessa papers.
39. Ibid.
40. Robert Culbertson to Dorothy Bracey, August 10, 1983. Edward Latessa papers.
41. Robert Culbertson to R. Paul McCauley, October 17, 1983. Edward Latessa papers.
42. Robert Culbertson to Dorothy Bracey, August 10, 1983. Edward Latessa papers.
43. See Dennis E. Hoffman, Jack C. Snell, and Vincent J. Webb, "Insiders and Outsiders in Criminal Justice Education," *Journal of Criminal Justice* 4 (1976), pp. 57-61.
44. Interview with Larry Hoover, March 29, 1984; with Jack Greene, March 30, 1984.
45. Robert Culbertson to Dorothy Bracey, March 11, 1984. Edward Latessa papers.
46. Ibid.
47. Robert Culbertson to R. Paul McCauley, October 17 and 19, 1983. Edward Latessa papers.
48. Robert Culbertson to Gilbert Bruns, September 30 and November 1, 1983. Edward Latessa papers.
49. Robert Culbertson to Richard Bennett, October 17, 1983; and Robert Culbertson to Vincent Webb, October 18, 1983. Edward Latessa papers.
50. Robert Culbertson to R. Paul McCauley, October 17 and 19, 1983. Edward Latessa papers.
51. Robert Culbertson to Dorothy Bracey, March 11, 1984. Edward Latessa papers.
52. *ACJS Today* (January 1984), p. 7.
53. Ibid. (September, 1984), p. 1
54. "Criminal justice Major Programs of Study in American Colleges and Universities by Type of Program, Level of Degree, and State, 1988-89," *Journal of Criminal Justice Education*, 1 no. 2 (Fall 1990), pp. 261-262.
55. Ibid. Membership figures for other academic professional organizations offer additional perspective. For example, the American Psychological Association had 55,000 members by 1983. The American Economics Association (with 19,200), the American Society for Public Administration (18,000), the American Historical Association (14,500), the American

Sociological Association (13,000), and the American Political Science Association (12,000) reflect the magnitude of academic membership in the older associations.
Denise S. Akey, ed. Encyclopedia of Associations (Detroit: Gale Research Company, 1984).

EPILOGUE

1. *ACJS Today*, (September, October 1988), p. 1.
2. Ibid. (January, February 1989), p. 1.
3. Minutes of the Executive Board of ACJS, March 9 1987.

Bibliography

PRIMARY MATERIALS

The material for this book came largely from primary sources. In 1982 the Academy of Criminal Justice Sciences commissioned me to write its history. I was granted access to personal papers and interviews with past presidents and other significant characters in the history of the organization. They all took part willingly and helpfully. (A list of those interviewed follows at the end of the bibliography.) At the time of their interviews they all understood that their comments would be used in this history. The research culminated in an unpublished monograph, *The Academy of Criminal Justice Sciences and the Criminal Justice Movement: Some History*.

A great deal of the information for this book came from (1) manuscripts in the possession of the original owners, (2) those given to me by the original owners, or (3) those found in library archives.

In the first category the greatest single source of manuscript information was the Gordon Misner papers; they are the most complete and richest set. They are privately held; interested researchers must contact Misner at the University of Illinois-Chicago. This is true as well of the Richard Ward papers at the same university. Also of importance are the papers of Earl Lewis and Robert Culbertson, all remaining in the possession of their original owners.

In the second category, I have in my possession the relevant papers of Larry Bassi and Edward Latessa.

Of course, the largest set of manuscript materials may be found in various libraries and archives. Most important for this work were the Vollmer papers and the O. W. Wilson papers at the Bancroft Library at the University of California. In addition, the Presidential Files in the University Archives of the University of California in the Bancroft Library were very useful. So were the School of Criminology Papers in the Office of the Chancellor's Archives at the University of California. Some of those papers were so important that I have titled them the Goolsby File, after the School secretary of the 1960s and 1970s; they all have been placed in the University Archives, Bancroft Library, since I first used them. The Albert Morris papers at the American Society of Criminology archives at the organization's secretariat office at Ohio State University were of some aid as well. The Richard Hankey papers at the John Jay College of Criminal Justice Archives in New York City; the David Duffee File of the Albany School of Criminal Justice Archives in Albany, New York; and the Richard Velde papers in the National Archives in Washington, D.C., were all of some aid. The proceedings of the International Association of Police Professors—particularly for 1964, 1965, 1966, 1969, and 1970—were helpful.

SECONDARY MATERIALS

By necessity, this bibliography is selective. For a more complete compilation see Carolyn Johnson *The Literature of Higher Education in Criminology and Criminal Justice: An Annotated Bibliography* (Chicago: The Joint Commission on Criminology and Criminal Justice Education Standards and the University of Illinois at Chicago, 1980.)

Books

Auerbach, Jerold S. *Unequal Justice: Lawyers and Social Change in Modern America*. New York: Oxford University Press, 1976.

Bopp, William J. *"O. W.": O. W. Wilson and the Search for a Police Profession*. Port Washington, NY: Kennikat Press, 1977.

Carey, James. *Sociology and Public Affairs: The Chicago School*. Beverly Hills:Sage Publishing, 1975.

Carte, Gene E., and Elaine H. Carte. *Police Reform in the United States: The Era of August Vollmer, 1905-1933*. Berkeley: University of California Press, 1975.

Clifford, Geraldine Jonach, and James W. Guthrie. *Ed. School: A Brief for Professional Education*. Chicago: University of Chicago Press, 1988.

Coakley, Leo J. *Jersey Troopers: A Fifty Year History of the New Jersey State Police*. New Brunswick, NJ: Rutgers University Press, 1971.

Connery, Robert H., and Gerald Benjamin. *Rockefeller of New York: Executive Power in the Statehouse.* Ithaca, NY: Cornell University Press, 1979.
Diner, Steven J. *A City and Its Universities: Public Policy in Chicago, 1892-1919.* Chapel Hill, NC: University of North Carolina Press, 1980.
Goldman, Erick F. *Rendezvous with Destiny.* New York: Vintage Books, 1956.
Grammage, Allen Z. *Police Training in the United States.* Springfield, IL: Charles C. Thomas, 1963.
Haber, Samuel. *Efficiency and Uplift: Scientific Management in the Progressive Era, 1890-1913.* Chicago: University of Chicago Press, 1964.
Hays, Samuel P. *The Response to Industrialism.* Chicago: University of Chicago Press, 1963.
Hofstadter, Richard. *Social Darwinism in American Thought.* Boston: Beacon Press, 1963.
Karl, Barry D. *Charles E. Merriam and the Study of Politics.* Chicago: University of Chicago Press, 1974.
Kenney, John P. *The California Police.* Springfield, IL: Charles C. Thomas, 1964.
Kruytbosch, Carlos E., and Sheldon Messinger. *The State of the University: Authority and Change.* Beverly Hills: Sage Publishing, 1968.
Lane, Roger. *Policing the City: Boston 1822-1885.* Cambridge, MA: Harvard University Press, 1967.
Link, Arthur S. *Woodrow Wilson and the Progressive Era, 1890-1920.* New York: Harper Torchbooks, 1954.
Lubove, Roy. *The Professional Altruist: The Emergence of Social Work as a Career, 1889-1930.* New York: Atheneum, 1971.
Miller, Wilber R. *Cops and Bobbies: Police Authority in New York and London, 1830-1870.* Chicago: University of Chicago Press, 1977.
Mohr,James C. *Abortion in America: Origins and Evolution of a National Policy.* New York: Oxford University Press, 1978.
Morn, Frank. *The Eye That Never Sleeps: A History of the Pinkerton National Detective Agency.* Bloomington: Indiana University Press, 1982.
Mowry, George E. *The California Progressives.* Chicago: Quadrangle Books, 1963.
———. *The Era of Theodore Roosevelt and the Birth of Modern America, 1900-1913.* New York: Harper Torchbooks, 1958.
Musto, David F. *The American Disease: Origins of Narcotics Control.* New Haven, CT: Yale University Press, 1973.
Niederhoffer, Arthur. *Behind the Shield: The Police in Urban Society.* New York: Anchor Books, 1969.

Oberschall, Anthony (ed.). *The Establishment of Empirical Sociology: Studies in Continuity, Discontinuity and Institutionalization*. New York: Harper & Row, 1972.

O'Neill, William. *Coming Apart: An Informal History of America in the 1960s*. Chicago: Quadrangle Books, 1971.

Richardson, James. *The New York Police: Colonial Times to 1901*. New York: Oxford University Press, 1970.

Rothman, David. *Conscience and Convenience: The Asylum and Its Alternatives in Progressive America*. Boston: Little, Brown, 1980.

Schneider, John C. *Detroit and the Problem of Order, 1830-1880: A Geography of Crime, Riot and Policing*. Lincoln: University of Nebraska Press, 1980.

Schwartz, Tony. *Media: The Second God*. New York: Random House, 1981.

Sellin, Thorsten. *Culture, Conflict and Crime*. New York: Social Science Research Council, 1938.

Sinclair, Bruce. *A Centennial History of the American Society of Mechanical Engineers, 1880-1980*. Toronto: University of Toronto Press, 1980.

Somit, Albert, and Joseph Tanenhaus. *The Development of American Political Science: From Burgess to Behavioralism*. Boston: Allyn & Bacon, 1967.

Underwood, James E. and William J. Daniels. *Governor Rockefeller in New York: The Apex of Pragmatic Liberalism in the United States*. Westport, CT: Greenwood Press, 1982.

Veysey, Laurence R. *The Emergence of the American University*. Chicago: University of Chicago Press, 1965.

Walker, Samuel. *A Critical History of Police Reform* Lexington, MA: Lexington Books, 1977.

———. *Popular Justice: A History of American Criminal Justice*. New York: Oxford University Press, 1980.

Ward, Richard H., and Vincent J. Webb. *The Quest for Quality*. New York: University Publications, 1984.

Articles

Adams, Reed. "Criminal Justice: An Emerging Academic Profession and Discipline" *Journal of Criminal Justice* 4 (1976): 304-314.

Bassi, Larry, and Ronald H. Rogers. "The Road to Accreditation" *Journal of Criminal Justice* 4 (1976): 243-252.

Bekman, Erik. "Police Education and Training: Where Are We? Where Are We Going?" *Journal of Criminal Justice* 4 (1976): 315-322.

Bennett, Richard R., and Ineke H. Marshall. "Criminal Justice Education in the United States: A Profile." *Journal of Criminal Justice* 7 (1979): 147-172.

Blumer, Martin. "The Chicago School of Sociology: What Made It a 'School'?" *History of Sociology* 5 (1985): 61-71.

Brandstatter, Arthur. "A Career Concept for Police" *Journal of Criminal Law, Criminology and Police Science* 61 (1976): 438-445.

———."The School of Police Administration and Public Safety," *Journal of Criminal Law and Criminology* 48 (1958): 504-506.

Brereton, George H. "The California Plan for Police Officer Training" *Journal of the American Institute of Criminal Law and Criminology* 30 (1939): 370-378.

Caldwell, Lynton. "Public Administration and the University: A Half Century of Development" *Public Administration Review* 25 (1965): 52-60.

Camfield, Thomas. "The Professionalization of American Psychology, 1870-1917" *Journal of the History of the Behavioral Sciences* 9 (1973): 66-75.

Coats, A. W. "The First Two Decades of the American Economics Association" *American Economic Review* 50 (1960): 555-574.

Cravens, Hamilton. "The Abandonment of Evolutionary Social Theory in America: The Impact of Academic Professionalization upon American Sociological Theory, 1890-1920" *American Studies* 12 (1971): 5-10.

Diner, Steven J. "Department and Discipline: The Department of Sociology at the University of Chicago, 1892-1920" *Minerva* 13 (1975): 514-553.

Egger, Rowland. "The Period of Crisis, 1933 to 1945" In *American Public Administration: Past, Present, Future*, Fredrick C. Mosher (ed.). Tuscaloosa: The University of Alabama Press, 1975.

Felkenes, George. "Accreditation: Is It Necessary? Yes!" *Journal of Criminal Justice* 8 (1980): 77-87.

Friedman, Lawrence M. "The Law and Society Movement" *Stanford Law Review* 38 (1986): 763-780.

Fry, Lincoln, and Jon Miller. "The Organizational Transformation of a Federal Education Program: Reflections on LEEP" *Social Problems* 24 (1976): 259-270.

Germann, A. C. "Law Enforcement Education and Training in the United States" *Police Chief* 24 (1957): 22-28.
Glazer, Nathan. "The Schools of Minor Professions" *Minerva* 12 (1974): 346-364.
Gourley, G. Douglas. "In-Service Training of Policemen by Universities and Colleges" *Journal of Criminal Law, Criminology and Police Science* 44 (1953-54): 229-238.
Hiner, N. Ray. "Professions in Process: Changing Relations among Social Scientists, Historians and Educators, 1880-1920" *History Teacher* 6 (1972-1973): 201-218.
Hoffman, Dennis E., Jack C. Snell, and Vincent J. Webb. "Insiders and Outsiders in Criminal Justice Education" *Journal of Criminal Justice* 4 (1976): 57-61.
Jacob, James B., and Samuel B. Magdovitz. "At LEEP's End: A Review of the Law Enforcement Education Program" *Journal of Police Science and Administration* 5 (1977): 1-18.
Johnson, William P. "Education and Professional Life Styles: Law and Medicine in the Nineteenth Century" *History of Education Quarterly* 14 (1974): 185-207.
Karl, Barry D. "The Power of Intellect and the Politics of Ideas" In *Philosophers and Kings: Studies in Leadership*, Dankwart A. Rustow (ed.). New York: George Braziller, 1970.
Kuykendall, Jack L. and Armand P. Hernandez. "Criminal Justice Programs in Higher Education: Course and Curriculum Orientations" *Journal of Criminal Justice* 5 (1977): 149-163.
———. "Undergraduate Justice System Education and Training at San Jose State University: An Historical Perspective" *Journal of Criminal Justice* 3 (1975): 111-13
Levine, Felice J. "Goose Bumps and 'The Search for Signs of Intelligent Life' in Sociolegal Studies after Twenty-five Years" *Law & Society Review* 24 (1990): 7-33.
MacQuarrie, T. W. "San Jose State College Police School" *Journal of the American Institute of Criminal Law* 26 (1935): 255-261.
Markowitz, Gerald E., and David Karl Rosner. "Doctors in Crisis: A Study of the Use of Medical Education Reform to Establish Modern Professional Elitism in Medicine" *American Quarterly* 25 (1973): 83-107.

McCandless, David A. "Southern Police Institute at the University of Louisville" *Journal of Criminal Law, Criminology and Police Science* 42 (1951-52): 105-111.

Morris, Albert. "American Society of Criminology: A History, 1941-1974" *Criminology* 13 (1975): 123-167.

Parrish, John. "Rise of Economics as an Academic Discipline: The Formative Years to 1900" *Southern Economic Journal* 34 (1967): 1-16.

Robinson, Elmo A. "The Seven State Colleges of California" *School and Society* 53 (1941): 640-650.

Ross, Dorothy. "The Development of the Social Sciences" in *The Organization of Knowledge in Modern America, 1860-1920*, Alexander Oleson and John Voss (eds.). Baltimore: Johns Hopkins University Press, 1979.

Ross, Hugh. "University Influences in the Genesis and Growth of Junior Colleges in California" *History of Education Quarterly* 3 (1963): 143-152.

Senna, Joseph J. "Criminal Justice Higher Education--Its Growth and Directions" *Crime and Delinquency* 20 (1974): 389-397.

Swyget, Michael I., and Nathaniel E. Gozansky. "Senior Law Faculty Publication Study: Comparison of Law School Productivity" *Journal of Legal Education* 35 (1985): 373-394.

Tracy, Charles A. "Survey of Criminal Justice Subject Matter Baccalaureate Programs" *Journal of Criminal Law, Criminology and Police Science* 61 (1970): 576-579.

Veysey, Laurence R. "The Plural Organized Worlds of the Humanities" In *The Organization of Knowledge in Modern America, 1860-1920*, Alexander Oleson and John Voss (eds.). Baltimore: Johns Hopkins University Press, 1979.

Vollmer, August, and Albert Schneider. "The School for Police as Planned at Berkeley" *Journal of the American Institute of Criminal Law and Criminology* 7 (1917): 877-898.

Index

About the Author

FRANK MORN is Professor of Criminal Justice Sciences at the Illinois State University. A respected educator and thinker in the field of criminal justice, he is the author of a history of the Pinkerton Detective Agency and numerous articles.

www.ingramcontent.com/pod-product-compliance
Ingram Content Group UK Ltd.
Pitfield, Milton Keynes, MK11 3LW, UK
UKHW020805290926
15470UKWH00003B/975

9 780313 2931